blindsided

JONATHAN GIFFORD

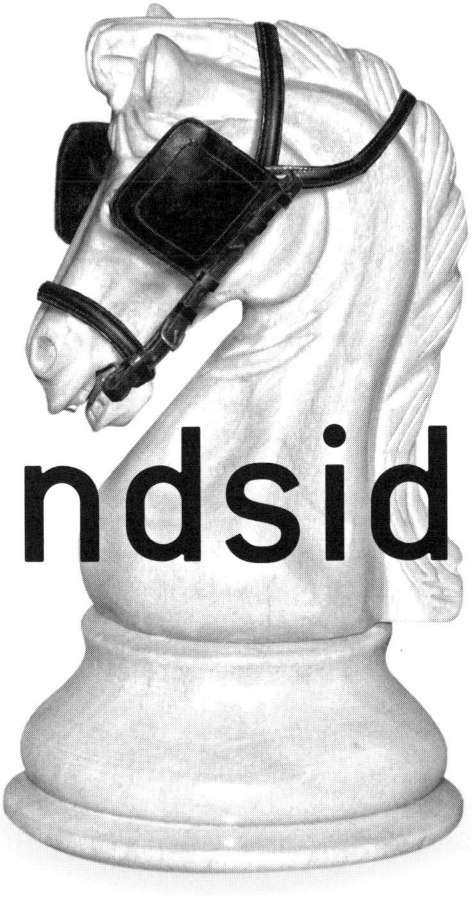

blindsided

How business and society are shaped
by our *irrational* and *unpredictable* behaviour

Published by Marshall Cavendish Business
An imprint of Marshall Cavendish International

PO Box 65829
London EC1P 1NY
United Kingdom
info@marshallcavendish.co.uk

and

1 New Industrial Road
Singapore 536196
genrefsales@sg.marshallcavendish.com
www.marshallcavendish.com/genref

Marshall Cavendish is a trademark of Times Publishing Limited

Other Marshall Cavendish offices:
Marshall Cavendish International (Asia) Private Limited, 1 New Industrial Road, Singapore 536196 • Marshall Cavendish Corporation, 99 White Plains Road, Tarrytown NY 10591–9001, USA • Marshall Cavendish International (Thailand) Co Ltd, 253 Asoke, 12th Floor, Sukhumvit 21 Road, Klongtoey Nua, Wattana, Bangkok 10110, Thailand • Marshall Cavendish (Malaysia) Sdn Bhd, Times Subang, Lot 46, Subang Hi-Tech Industrial Park, Batu Tiga, 40000 Shah Alam, Selangor Darul Ehsan, Malaysia

A CIP record for this book is available from the British Library

ISBN 978-981-4351-29-4

Cover design by OpalWorks
Printed and bound in the United Kingdom by TJ International Ltd, Padstow, Cornwall

To my wife Mary, who makes everything possible

Contents

INTRODUCTION 1

We Should Have Seen This Coming ... Rushes and Booms ... Brave New Worlds ... Riots and Credit Crunches ... Dust Bowls and Plagues ... In Search of Self-Knowledge

1 SOONERS, BOOMERS AND BOO 11

The Race to be First ... On the Edge of a New Frontier ... Boom, Bubble and Bust ... Boo.com ... Grow Now, Make Profits Later ... A Runaway Locomotive, Fuelled by Banknotes ... Hire Now, Ask Questions Later ... Miss Boo's Bad Hair Day ... Soft Launch, Hard Landing

2 BUBBLES AND CRASHES 31

To Market, To Market ... The Rational Market ... A Never-Ending Cycle ... A Licence to Print Money ... House of Cards ... A Very Big Baburu ... If the Price is Right ... Oscillations Around a State of Equilibrium ... Drift, Momentum and Irrationality ... Irrational Exuberance ... Short Memories

3 THE SCIENCE OF DESIRE 57

The Id, the Ego & the Ad ... Selling a Cure ... A Broken Trust ... Consumption Engineering ... Techniques of Mass Persuasion ... The Id Goes Shopping ... Insights and Insults ... Playing to Our Emotions ... Selling Politicians to the People ... 'Eisenhower Answers America' ... The Consumer Society

4 NEW LAMPS FOR OLD 78

New Driver ... Banking On Gas ... 'The Death Knell of Every Traditional Integrated Firm' ... Virtual Integration ... One Side of Every Trade ... Better Than the Market? ... An Environment Ripe for Abuse ... A Cool New Kind of Company ... The Unthinkable Happens ... Handsomely Rewarded for Losing Billions ... Accounting Held to Account ... The Slippery Slope ... Why Were We So Blindsided by Enron?

5 THE GUNFIGHT AT THE OK CORRAL 114

People Power ... When Tyrants Fall ... Walls Come Tumbling Down ... Rights, Rents and Total Democracy ... Law and Fair Play ... The Gunfight at the OK Corral ... The Earp Vendetta Ride ... Law and Peace ... Us and Them

6 WEAPONS OF MASS FINANCIAL DESTRUCTION 136

Anything Except Onions ... Transition and Trauma ... Why Did No One See It Coming? ... Infinity and Beyond ... Subprimes, Teasers and Balloons ... Mortgage Madness ... Originate and Sell ... The Financial Instruments Formerly Known as 'Bonds' ... Rating Risk ... Repackaged Bonds ... Weird Beasts from the Wall Street Jungle ... A Collection of Betting Slips ... Synthetic Bets, Synthetic Assets ... At the Heart of the Credit Crunch ... Survival of the Greediest

7 DUST BOWL AND THE DIRTY THIRTIES 166

The Sale of the Century ... The Louisiana Purchase ... The Wrong Sort of Country ... Wild and Untamed ... Rain Follows Plough ... Wrong Side Up ... Black Sunday ... Sustainability ... The Tragedy of the Commons ... 'We Know This Won't Last Forever'

8 THE BLACK DEATH 188

Going Viral ... The Great Plague ... A Twentieth-Century Plague ... Not If, But When

9 THE BLINDSIDED BRAIN 200

Fast and Slow Thinking ... Blind to the Obvious ... Unconscious Influences ... The Emotional Brain ... Iowa Gambling Task ... Fear and Reward ... The Left & Right Hemispheres ... Big Picture, Little Picture ... Two Different Ways of Experiencing the World ... Split-Brain Experiments ... Cognitive Neuroscience ... Right Hemispheres Do Empathy, Left Hemispheres Do Denial ... Who Are We? ... Taking Charge

Acknowledgements 225

Notes 227

Bibliography 239

About the Author 245

INTRODUCTION

Blindsided. It's strange. We seem to have woken up on a surprisingly large number of mornings in the few millennia of our existence as a species and thought: 'Did we really do that? How could that happen? How could we have been so stupid? Why were we so completely *blindsided* by that particular set of events? Why, for goodness sake, didn't we see it coming?'

It's a very good question, and it has a very simple answer – and one that we should not be particularly ashamed of. It is, I am confident, because we are human.

We Should Have Seen This Coming

Being blindsided, in the context of this book, is something that happens to us. A particular set of events unfolds and the end result is not what we would have wished for. But there is another component to this interpretation of being blindsided. It is not just that the outcome is not what we wanted, it is that we feel, in some way, that we should have predicted it; that it fits a pattern we should have recognised; that, although the set of events was highly unlikely, we should have known from our own experience or from the records of our ancestors that these things can happen, and that we have been foolish not to have prepared for it, like squirrels who have failed to gather nuts for the coming winter.

Intriguingly, it is impossible to imagine animals being blindsided in this way. The animal who behaves like our hypothetical foolish squirrel does not survive, and neither do his or her genes. We do not seem to find our cousins, the great apes – chimpanzees, gorillas, orang utans – tidying up after some disaster in the forest and muttering, ruefully, 'We really should have seen that one coming. What were we thinking of?' To be blindsided, it seems to be necessary to be human. It also seems to be necessary to belong to the same group.

We are, after all, highly social animals. Some scientists believe that the complexity and size of the brain of any species is a function of the complexity of the social networks within which that species has evolved. To be able to reconcile the interests of the individual and the group successfully, it is argued, is uniquely demanding in terms of brain power. The 'social brain hypothesis' suggests that being able to survive and reproduce more efficiently in a group requires demanding mental mechanisms for social cohesion that create an evolutionary pressure towards increased brain size. Being sociable, it seems, is difficult – which is believable.

Being sociable also creates problems for modern social animals like mankind. We tend to exhibit 'herd-like' behaviour. After all, if we stand out too much from the herd, then the herd begins to worry that we might be genuinely 'different' – that we might actually be a predator. Such individuals tend not to survive in herds. Our very sociability, once established, tends to drive us to behave in the same way as the rest of the group.

In this, however, we are very much like our primate cousins, and indeed like most mammals and birds: we are capable of individual, intelligent initiative, but, when everybody else flocks or stampedes, we find it very hard not to join in. What sets humans apart – what creates the possibility of being blindsided in ways that other species are not – is our unique ability to create belief systems that persuade us that what we are doing is sensible and far-sighted, despite all of the evidence to the contrary. Other species are not surprised when they have eaten all of the berries on the bushes. They move on, and eat something else. We, in sharp contrast, seem to find ourselves bewildered and astonished when the berries run out. 'There's plenty here for everyone,' we seem to have persuaded ourselves. 'These good times will last forever!' There is a sense that one needs a community of believers to create the possibility of being blindsided – a collection of people in relatively close connection with one another who begin to sustain a myth about what is really happening.

This, however, is to prejudge the issue. This book will demonstrate – and in the last chapter analyse in detail – the proposition that we human beings are far less rational than we like to believe. Research in the field of psychology suggests that we make a large number of our decisions very quickly, based on previous experience. There is a very good evolutionary reason for this: most decisions that are relevant to our survival, to our ability to evaluate threat and opportunity, are best taken quickly. Our brains, as a result, are now hard-wired for this. But while this quick decision-making process works well in the majority of cases, it is prone to biases and systematic errors, which lead us, without our knowledge, into making some spectacularly bad choices.

Emotions have been found to play a far bigger role in our decision-making than we like to believe, given our vision of ourselves as rational beings who make decisions as the result of having weighed up various alternatives in the 'light of pure reason'. This model of our own decision-making process seems, sadly, to be another delusion of ours. Discoveries in the field of neuroscience are beginning to confirm that every idea that enters our minds is given an emotional value, so that we can instantly assign it a value in terms of our most important emotional responses: friend or foe, fight or flight, disgust or anticipation. This works very well (of course), but it cannot be described as a rational thought process.

Rushes and Booms

One of the major causes of our downfall throughout history has been our all-too-human inability to resist a 'rush'. Chapter 1 ('Sooners, Boomers and Boo') looks at the rushes that have blindsided us, starting with the remarkable 'land rushes' in America's newly opened Oklahoma Territory in the late nineteenth century. When all around us are grabbing their share of something, we find ourselves irresistibly drawn to join in. You probably recognise something of this in your own behaviour. When there is a shortage of any commodity, whether it's petrol, candles, water or sugar, if it is due to some expected disruption of supply, your first reaction is probably to think, rightly, that you will last until the temporary crisis has passed and normal supply is resumed. But if you were to see a long queue at the petrol station or at the water bowser, or large numbers of people leaving shops with boxes of candles under their arms, I suspect that you would find it very hard not to join in, and start panic buying. We are, most likely, schooled by evolution to want to grab a share of any resource that our neighbours are helping themselves to; not to do so might well have been life-threatening.

Fascinatingly, this instinct still kicks in when people are acquiring less obviously essential resources – such as shares in tech companies during the dot-com boom of the late 1990s. It takes a strong will to stand by when all your peers are making money from stocks that are increasing in value on a daily basis. Business people are not immune to this urge. The founders of the internet retail company boo.com spent – and lost – outrageous amounts of investors' money because they believed that launching quickly was more important than launching efficiently. The rush was on, and the laggards would miss the boat. This, as we shall see, is one of the easiest ways for us to be blindsided.

Chapter 2 exposes another set of perennial blindsiders: bubbles and crashes. Surely we have seen enough of these to recognise a new bubble when it comes our way? Sadly, it seems we have not. From eighteenth-century France to twentieth-century Japan, we have been swept up by bubbles and left despondent by crashes. The chapter then looks at a theory about market behaviour first forwarded in the 1960s and thereafter widely embraced: the efficient-market hypothesis. According to this theory, the price for any item traded on a market with a high volume of trades was, in fact, the 'correct' price in the light of all of the available information about that item. If the price was wrong, then some clever arbitrageur, the theory argued, would make a killing and by so doing adjust the price back to its correct level. This theory struggles, however, to account for the observable fact that the market price can apparently be 'correct' one day, and have dropped by 20% or more the following day. A belief that the market must be 'right' is a well-tested way to find oneself blindsided – though the theorists manage always to rise above the fracas, pointing out that a sudden crash in prices is, in effect, meaningless: a minor adjustment as markets continue to determine the 'right' price for all traded goods. Which is not very useful if you have just lost all of your money.

Brave New Worlds

The world of advertising, which Chapter 3 explores, provides us with a demonstration of how being blindsided is intimately intertwined with our desires, and especially with our 'unconscious' desires. American consumers in the 1960s became increasingly concerned that advertisers were using new 'psychological' techniques to tap into their subconscious, to manipulate them into making purchases that they would not otherwise have made. Even more alarming were the emerging theories of 'conditioned responses' which could be used to programme consumers to respond to 'triggers' hidden in advertising messages. Advertisers dreamed of compliant consumers, and consumers had nightmares about mad scientists enabling advertisers to take control of their minds.

These concerns look amusing now, but accounts of how the advertising men took over Dwight D. Eisenhower's presidential campaign in 1952, using all of their recently acquired sales techniques to sell Ike to the American public, are rather more unsettling. Still — that couldn't happen now, could it? Surely we are not still blindsided by advertising?

Desire also lies at the heart of the shocking collapse of America's giant energy corporation, Enron: our desire to believe that Enron had found some magical new way of making money, and Enron's desire to persuade us that this was true, so that the directors of Enron could, indeed, make personal fortunes at the expense of the company's shareholders who, in turn, had hoped that owning shares in Enron was in itself a new route to magical riches.... As Chapter 4 ('New Lamps for Old') shows, we are especially prone to the idea that some new way of doing things has been discovered that will make life much easier, and all of us much richer. Enron's vision of 'virtually integrated' companies seemed to fit the bill. We allowed our belief in this radical 'new economy' way of doing business to explain the fact that Enron could apparently deliver ever-increasing levels of profitability despite the figures published in its quarterly reports not adding up.

In instances like this, we are blindsided by our wish to believe that the new magic is real and that we are entering a brave new world. In a less elevated sense, we are blindsided by our old friends, greed and selfishness; by our deeply ingrained habit of trusting people who are at the top of social hierarchies (as successful corporate executives are seen to be, especially in American culture); by our drive not to lose out on our share of good things when they are on offer; and by the fact that the experts that we look to for advice also live in social 'herds' and have their reasons (self-preservation and -enrichment) for following the accepted wisdom.

Riots and Credit Crunches

Chapter 5 ('The Gunfight at the OK Corral') moves into the realm of sudden breakdowns in law and order. An exploration of the development of law and order in America's Wild West reveals, surprisingly, that groups of people embarking on perilous undertakings (like gold miners, or people on the early wagon trains) are instinctively law-abiding. So why does lawlessness break out when lawfulness seems to be our first instinct?

The constant tension between trust within the group and mistrust of outsiders may explain why we are so often blindsided by outbreaks of violent disorder. The leaders of North African countries were as blindsided by the Arab Spring as, apparently, were all political commentators; but nobody was more blindsided than the people of London when the city erupted into an orgy of violent looting just weeks after the city had come together to celebrate a royal wedding. Houses and shops burned, citizens were terrorised, and beleaguered dictators such as Libya's Colonel Gaddafi were able to draw unflattering comparisons between 'unrest' in Libya and rioting in the United Kingdom – home to the Mother of Parliaments. No government, it seems, is immune to the belief that every citizen is contented and that dissent will always be minor and containable.

We tend to see our capacity to be caught unawares by political and social upheavals as our worst examples of being blindsided: history is largely written as an account of riots and revolutions. The increasingly complicated world of our financial infrastructures, however, creates a kind of parallel – and largely unaccountable – world in which the conditions for being blindsided on a truly global scale can be created without the clear warning signs created by political unrest, such as stone-throwing rioters and burning cars. Chapter 6 ('Weapons of Mass Financial Destruction') explores the most shocking and far-reaching financial disaster of modern times: the collapse of the American sub-prime market and the ways in which America's financial institutions encouraged reckless and irresponsible lending practices, and then turned a disaster into a crisis by means of obscure and arguably meaningless financial derivatives, which served not only to multiply the effect of the crash but to spread it throughout the global financial markets.

Key to this story is the way in which efficient-market theory persuaded America's leaders that it was a mistake to regulate any market for fear of interfering with its magic. The 'over-the-counter' bond market was duly deregulated. We were won over by a theory that argues that unfettered greed will generate an infinity of clever financial products, and that the efficiency of the market will ruthlessly weed out those that do not have any beneficial function. Unfortunately, there is no meaningful 'market' in over-the-counter bonds. These products are traded, for very high stakes, amongst a very small number of institutions. It is not obvious that they serve any function other than to generate huge commissions for their originators. Astonishing losses in this rich man's casino led directly to a global credit crunch, the effects of which we are still suffering from.

Dust Bowls and Plagues

We return to America's Midwest in Chapter 7 to consider the environmental disaster in the 1930s that became known as the Dust Bowl — a tragic mixture of muddled government policy and human short-sightedness. The farms of the Midwest have since recovered from the Dust Bowl years, relying on water from the aquifer that lies beneath the Great Plains. Unfortunately, this aquifer is not replenished by rainwater at a rate anywhere near the rate of extraction. Soon, the water will all be gone. We are especially bad at considering what effects our current actions may have on future generations. We tell ourselves that if we don't help ourselves to the water, the other farmer down the road will still help himself to it, and nobody will be any better off. The tragedy of the commons continues to blindside us all.

Chapters 8 ('The Black Death') takes us to a different way of being blindsided – one that cannot be ascribed to poor decision-making on the part of *individuals*. Mankind, like all living creatures, is subject to disease. The Black Death is believed to have killed half the world's population in the fourteenth century. In the twentieth century, an outbreak of Spanish Flu resulted in more deaths than were caused by the First World War. It ranks as one of the world's greatest natural disasters, and we can expect a similar outbreak at any time. And yet this is not at the top of our minds (except when there is a temporary scare about an outbreak of bird flu). As individuals, we are incapable of living our lives in expectation of the next disaster, for obvious reasons, and rightly so. It is only at the most advanced organisational level that mankind is capable of keeping these things in mind. Our unique strength as a species has been our creation of organisations capable of keeping our collective memories in mind and of making preparations for disaster. But this will not prevent us, at an individual level, from being blindsided when the disaster does strike.

In Search of Self-Knowledge

It is becoming increasingly clear that we are not the rational, predictive decision-makers that we believe ourselves to be. In the last chapter of the book, we turn to look at the fascinating developments in psychology and neuroscience that are beginning to make sense of the ways in which we actually make decisions. Our choices, it turns out, are driven by older instincts, emotions and drives, while what we take to be our 'self' gaily rationalises what we have done *after the event*. We create narratives – always, effectively, false narratives – that persuade us to believe we are in control of the situation.

These theories offer a clear underpinning for the experience of being blindsided. More than that, they suggest that 'being blindsided' is a fundamental and perhaps unavoidable aspect of being human; that we make most of our decisions using a fast, 'instinctive' set of responses, whereas we reflect on our actions via a far slower, less frequently used, and more energy-consuming set of mental processes. Unfortunately, the fast system is highly susceptible to being undermined by a wide range of influences. Even more unfortunately, it is the latter, slow, processes that we see as being 'us'; as a result, 'we' are frequently blindsided.

Neuroscientists are finding, furthermore, that our ideal of 'rational' thought – thought that takes place away from the disturbing influence of emotions; cool, calm, *dispassionate* thought – is a myth. Everything that enters our minds is ascribed an emotional value, so that our minds can very quickly (too quickly for the decision that is about to be made to enter our conscious minds) assess it in terms of what really matters to the mind: friend or foe, fight or flight. We may be able to reflect on the issue at our leisure (if it even 'comes to mind' at all), but the initial emotional decision, the 'gut reaction', has taken place within milliseconds of the idea entering our brain.

Finally, the fields of both neuroscience and psychology continue to probe the significance of the demonstrable differences between the left and right hemispheres of our brains. The right hemisphere, which deals with our relation to the outside world, is empathetic and engaged. The left hemisphere, in contrast, seeks to break down its impressions of the outside world into units that it can analyse and categorise. It also believes that it is 'us' and, on this analysis, it is beginning to assert itself over the right hemisphere, whose influence and input it refuses to recognise.

This remarkable theory opens up intriguing lines of thought that illuminate many of the dysfunctionalities of modern life. At the same time, it offers us a potential route back to a way of engaging more directly with the real world, a way of avoiding the dangers of our overwhelming tendency to false rationalisation and self-deception – those tendencies that, amongst many others, lead us so often to the feeling of being blindsided, of having got ourselves into a fine mess – again.

1 SOONERS, BOOMERS AND BOO

At the end of the nineteenth century, following the American Civil War, a large piece of territory in America's Midwest was argued by settlers to be 'Unassigned Lands'. The various treaties with Native American tribes were said to have left an area that was public land, which should be made available for settlement by anyone, not just Native Americans. The government disagreed, arguing that the land was still part of Indian Territory, and issued a proclamation forbidding settlement of the land, but a popular campaign for settlement continued. The advocates of settlement became known as 'boomers'. Boomers set up illegal homesteads in Indian Territory and were evicted by the army. A case finally came before a district court, which ruled that settling in Unassigned Lands was not a criminal offence.

The federal government refused to accept this but, in 1889, a treaty was signed with the Creek Indians, who ceded title to all of the lands in the western half of the territory, which was now to be known as Oklahoma Territory. All existing settlers were evicted from the territory: settlement was to take place under the terms of Abraham Lincoln's Homestead Act of 1862, which granted parcels of land to anybody who would farm the land for a period of five years and build a small dwelling place.

The land was to be allocated in a remarkable process of 'first come, first served'. Would-be settlers were to gather on the borders of Oklahoma Territory and, at midday on 22 April 1889, at a given signal, could race into the interior in search of the best lands. The first 'land run' in history was about to take place. William Willard Howard, a reporter for *Harper's Weekly*, recorded the scene:

> The lieutenant had caused all the boomers' watches to be set by his own, in order that there might be no false start. Just as the second hand of his watch touched the hour of twelve he gave the signal, and before the stirring notes of the bugle had found an echo ... the foremost horsemen had dashed into the fords. Spurred on by yelling and wildly excited riders, the horses made a furious dash through the water, throwing sand and spray on all sides like a sudden gust of rain and hail.[1]

Others arrived on crowded trains, many jumping off – and concussing themselves – before the trains had stopped at the empty spaces that were about to become towns. Howard also recorded that boomers who made for desirable stretches of land – land near the major rivers and their tributaries – found, to their dismay, that others had got there first: the so-called 'sooners', who had got there 'sooner' than they legally should have done by moving quietly into the territory on the previous day and hiding in woods and ditches until the official start time for the run.

In the towns, the boomers rushing off the trains were amazed to find deputy marshals quietly laying claim to lots on what were about to become prime locations in the new towns springing up from the soil. The deputies were allowed to enter the territory, and had been sworn in for that very purpose, but they were forbidden from making claims – a technicality that the new deputies were now deliberately and brazenly ignoring.

Despite the many arguments that broke out, what came to be known as the Oklahoma Land Run was remarkably peaceful, which Howard, the *Harper's Weekly* reporter, believed was entirely due to the ban on the sale of any intoxicating liquor. 'Had whiskey been plentiful,' he wrote, 'the disputed lots might have been watered in blood, for every man went armed with some sort of deadly weapon.'[2]

As the excitement of the rush wore off, Howard also recorded the fact that many boomers were soon to leave Oklahoma, disappointed by the poor, sandy soil and the scarcity of water, or simply unable to afford the high prices of food even for the first few weeks of their settlement.

Nevertheless, wells were sunk and food supplies established, and soon the new towns were no worse off than any other frontier town. The new settlers had established themselves; they now faced years of toil to establish farms, communities and services. Many were ill-equipped for this struggle, as Howard noted:

> Men with large families settled upon land with less than a dollar in money to keep them from starvation. How they expected to live until they could get a crop from their lands was a mystery which even they could not pretend to explain. Like unreasoning children, they thought that could they but once reach the beautiful green slopes of the promised land, their poverty and trouble would be at an end. They are now awakening to the bitter realization that their real hardships have just begun.[3]

The Land Runs in Oklahoma, of which there were to be six more, were a remarkable piece of social engineering, requiring settlers to build whole communities from scratch, and with an incomplete railway line as the only piece of infrastructure in place in a territory of some 3,000 square miles (7,770 km^2). For many settlers, the rush to take part, driven by their hunger for a piece of land to call their own and the natural fear of losing out in the race, was arguably a bad decision. Those without sufficient resources were doomed to fail. Those who succeeded in establishing going concerns paid for their eventual success with hardships that would have been avoided by a more planned – or even simply a less sudden – development.

The land runs perfectly fulfil the likely criteria for the development of a rush: the cost of entry was low and there were many eager participants. A lot of people were swept along by the irresistible feeling that they were in danger of missing out on something that everybody else was getting – something good (and free!) – and that they would be sorry for the rest of their lives if they didn't join in, right away.

Nevertheless, the rush was for a real and finite asset: land. Rushes like the Oklahoma land rush, or the gold rush in California that had begun some 50 years earlier, nearly always make a very few lucky people very rich (enough to ignite the spark of hope and envy in the rest of us), while making most people not very much money or none at all, and ruining an unfortunate few. For some lucky boomers, the land rush did indeed give them the opportunity that they and the government wanted: the chance to set themselves up as self-sufficient farmers and build a settled community around them.

The Race to be First

There is, however, another kind of rush: a rush to be first in a race for something that turns out *not* to be finite; a rush to be first when it turns out that it didn't actually matter whether one was first, fiftieth or two-thousand-and-fiftieth. A recent perfect example of this was the dot-com boom and bust. People seemed initially to envisage the internet both as a piece of territory where it was vital to stake one's claim: a kind of virtual high street where the 'first movers' who staked their claims would prevent other significant entries. 'Get big fast' was the mantra of Jeff Bezos, founder of Amazon. Bezos and hundreds of other internet entrepreneurs were proved wrong. Amazon survived because it abandoned 'get big fast' – when the astonishing flow of funds that investors were initially prepared to throw at the internet started to dry up – and began to focus on the old-fashioned virtue of getting profitable. Amazon is a success because it established itself early in a new market – aiming to become 'the world's largest bookseller' by offering goods for sale online (books, and later

DVDs, CDs and other products) which were perfectly suited to a 'virtual' store that was able to offer a far higher range of products than any physical store could hope to carry. It offered people a service that they wanted and it began to make money after a supportable period of losses. With hindsight, the early 'high street' analogy was never apt. A high street is a small, central location with relatively high rents where you can hope to find your favourite stores. The internet was a high street, and a village store, and a tiny specialist boutique outfit shipping items out of their spare room, and a retail park, and an out-of-town warehouse operation. The internet was everything and everywhere.

Do retailers – even major retailers – come and go on the high street and elsewhere? Yes, they do. Could Amazon be overtaken one day by competitors, and even go out of business? Yes, it could. Were the assets that people rushed to grab, in this magical new thing called the internet, real assets? No, they were not. Being the first major retailer of pet food on the internet, or the first online florist, or the first virtual fashion outlet, was not the equivalent of sitting on a goldmine, or an oil well, or even on a piece of land. A very large amount of money was spent by a surprisingly large number of people who should have known better on establishing this painful truth.

On the Edge of a New Frontier

Business rushes depend on capital, but the suppliers of capital are no more immune to the infectious excitement of a rush than are the rest of us. Capital can become surprisingly available for rushes as investors become just as swept away by excitement as the pioneers. A good example from relatively modern times is the 'Railway mania' that took over nineteenth-century Britain.

Railway mania was a marvellous example of a rush caused by a significant technological advance – this time in the field of transport and communications. It paralleled the development of Britain's canals in the early days of the Industrial Revolution, and presaged the development of networks for road and air travel, as well as later examples of the communications revolution that we are still experiencing: radio, television, cellular phones, the internet.

Railway mania represented an entirely meaningful kind of rush. Britain is a small island; the rail network offered obvious and potentially dramatic economic benefits to the regions that it served; people felt that the railways would usher in a new age of possibility and prosperity. (This understandable sense of optimism recurs throughout the modern age: think of John F. Kennedy's 1960 presidential acceptance speech, 'We stand on the edge of a New Frontier – the frontier of unfulfilled hopes and dreams, a frontier of unknown opportunities.') The amount of railway track that Britain could possibly support was inevitably limited, but the intentionally laissez-faire attitude of the government of the day, under Prime Minister Robert Peel, allowed any number of railway companies to develop.

The rush to own Britain's precious railway assets began, and a speculative bubble – the almost inevitable partner of a rush – grew in earnest.

When the bubble burst, as Edward Chancellor notes in *Devil Take the Hindmost*, his account of financial bubbles through the ages, shares in railway companies 'declined from their peak by an average of 85%, and the total value of all railway shares was less than half the capital expended on them'.[4] Many railroads disappeared, their demise hastened by the arrival of the automobile. There was, however, a long-term advantage from the rush of railway entrepreneurs and the flood of capital that accompanied them: by 1855 Britain had over 8,000 miles (12,875 km) of track in operation, the highest density of railways in the world.[5]

Boom, Bubble and Bust

Rushes and their accompanying speculative bubbles would be entirely healthy ways of driving progress if they were not so invariably accompanied by a stage at which the frenzy of the rush creates a huge overvaluation of the underlying assets. The whole process can ensure the rapid commercial development of the resource in question but, along the way, a large number of people will pay too high a price for their share of the new resource, and a lot of business people will make some shockingly bad decisions.

The dot-com boom, or rush, was a classic example. People were very quick to realise the enormous potential of the internet – a potential that is currently being fulfilled. Some of our most important new technology companies were launched during this period. Unfortunately, the great success of a number of technology companies led to a belief that internet companies could do no wrong.

The early Internet Service Providers – the companies that provided public access to the internet – went to market with Initial Public Offerings (IPOs) in 1994 and 1995. Despite having never turned a profit, the companies' shares sold like hot cakes. Netcom On-Line launched their IPO in December 1994 and sold 1.85 million shares at US$13 each, valuing the company at US$85 million. Since the company made no profits, its value could be based only on the size of its subscriber base. At this valuation, the stock market was giving internet subscribers a substantially higher value – and therefore a supposedly higher 'worth' – than it traditionally gave to cable TV subscribers. As John Cassidy, author of *Dot.Con: The Greatest Story Ever Sold*, an account of the internet revolution and the dot-com bubble, notes:

> There was no obvious reason why internet users should be valued so highly, but even at this early stage internet stock valuation wasn't based on reason. It was based on hope and hype. The new valuation formulas were primarily an attempt to rationalize the fervor of the speculators.[6]

Another Internet Service Provider, PSINet, offered nearly 4 million shares at US$12 in May 1995, valuing the company at US$431 million. The shares doubled in value in the next twelve months.

UUNET, which had provided Microsoft with access for users to both the new Microsoft Network (MSN) and the internet, offered nearly 5 million shares at US$14, also in May 1995; the price rose to US$45 by July of that year.[7] UUNET's offering was underwritten by the prestigious Goldman Sachs merchant bank: internet shares were becoming not only profitable, but also mainstream.

As the number of people connecting to the internet began to grown exponentially, so did investors' visions of possible returns. It was the stock market launch of the web browser Netscape that was to really set the market alight. Netscape had planned to launch their shares at US$14 but, based on the increasingly feverish interest in internet-based share offerings, doubled this at the last moment to US$28. In the first day of trading, Netscape shares reached US$74, before closing at US$58.25, valuing the company at US$2.2 billion – about the same valuation as the giant defence contractor General Dynamics, a builder of jets and submarines.[8]

This was a new way to raise money. The conviction of investors that the internet would drive huge future profits meant that companies without any track record of profitability (or even, increasingly, companies that were losing frightening amounts of money) could still hope to achieve multimillion dollar valuations on the stock market. The investors of America – which would come to include an increasing number of people trading from their home computers – had become a host of mini venture capitalists, placing bets on an uncertain future in the growing belief that the internet represented a new machine for making money.

After the successful launch of the Internet Service Providers, who were, after all, offering a service (access to the internet) which was very likely to attract customers, came the launch of a bewildering array of companies, offering online versions of virtually every service known to man. The value of the earliest internet companies to go public went through the roof. In 1998 the shares of America Online rose by 593%, those of Yahoo! by

564%, and those of Amazon by 970%. Amazon's shares on 15 December at US$242 (they had launched on the in 1997 at US$18). Amazon did at least have a growing revenue stream, but in the previous quarter they had *lost* US$50 million. The relentless hyping of internet stocks, and the public's appetite for speculation, led to some astonishing launch capitalisations for companies that, unlike Amazon, had little or even no revenue stream and, very often, extremely dubious business plans. All that they had were hopes – but who could blame them?

Boo.com

Boo.com was a relatively late entry into the race to produce instant millionaires by creating new internet businesses that could gain enough credibility to launch an IPO. The young people who in 1998 conceived the ambitious start-up that was to become perhaps the defining example of 'dot-com madness' did not launch a company so much as an IPO. From the very outset, this was the goal, the purpose, of the organisation. Since the IPO would shower money on the new company, the founders' only concern was to get up and running.

This was the new economy; none of the old rules applied. Making money, proving that your business model made sense – those things didn't matter. And whatever it cost to be the first major fashion and sportswear retailer online didn't matter either, because the public valuation of the new leviathan would dwarf the few millions – tens, hundreds of millions, what did it matter? – that it cost to get to the all-important IPO. All that old-fashioned profitability stuff could come later, after the baby was born. To say that a company should show a profit before going public was to prove that you just didn't understand the new internet model of 'grow now, make profits later'.

The business plan of Boo.com, though light on detail, was not necessarily fatally flawed. The idea was to create a global retail empire, selling the most sought-after and powerful brands in fashion and sportswear. It is perhaps worth wondering why *fashion* (and high-end fashion at that) and *sportswear* should be offered at the same outlet – but never mind. The organisation would operate in many different countries, and in many different currencies. State-of-the-art 3-D graphics would allow customers to see how the clothes would look on the wearer.

If the business plan was not madness, it was nevertheless a complex retail model dependent on technologies (like 3-D graphics) that were in their infancy at the time. The tax implications of supplying goods across so many national boundaries proved to be eye-wateringly complex, and had not been thought through, let alone addressed. Boo.com promised their prestigious suppliers that they would not discount the goods on offer, so as not to upset the suppliers' vital and delicate relationship with existing key retail outlets. Visitors would be directed to their own 'national' website in their own currency and with different price structures, where necessary, to reflect the established market – fashion items were traditionally more expensive in some countries than in others, and Boo's prestigious fashion suppliers did not want to undercut their all-important retail network around the world.

There was the logistical challenge of handling thousands of product lines in different colours and sizes, all searchable by many different criteria, all viewable in every colour variation on the 3-D virtual mannequins (one male, on female), each with their own sales descriptions in multiple languages, each with their own prices in multiple currencies. (Unsurprisingly, the back end of the site struggled to cope with the sheer complexity of this database and ran frustratingly slowly for a site that was supposed to offer a cutting-edge internet experience.) Oh, and there were to be 24-hour call centres to handle customer problems in various languages.

A great part of the style and excitement of the site was to be generated by a stylish and thought-provoking online magazine, with an entirely independent editorial stance, contributed to by the major writers of the day. And launching in several different countries meant, of course, that most should have their own office: New York, London, Paris, Munich, Stockholm....

Grow Now, Make Profits Later

The founders of Boo.com were Ernst Malmsten and Kasja Leander. Ernst was a lover of Nordic poetry who found the excitement of organising poetry festivals at Lund University to be so great that he abandoned his studies in order to organise bigger and even more wonderful festivals. Kasja, whom Ernst had first met at kindergarten, was an ex-model who had appeared on the covers of *Vogue* and *Elle*, and who had been one of the faces of the ultra-cool fashion brand, Benetton. They became a couple, but as they began to explore their joint business interests, so their relationship cooled and developed into something that was still close, but now professional only. They were a PR agent's dream. If the intriguing Ernst and the beautiful Kasja had launched a new range of sausages, they would still have got coverage in glamorous magazines and prestigious newspapers.

Their first claim to fame had been to organise one of Ernst's beloved Nordic poetry festivals in New York City, where they were living at the time. They found sponsorship and support from Scandinavian governments and corporations, and created an event that became the talk of East Village. Flushed with success, they launched a new publishing house back home in Sweden, where they proved themselves once again to be brilliant publicists. They were, charmingly, rather surprised when their books of poetry failed to sell, and their new company found itself in financial difficulty. Further expansion in the world of publishing proved that they were high on style but low on substance: good at capturing the media's attention with lavish and expensive public events, bad at turning a profit. Nevertheless, Ernst and Kasja got venture capital funding for their publishing business.

And then they got the internet bug. With the help of further venture capitalist funding they launched an online book retailer called Bokus. However, they struggled to agree with their venture capital shareholders and could not persuade them that the new company's lack of profitability was no reason not to raise more money from an IPO. Amazon, after all, had then just recently launched a successful IPO without ever having made a profit. 'The problem was,' wrote Ernst, 'our grey-haired venture capitalist shareholders couldn't seem to get their heads around the prevailing internet logic of "grow now, make profits later."'[9] In the end, Ernst and Kasja sold their shareholdings to the giant Swedish supermarket-to-publishing cooperative KF for a handsome sum. The two youngsters were millionaires. They had launched an internet company and sold it for a good price. They had a track record. And now they had even bigger ideas.

Boo.com was to be Europe's first major internet venture, and it would take on the world. 'What we had in mind,' said Ernst, 'was a virtual hybrid of a department store like Harvey Nichols in London or Bloomingdales in New York, where the name of the store itself was as significant as anything you could buy in it. Most of the early American internet companies had sprung from the minds of technologists. All they cared about was functionality and cost.'[10] Ernst was to always keep this early insight in mind as the saga of Boo.com unfolded: he and Kasja never allowed themselves to become embroiled in issues such as functionality or cost.

A Runaway Locomotive, Fuelled by Banknotes

Though the founders of Boo.com believed differently, they didn't actually know anything about retail. Or about the internet's underlying technology. Or about project management. Or about magazine publishing. Or about business. It was the internet equivalent of planning to launch a luxury car in several different markets whilst needing to build a new and revolutionary production line from scratch, without any previous experience in the automobile industry. And then, of course, of persuading the public to buy shares in this operation before any cars had finally made it off the struggling new line and without any clear indication of how many people might actually buy them.

The whole undeniably exciting saga of Boo unfolded with astonishing speed, like a runaway locomotive fuelled not by coal but by banknotes, with young, intelligent and beautiful people – the masters of the new universe – shovelling dollar bills into the furnace with wild abandon. The founders persuaded the London office of one of the most prestigious merchant bankers in the world, J.P. Morgan, to raise their start-up capital. In the real world, you don't even get to talk to the likes of J.P. Morgan until you have a very successful business in place. But no European bank had yet staked out a major position in the internet and the global aspirations of Boo.com gave the company the potential to go big, which would put J.P. Morgan's London office at the heart of the growing internet revolution in Europe. The bank recommended raising US$100 million over 18 months, with the first round of funding completed within four months (Ernst and Kasja had imagined that funding of around US$2 million would be enough to get the company up and running).[11]

At the initial meeting, the Swedish founders had been affronted to be asked a number of tough financial and business questions by their putative bankers. 'I couldn't help feeling the bankers' toughness was an attempt to compensate for their lack of knowledge. I doubted if they had ever worked with an internet company before,' said Ernst. Their banking inquisitors also displayed their naivety by asking if the founders had done any market research. 'Market research?' gasped Ernst, disturbed and alarmed. 'That was something Colgate did before it launched a new toothpaste. The internet was something you had to feel in your fingertips.'[12]

At this stage, the young Swedes had spent many hours

agonising over the new name of 'Boo', but they had not yet actually registered the company name, nor incorporated the company. J.P. Morgan had just agreed to raise US$100 million for a company that didn't actually exist. They suggested, politely, that the incorporation of the company was a matter of some urgency.

It was decided that Boo.com would launch less than a year later, in May 1999. Speed was of the essence; the key to success was to be the first to occupy this particular piece of internet territory. The company would go public a mere six to nine months after launch. J.P. Morgan's fee was to be 7% of the hoped-for US$100 million raised. They also wanted the option to transfer their fees into shares, giving them a bigger return from the expected share sale bonanza. Then, of course, there would be their fees for the IPO itself. The company's new bankers were also about to become shareholders.

Hire Now, Ask Questions Later

As the saga of Boo began to unfold, an ominous pattern of events emerged. As investors were found to supply the seed capital for the venture, so it was quickly spent with strange priorities and to little effect. By April 1999, Boo.com had spent US$4 million, of which US$436,000 had already gone on salaries and US$586,000 on headhunters' fees. As Ernst himself said:

> If there was a catchphrase that summed up the weeks that followed the first round of funding, it was 'Hire now, ask questions later.' How many people did we actually need? More than 100 in London alone. Then there were our new offices in New York, Stockholm, Munich and Paris. It was a build-up that headhunters are probably still talking about in wistful tones.[13]

On the all-important technology front, the Boo team met with, but were unimpressed by, IBM. 'IBM in Europe had designed the website for the English retailer Sainsbury's, but hadn't done much else that I could see.' IBM also 'seemed more interested in selling us their products. Like two of their RS/6000 servers.' (As Boo finally came close to launching, they realised that they did indeed need to acquire some heavyweight servers before they could go live, which they bought from Sun, at the cost of millions of pounds, as we shall shortly see). Then, by prioritising meetings with potential fashion suppliers, the founders postponed three meetings with software giant Oracle, which finally declined to become involved with Boo unless they could provide a plan (which, of course they could not) and (which should have been easier) could demonstrate some professionalism in respecting meeting arrangements.[14] Finally, Boo teamed up with Swedish telecoms giant Ericsson, who were keen to break into internet technology and who promised to field a global team of their own people and to pull in outside expertise where necessary.

The company finally employed three different external companies to develop the all-important website. However, a newly-recruited chief technical officer failed to properly coordinate the activities of designers, e-commerce programmers and back-end database developers. A fourth technology company was tracked down when Boo realised that they needed 3-D images for an online product catalogue of around 5,000 items 'within weeks'. A small, pioneering company based in Los Angeles said they could take on the challenge. Unlike the founders of Boo, they had done their sums. In order to deliver the necessary results by the May launch deadline, they would have to take on a team of 60 people. The small company needed US$1.5 million for the task, with US$500,000 up front. Boo had no option but to agree.

The rest of the increasingly sorry saga proceeds with a sad inevitability. At every stage, prodigious amounts of money were spent in 'fire-fighting': finding immediate solutions to keep the company afloat because a complete lack of foresight and planning had resulted in some new crisis. Easily foreseeable issues landed on the founders' desks (to their astonishment) on a daily basis. The product database, for example. 'It was an enormous job,' says Ernst. 'Each product needed something like 50 pieces of descriptive information. There were such things as brand, colour and size, not to mention the prices in 18 currencies, but there were also the different search categories to which the product belonged. You could, for example, search by activity. So we had to know if a particular shoe was a hiking, running, tennis or basketball shoe.'[15] And when they finally got the information from suppliers, it had to be turned into 'Boo' language. 'Who's going to do the writing for thousands of products?' asked the assistants. 'You'll have to hire some writers,' said Ernst. 'See if you can get people from magazines like *Arena* or *Face*.' (Employing established writers from successful style magazines is not, as you may have guessed, the cheapest way of finding writing talent.) Even the relatively small Scandinavian office realised that, in order to meet the May 1999 launch deadline, they would have to create 500 translations per week. One person could achieve about 80 translations per week. More translators were needed.[16]

Miss Boo's Bad Hair Day

Ernst and Kasja's obsession with marketing and hype caused them to create a hugely valuable PR wave – at a time when the company was uncertain as to when, or even if, it would be able to launch its website. The PR was exciting, glamorous and glittering. It raised expectations to a dangerous level. Huge amounts of money were wasted in cancellation fees for postponed ad campaigns. One outdoor campaign for the launch in Sweden that could not be cancelled actually ran with the words 'Coming Soon!' inserted at the bottom of the posters. The PR campaign could not now be put back into its box; the interviews kept coming. The bold new start-up got increasingly impressive coverage in prestigious magazines and newspapers – including the *Financial Times*, who quoted Boo.com's potential valuation at US$125 million, a record for a European internet start-up.

Boo missed their launch deadline of July 1999. In August, the

Boo team were told by new technology consultants that they were in big trouble. The lack of any central control meant that several companies had been tinkering with the site at will, adding bits here and there. No central core had been steadily tested, documented and then developed further. The system was riddled with bugs. The three core databases weren't talking to each other; there was no overall view of content. Customers were unlikely to be able to buy anything, or were likely to receive the wrong product if they succeeded in making a purchase. A staffer given the role of launch manager drew up a list of 10,000 tasks that needed to be accomplished.

In August 1999 the founders gathered the London employees at the Café Royal in London's Regent Street, just a short walk from the company's now cramped Carnaby Street offices and, without any apparent sense of irony, announced 'Project Launch'. They aimed to launch on 1 November 1999 – 'And this time we're going to stick to it.'[17]

Boo was now burning money at the rate of US$10 million a month. The money they had raised had been meant to last until mid-October, by which time the website would, in principle, have been up and running and generating some income. Now they needed another US$12 million just to survive until the November launch. They decided to raise US$15 million. J.P. Morgan advised them not to open another investment round, but to go back to the previous investors. The team were upset to discover that the company valuation used for the continuation investment round would not change (higher valuations had been dangled in front of the founders' eyes by other bankers). J.P. Morgan reminded the crestfallen team that the situation had deteriorated since the previous round. They were lucky the valuation wasn't going down.

Boo found a new chief technical officer to replace their original man. 'Launch-critical' activities began in earnest. The company now had 4,000 products sitting in its warehouses, but database problems were such that only 100 or so of these could be successfully ordered via the website. A team of 50 (including some new technical recruits) set to work sifting through the thousands of product entries, reconciling differences and sorting technical issues.

The founders, however, had more pressing concerns: the website's virtual shop assistant, Miss Boo. Was she cool enough, or even too cool? Did she say cool things? Was she the right age? Most worryingly, was her hair right? A journalist was flown over from New York to work on Miss Boo's script. A top Hollywood hair stylist was flown over to London to 'get to know' Miss Boo, and then flown back to America to work with the 3-D graphics designer on her new hair look. This turned out to be striped red and black, with four upright corkscrew curls on top. Kasja didn't like it, so they went back to a fringe and ponytail. 'There was a frustrating sense of having expended huge energy to get hardly any distance at all,' says Ernst.[18]

Soft Launch, Hard Landing

As the launch date approached, it became clear that the site, which was at least beginning to function, was running horribly slowly: all of the things that were supposed to create such a unique shopping experience – the graphics, animation and sound, to say nothing of the multi-language, multiple-option database – were slowing things down. And this was before the site was being asked to handle the expected tens of thousands of simultaneous users once it went live. The quick fix was to buy five more Sun servers at a cost of almost £1 million. That didn't work well enough, so they bought the biggest machine that Sun had – the 'Starfire' – which handled 64 processors and cost £1.3 million. The floors of the data-handling centre in London's Docklands had to be assessed by Sun surveyors to ensure that they could hold the monster's weight.[19]

In October, the team achieved a 'soft' launch, opening the site to employees and suppliers and inviting feedback. The fully staffed call centres, which for many months had been filling their time with training, were finally able to answer calls and emails and to report back on users' experiences of the site.

On 3 November 1999, Boo.com opened for business to the world. In the headiest of heady days, there had been talk of the site attracting one million users on Day One. In the event, it attracted 50,000. The rush to launch had unfortunately introduced a bug that blocked the purchase path for Apple users – which included most journalists. One journalist spent 81 minutes trying to order a pair of shoes, and only succeeded after ringing the call centre several times. He was not impressed.[20]

Boo was not a complete failure. The website began to make sales; orders were fulfilled. But the profligate early spending meant that nothing remained to plug the gap left by the disappointing revenues. In early 2000, J.P. Morgan postponed the planned IPO; the market was beginning to cool, Boo's revenues were too low and its burn rate was still too high; institutional investors, in a new mood of cautiousness, were not prepared to buy in. A drastic cost-cutting plan was, finally, put in place. Staff numbers were reduced radically, customer service teams were scaled back, local offices were streamlined. The magazine was abandoned – which proved almost too much for Kasja, who threatened to resign. Without the magazine, she wailed, Boo was 'just a place to sell stuff'.[21]

The Nasdaq technology index reached a peak on 10 March 2000 and soon began to slide. On 14 April, the index lost 10%, or 355 points. On 18 May, Boo.com was liquidated. The company had burned through US$135 million in 18 months. At the very end, Ernst and Kasja hit the phones trying to raise a mere US$20 million by midnight. They were incredulous that it should have come to this: sales, after all, were on target for US$1 million per month, well up from US$1.1 million in the company's first trading quarter. They had a 'healthy, thriving business'.[22] Well, they would have, if they had not managed to spend all of the US$135 million of investment to arrive at that point at exactly the time when investor confidence was beginning to drain away from the dot-com boom.

Many lessons were learned during the technology boom, and some of these – at great expense to investors large and small – will have benefited business and society as a whole by taking us through a steep learning curve at an incredible pace. Ernst Malmsten has recently returned to high-end retail: he is now the chief executive of luxury goods company Lara Bohinc. 'This time we have done it by the book, step-by-step,' says Ernst. 'The internet was new back then: we were the pioneers. Today the technology is so accessible – lots of things are free on the internet and open-source. We have spent maybe £10,000 on the website. Back in the Boo days, I'm a bit embarrassed, we spent £30m.'[23]

Well, Ernst, it was a rush, in every sense. We all joined in. We were all blindsided.

2 BUBBLES AND CRASHES

A good market is a marvellous thing. A market is a celebration of the earth's riches and of mankind's husbandry and ingenuity. The very existence of markets has allowed us to lift ourselves above subsistence and has paved the way for the one human activity that, more than any other, has been the driver of our progress towards civilisation: trade. If you have an abundance of peaches and cherries but you don't keep livestock, you can take your fruit to the market and return with a leg of lamb for supper. We've been doing it for millennia, and it is of fundamental importance to human society. As William J. Bernstein wrote in *A Splendid Exchange*, about the history of global trade:

> World trade has yielded not only a bounty of material goods, but also of intellectual and cultural capital, an understanding of our neighbours, and a desire to sell things to others rather than annihilate them.[1]

Trade has been the driving force for the exchange of goods and ideas since the earliest times: the export of stone axe and adze blades from the Balkans to the Black Sea and the Baltic around 7,000 years ago; the silk trade between China and the West, beginning during the Han Dynasty around 2,000 years ago; manufactured goods of every kind from the factories of Britain to much of the rest of the world at the dawn of the Industrial Revolution a few hundred years ago. With this trade in goods have come ideas, technologies and religions, and it has been in the great markets of the world that this real and intellectual capital has been exchanged.

To Market, To Market

The thing about markets is their remarkable reactivity. Prices change very quickly. They change, obviously, based on those immutable laws of supply and demand: if there is a glut of silk, the price of silk falls. If there is a shortage, the price rises. Market prices also change on the basis of *information:* the price of silk may rise if there is the expectation of a shortage in the supply of silk, or fall if there is the expectation of a shortage in potential buyers for silk (as the Roman Empire began to collapse, for example). As Bernstein reminds us, even in the earliest days of trade, the intrepid merchant, having endured great hardship and been fortunate enough to survive the great perils of an arduous journey across oceans or deserts, could still face 'ruin ... at the hands of a fickle marketplace' because 'prices were wildly unpredictable.'[2]

Ever since traders first took their goods to market and were disappointed (or delighted) by the price offered for their wares, the ability to predict market movements has been an obsession. A millennium or two has passed, and a lot of very clever people have spent a lot of time studying market movements. Some interesting ideas have emerged, along with a very clear understanding of why it is (virtually) impossible to beat the market, but nobody has found a way to predict the market. Indeed, in a slightly perverse way, the unpredictability of markets has been taken as a proof of the infallibility of markets. You can't beat the market, runs the argument of many modern economists, because the market is cleverer than you; and the reason that the market is cleverer than you is that the market price, in a large and sophisticated market, is arrived at via the informed judgements of perhaps hundreds of thousands of individual buyers and sellers.

This developing belief in the infallibility of markets began to lead us into some rather strange intellectual places, the end result of which was a number of cases where we were very effectively (and painfully) blindsided by various stock market crashes; meanwhile the true believers in the rationality of markets argued that (a) they had been perfectly right in saying that the market prices just before each crash did in fact reflect the correct price for the stocks quoted on the market at that time and that (b) the crash was merely 'an adjustment' (probably caused by some foolish actions taken by governments that had disturbed the free action of the market) and that we shouldn't make such a big fuss about it. The theory, after all, was right, and mere inconveniences like the Great Depression should not be allowed to disturb our belief in the theory. At which point you might very well, like me, begin to wonder if the theory is actually very much use.

The Rational Market

The rational-market argument is more subtle than it might seem at first glance. According to this new economic orthodoxy, which is known as the 'efficient-market hypothesis', the market price does not merely reflect all of the informed judgements of large numbers of buyers and sellers: all of these judgements might, after all, be wrong or, more likely, and as seems to happen often in real life, to be coloured by unreasonable optimism or pessimism. The efficient market hypothesis takes us way beyond the notion that a market price is an extremely good indication of what a large number of people feel to be the right price for any particular asset. The problem word in that last sentence, for efficient-market economists, would be the word 'feel'. There is no room in their world for the feelings of the individual players in any market, because this would imply that markets were at the whim of people's emotions. Economic theory is based on the assumption that everyone involved in a market is a 'rational agent'.

What is truly strange is that efficient-market economists have developed mathematical models of great subtlety and complexity which argue that the market is, in a rather mystical kind of way, a kind of hyper-rational entity that absorbs and reflects all known information about the assets that are being traded and reflects all of that information in the price – the 'correct' price. Oh, by the way, you can't predict where the market will be at any point in time because market prices fluctuate randomly around the 'inherent' price – and you can never know at any point in time where the price is on this unpredictable journey around its correct level.

Which for me rather spoils all of the glorious and supposedly scientific theorising about how markets work. The test of any scientific theory is, after all, not whether it successfully describes a system, but whether you can make predictions about the future based on that theory. The 'random walk' theory of market behaviour takes it as a fundamental principle that market trading results in an essentially random distribution of prices around the elusive 'inherent value' of the assets in question, which means that it is impossible to predict what the state of the market will be at any point in time. Otherwise, one would be able to beat the market, which is impossible. So the efficient-market hypothesis may or may not be a perfect description of how markets work (it isn't, but we'll get to that later). But even if it was, it wouldn't be much use to anybody. All we seem able to do is watch the enigmatic movements of the market with awe and wonder, muttering, from time to time, 'It's amazing!' or, 'Who would have expected that?' or similar ineffectual sentiments.

You may have noticed that I managed to use the words 'mathematical', 'rational' and 'mystical' in the same sentence in the previous paragraphs. This may be because the higher realms of mathematics (which is an entirely rational activity) enter into some surprisingly mystical realms (or so I am told), or it may be that the use of complex mathematical models has blindsided economists to the fact that human beings' behaviour has never yet proved reducible to mathematical equations. There are clever statistical things that one can do – as with actuarial models, for example – that deliver a good approximation of whether people will die of diseases, fall out of trees or kill themselves with petrol-driven gardening implements, but these approximations are based on large amounts of data about the rate at which people have died from diseases or killed themselves with petrol-driven garden implements, et cetera, in the past.

A complex system like a financial market, which depends on the interactions of thousands, or hundreds of thousands of people, constantly reacting to shifts in available information and (dare one say it?) sentiment, is unlikely to be capable of being reduced to mathematical formulae. The fact that economists believed they had acquired such a magical formula is, perhaps, at the heart of the reason why they also acquired such a mystical belief in their theory's power. The theory was *right* – in the way in which religious dogma is believed to be right – and the world should therefore be changed to fit the dogma, rather than the other way round. As Paul Krugman, economist and efficient-market sceptic wrote in his *New York Times* column in 2009:

> Unfortunately, this romanticized and sanitized vision of the economy led most economists to ignore all the things that can go wrong. They turned a blind eye to the limitations of human rationality that often lead to bubbles and busts; to the problems of institutions that run amok; to the imperfections of markets – especially financial markets – that can cause the economy's operating system to undergo sudden, unpredictable crashes; and to the dangers created when regulators don't believe in regulation.[3]

Ah, regulation. All of this debate about efficient markets would not be so important if adherents of the efficient-market hypothesis had not argued so fiercely that the perfection of markets led inexorably to the conclusion that all regulation was a bad thing. Markets should be – must be – left to do what it is that they magically do, or else the magic will be ruined. Which rather glosses over the unfortunate fact that markets, when left alone, repeatedly boom and crash.

A Never-Ending Cycle

There have always been bubbles and crashes. History has surely now proven that economies move in cycles of boom and bust. Nevertheless, when good times arrive, we persuade ourselves that the good times are here to stay. There is some clear reason, we are certain, why this time it will not all end in tears: we have learned more; our financial systems are more sophisticated; the information technology revolution means that we know everything that we need to know in order to make fully-informed and rational decisions. Markets themselves are rational and brilliantly sophisticated mechanisms that ensure that every asset will be priced at its correct value – it is impossible for the markets to ascribe an inflated value to any asset. This last statement may well, in fact, true – but only in the long term.

In the short and even medium term, because we are acquisitive, competitive, jealous and greedy – in short, because we are human – we will from time to time be swept away in some bout of speculative madness. As historian, investment banker and journalist Edward Chancellor, author of *Devil Take the Hindmost,* writes: 'Speculation never changes, because human nature remains the same.' He quotes the eighteenth-century philosopher and moralist David Hume: 'Avarice, or the desire of gain, is a universal passion which operates at all times, in all places, and upon all persons.' And to this most basic of human emotions, Chancellor adds other contributing factors: 'the fear of loss, emulation of one's neighbour, the credulity of the crowd, and the psychology of gambling'. Taken together he argues, all of these oh-so-human factors 'explain why all great speculative events seem to repeat themselves'.[4]

In another book on the same theme, *This Time Is Different*, economists Carmen Reinhart and Kenneth Rogoff assemble an overwhelming body of historical statistical evidence about financial crises over the ages. Having studied the financial booms and crashes of nearly a millennium, the economists' conclusion is stark: 'Each time, society convinces itself that the current boom, unlike the many booms that preceded catastrophic collapses in the past, is built on sound fundamentals, structural reforms, technological innovation and good policy.'[5] Reinhart and Rogoff's recipe for disaster is alarmingly simple: the taking on of excessive debt, especially government debt, in good times, invariably precedes and exacerbates the inevitable crash, while people simultaneously persuade themselves and others that there are compelling reasons why 'this time is different'.

A Licence to Print Money

Speculative 'bubbles' in which assets of various kinds are traded up by increasingly frenzied buying and selling are the frequent companions of economic booms – though it is quite possible to have a speculative bubble even when a country is in the middle of an economic crisis.

In eighteenth-century France, for example, the death of Louis XIV (the great 'Sun King' and creator of the Palace of Versailles) left France on the verge of bankruptcy, partly as a result of his palace-building habit, but also because of the incessant wars he fought with his European rivals. Louis outlived his immediate descendants, so that his great-grandson became Louis XV at the age of five, and France was ruled on behalf of young Louis by a Regent, the Duke of Orleans, who took quick recourse to the staple financial remedy of European monarchs, and debased the currency – replacing all gold and silver coinage with reissued coins containing 20% less metal.

By chance, the Duke had made the acquaintance of a charming and intelligent Scotsman called John Law, whose understanding of the mathematics of probability had brought him some success at the card tables, which provided his income for many years after he fled England, having had the misfortune of killing the husband of a lady of his acquaintance in a duel. Law was an early advocate of the benefit of paper currencies: he had realised, correctly, that money was a medium of exchange, and not something that needed to have an intrinsic value of its own. He did, however, grasp that currency needed to be underpinned by something real. (He had been an unsuccessful proponent of 'land banks' – national banks that would issue paper currency with a value backed by the value of state-owned lands.)

He gave the Duke – his old acquaintance from the card tables of high society – two papers that argued the benefits of a paper currency and the extension of credit to stimulate commerce. The Duke of Orleans was intrigued by this opportunity to break free from the shackles of precious metal, of which France at the time had precious little. In 1716, Law was granted the right to open a bank, three-quarters of the capital for which was provided by government *billets d'état* (securities issued by the state). Law had quite rightly seen that 'currency' could encompass coinage, paper money, credit notes, bonds and other promissory notes. He quickly established his bank's credentials by offering payment for his bank notes on demand and in the coinage current at the time they were issued. This was a masterstroke – Law's notes now held their value better than the nation's frequently debased coinage: new silver coins might be lighter and less valuable than the old; Law's notes would buy back the old coins.

Law's remedy worked: trade picked up, tax revenues improved. Law then started up a company – the Mississippi Company – to trade with the French territory of Louisiana in America (the whole of the Mississippi basin had been claimed for France by the explorer, La Salle, and the territory had been called 'Louisiana' in honour of Louis XIV). The new company was granted exclusive rights to trade with the territory, which was imagined to be rich in precious metals and other valuable raw materials. Shares in the Mississippi Company could be bought with *billets d'état* at their face value, even though these were actually trading at a fraction of that value – meaning that shares in the new company could be bought at a discount, and that people could invest their rapidly devaluing state bills at face value in a hopeful (and state-sponsored) new venture.

Both bank and company prospered. Their success in stimulating the economy and in collecting taxes led the Prince Regent to bring together the company and the bank into a new entity – the Royal Bank of France. To the Mississippi Company were later added the French East India Company and the China Company. The expanded company took over the national debt, the collection of all taxes and the minting of all coins.[6] (Using a private company to collect taxes may seem surprising, but France had long used the ancient Roman practice of collecting taxes via licensed 'tax farmers' or 'farmers-general'; these individuals, understandably, had come to be widely hated under the heavy tax regime of the spendthrift Louis XIV.)

In the early days of his bank, Law had declared that 'a banker deserved death if he made issues without having sufficient security to answer all demands'.[7] Sadly, the all-powerful Prince Regent realised very quickly that the new Royal Bank was, to use a modern phrase, a license to print money – which he began to do, with gusto. Law himself may have protested, but to no effect. Law soon issued further shares in the Mississippi Company, offering a dividend of 200 livres (the old French pound) for each 500-livre share. Since the shares could again be bought with *billets d'état* at their face value, the effective rate of dividend was well over 100%. Not surprisingly, demand for the shares soared. As the nineteenth-century journalist Charles Mackay wrote in his best-selling *Extraordinary Popular Delusions and the Madness of Crowds*:

> At least 300,000 applications were made for the 50,000 new shares, and Law's house in the Rue de Quincampoix was beset from morning to night with eager applicants. As it was impossible to satisfy them all, it was several weeks before a list of the fortunate new stockholders could be made out, during which time the public impatience rose to a pitch of frenzy. Dukes, marquises, counts, with their duchesses, marchionesses, and countesses, waited in the streets for hours of every day before Mr Law's door to know the result.... Every day the value of the old shares increased, and the fresh applications, induced by the golden dreams of the whole nation, became so numerous that it was deemed advisory to issue no less than 300,000 new shares, at 5,000 livres each, in order that the regent might take advantage of the popular enthusiasm to pay off the national debt.[8]

House of Cards

A little mental arithmetic shows that this new share issue alone would call for a sum of 1.5 billion livres from the French public. Law began printing money to provide loans to supply the necessary cash. This was his fatal mistake. 'Law's great error was his confusion of shares with money,' points out Chancellor. 'Since rising share prices led to the printing of more money, which in turn was ploughed back into shares, there was no potential limit to the ensuing asset inflation.'[9] It was during this boom that the term 'millionaire' was invented.

The whole edifice, of course, came tumbling down. One enemy of Law's, the Prince de Conti, upset because he had been refused a new issue of stocks, demanded that Law's bank convert such a vast number of his banknotes into cash that three wagons were needed to take home the resultant coinage. It was fortunate for Law that the medium of television had not yet been invented in order to make this spectacle available to a wider audience, but the risk of a run on the bank was clear. Law appealed to the Regent, who made the unpopular prince return two-thirds of the cash, and the event was seen as no more than a piece of malicious and petulant behaviour.

Some canny speculators, however, began to encash their paper wealth in less ostentatious amounts, and to secrete away coinage, or to convert it into jewellery, plate and the other valuables. Some moved wagon-loads of goods quietly over the borders to Holland, Belgium or England. One enterprising stockjobber disguised himself as a peasant and carted one million livres of coin, hidden beneath a load of manure, across the border to Belgium, from whence he quietly moved his fortune on to Amsterdam.[10]

Very soon, a popular run on the bank began in earnest. Heavy-handed legislation forbade citizens from having more than a certain amount of coin in their homes, or to buy jewellery or other valuables, on pain of fines and confiscation. Informers were encouraged to tell tales on their neighbours for a percentage of the fine. Ordinary citizens found themselves on the wrong side of the law for having a few gold coins in their purses. There was rioting in the streets. France teetered on the edge of revolt.

The attempt to introduce a paper currency through the over-printing of banknotes and the 'fatal flaw' of linking money to the value of shares ended in utter failure. Law was forced to flee Paris, disguised as a woman. He seems to have been, within his limits, an honourable man: he had made no attempt to smuggle his money out of France and had invested his one-time fortune in French landholdings, which he abandoned on leaving the country. In his farewell to his benefactor, the Prince Regent, he said: 'I confess that I have committed many faults. I committed them because I am a man, and all men are liable to error; but I declare to you most solemnly that none of them proceeded from wicked or dishonest motives, and that nothing of the sort will be found in the whole course of my conduct.'[11] He died in Venice, in 1729, in relative poverty.

A Very Big Baburu

Many key elements of this eighteenth-century French bubble and other early financial bubbles have recrudesced in subsequent crashes. The Japanese bubble economy of the 1980s, for example, exhibited several striking similarities, in particular the existence of a number of dangerously 'circular' share-based arrangements.

In the 1980s, Japan's ministry of finance allowed Japanese corporations to enhance their ordinary earnings with profits derived from speculation. This concept was called *zaitech* – a word meaning 'financial engineering' or 'financial technology'. The term is derived from the Japanese words *zaimu* (financial dealings) and *tekunorojii* (the charming Japanese adaptation of 'technology'). The Japanese also developed their own delightful word for 'bubble': *baburu*.

Zaitech not only allowed Japanese companies to show profits from speculation on their bottom line, it also exempted them from capital gains tax on those profits. To make matters worse, the ministry had also given Japanese corporations the right to issue 'warrant bonds' in the Eurobond market. These bonds not only represented the usual loan secured against the issuing company at an interest rate that reflects the market's assessment of the company's financial security, they also included an option ('warrant') to buy shares in the company at a fixed price at some later time. Since shares in Japanese companies were rising strongly at the time, this made the warrant bonds very attractive: they could be offered at very low interest rates. As a result, Japanese companies were able to raise money cheaply on the international market in order to fund speculative investments. These *zaitech* investments increased the profitability of the companies concerned, raising their share price. This raised the value of their warrant bonds, which helped them raise more money that could be invested in further *zaitech* activities....

Another disturbingly circular arrangement was inadvertently created by the international financial community with the Basel Agreement of 1987. Because Japanese banks were guaranteed by the Japanese government, they were able to operate with lower levels of capital than their international competitors. To level the playing field, it was agreed at Basel that Japanese banks would raise their loan-capital ratio to the more internationally typical rate of 8%. A distinctive characteristic of the Japanese financial system is the number of cross-shareholdings that most major companies have with each other, Japanese banks being no exception. As a concession, it was agreed that Japanese banks could count a proportion of the profits from these shareholdings in other companies towards their capital. The amount of money that Japanese banks could lend was now linked to the (rising) values of their outside shareholdings which, on a relatively small island, were also increasingly tied to the value of land and property that companies owned. As the banks lent money to property developers and businesses, the price of land and shares rose, and the amount that the banks could lend rose with it. What could possibly happen next?

When this particular bubble burst – slowly rather than dramatically, but very painfully, after the ministry of finance raised interest rates in recognition that the boom was unsustainable – banks and securities brokerages failed. As the stock market fell, so the banks' shareholdings in other companies became a liability, rather than an asset. Loans made by banks proved to be riskier than originally imagined. In 1998, it was estimated that Japanese banks had lost ¥5 trillion (US$38 billion) on the value of cross-shareholdings and that bad loans in the banking system still amounted to perhaps ¥150 trillion (US$1.1 trillion), despite massive write-offs before that date.[12] The country began to experience a credit crunch as investment capital dried up; savers fled from the stock market and invested their savings in low-interest cash accounts.

Japan's 'lost decade' had begun.

If the Price is Right…

It was in the late nineteenth and early twentieth centuries that people – and economists in particular – began to become interested in the workings of financial markets. The world was becoming rapidly wealthier, and that wealth was increasingly being 'managed' by the great financial markets. Whereas in ancient times capital could only be got from merchants or moneylenders or from banks (beginning with the great bankers of Renaissance Italy), corporations could now raise money by offering their bonds or stocks to a much wider range of people, culminating, in recent history, with the raising of huge amounts of capital from initial public offerings (IPOs), which raise money from, in effect, the general public, or from the people who manage the general public's money. The vital question thus became, for a growing number of people, whether the price that they had paid for their new assets, their bonds or shares, was the right price.

At the outset, it was bonds that were bought and sold. Bonds were the means by which governments and corporations raised money: they paid variable rates of return, which reflected the likelihood that the lender (the corporation or government) would still be around at the end of the period of the loan in order to hand back the capital. Once bonds had been issued, changing financial circumstances would mean that their likely worth to the holder would be more or less advantageous in the existing conditions, and so bonds would change hands at varying prices. Because bonds paid fixed rates of interest, an investor could make a relatively good estimation as to whether these represented a good or a poor use of his capital.

Company stocks, on the other hand, were seen as being a far more uncertain purchase: the amount of dividend that a company chose to pay depended on its fluctuating fortunes, and the future earnings from any particular stock were seen as being very difficult to estimate. Dealing in stocks, in the early twentieth century, was seen as a highly speculative activity.

However, a brilliant mathematician and economist called Irving Fisher realised that these differences were best seen merely as differences of degree rather than of principle. A bond issuer, for example, could go bust and never repay the capital. Different levels of inflation could eat into a bond's interest rate to varying and unpredictable degrees. The uncertainty surrounding the future earnings from the dividends on a share-holding were merely a different level of uncertainty. It was perfectly possible to create a formula that would estimate the likelihood of a dividend under- or over-performing the commonly expected level of payment.[13] The purchase of company stocks should therefore be put onto the same mathematical footing as the purchase of bonds – and market analysts were just beginning to discover that, over time, stocks were outperforming bonds. The age of the mathematical analysis of stock markets had dawned.

Oscillations Around a State of Equilibrium

Irving was undoubtedly a great economist, and his mathematical approach to financial markets influenced a future generation of 'neo-classical' economists (whose thinking had evolved from the 'classical' economic theories developed in the eighteenth and nineteenth centuries by people such Adam Smith, David Ricardo, John Stuart Mill and Thomas Malthus). The neo-classicists made certain key assumptions, which underpinned the increasingly mathematical work of the movement in the twentieth and twenty-first centuries.

It was assumed that people made rational decisions in their purchases, based on the 'utility' of what they were buying (for corporations, personal 'utility' is replaced by corporate profits – companies do things if they believe this will increase their profits), and that they acted independently and on the basis of full information. Fisher's doctoral thesis had dealt with one of the core beliefs of the utilitarian model of economics: that all of the various pushes and pulls of the marketplace are merely oscillations around a state of equilibrium, which represents the appropriate, the *rational,* price for any particular asset.[14]

This is all interesting stuff – though it led some intelligent people into some very strange intellectual places – and it is worth remembering that Irving Fisher, one of the founding fathers of neo-classical economic thinking, lost all of his money in the stock market crash of 1929. I don't want to bang on about this, but I think it does remind us that it is quite useful if theories of any kind actually stand up to being tested in the real world. Fisher, whose economic theories could be said to be in their infancy, completely miscalled the crash of 1929. This would not matter so much if the school of economic thought that Fisher effectively founded was not, to this day, trying to persuade us that inconveniences such as the Great Depression do not in fact throw any doubt on the general correctness of their economic theories.[15]

Despite the compelling examples from history of the wild, unpredictable and apparently irrational fluctuations in the value of markets of every kind, efficient-market economists managed to persuade themselves and others that markets had the remarkable ability to ensure that the price of any asset traded in a sophisticated market was, in fact, correct. Here's how the argument runs.

The decision to buy a share in a corporation is, in principle, a rational decision based on the expected future returns from that investment. Based on the assumption that everyone knows all of the relevant facts about that corporation's hopes of prospering in its chosen market, not only will the laws of supply and demand tend quickly to reach an agreement about the correct value of that share, but the very fact of trading – of the buying and selling of shares – will exert its own remarkable force on the price of that share.

Supposing, for example, that some investors had information that suggested strongly that the corporation's prospects were not as rosy as most people had hoped, or, conversely, that some expected event would greatly improve those prospects. Those investors would then sell the overvalued shares or buy the undervalued shares, and in the process of doing this they would move the share to a new level that reflected the new information.

Taken to its logical conclusion, this constant process, repeated in a large and sophisticated market thousands of times per day, would mean that, in effect, the price of an asset fully reflects all of the available information about that asset.

It is a seductive argument. But if the price is right one day (and contains every piece of information that is relevant to that price), how can it be that we all wake up the next day and find that the price was very wrong – that a bubble has burst? 'Ah ha', say the economists, 'your thinking is too short-term; this is merely a necessary adjustment. Over a period of time, you will find that the price has returned to its intrinsic value.' Unfortunately, that period of time (as with the Great Depression) might be inconveniently long.

And what does this mean for real-life investors? If we can never know whether we are in a bubble and that a sudden 'adjustment' might be about to take place, when can an investor know that the price that the market is offering at any point in time is, indeed, the 'intrinsic value' of the item? How does this help individuals and companies to make the correct investment decision, which is what the adherents of this 'efficient-market hypothesis' argue is what markets so helpfully do? How – since markets are apparently so astonishingly efficient that we can be certain that the prices we are being offered represent the correct price – can there even *be* bubbles and crashes? 'How come,' an unlucky investor might reasonably complain, 'I have just lost all of my money?'

At the same time that the efficient-market hypothesis was being accepted by economists, politicians, company executives and bankers around the world, some economists were pointing out interesting discrepancies which seemed to prove, at a more mundane level than the quantum physics-level mathematics that the efficient-marketers used to 'prove' their theorems, that investors did not always make decisions based on a rational assessment of the returns from that investment. Individuals' decisions were sometimes influenced to a considerable extent by the decisions of others, something which is simply ruled out by the efficient-market theory as being impossible: even if many people act irrationally in this way and value an asset wrongly, a speculator somewhere will step in to take advantage of this wrong valuation and bring the market back to its correct value.

Drift, Momentum and Irrationality

Let's look at some examples that were being explored, even as efficient-market thinkers protested that these were minor aberrations that the master theory would soon find an explanation for, rather than being a fundamental proof that the 'rational agent' assumption at the heart of the theory was fatally flawed.

One of the ways in which the market could be shown not to be efficient was that it clearly was not the case that information was 'instantly' absorbed by the market and reflected in prices. The market could, in fact, be a little slow to absorb some new information. The phenomenon was well-enough documented to acquire its own terminology: when companies issued earnings statements that differed significantly from general expectations, it would take some time for the stock price to fully reflect this new information, and this became known as 'earnings surprise' or 'earnings drift'. If these effects were real (which they clearly were), then even though the prices later returned to their correct equilibrium, the changes indicated that complete information is not fully reflected in prices *at any particular moment in time.* Rather, it proves, if accepted, that at any particular moment, prices might be wrong and stocks over- or under-valued (which was supposed to be impossible).

Then there were demonstrable examples where human psychology, rather than reason, could be shown to be affecting prices. Some economists demonstrated that if a particular stock was moving up or down in price, it was more likely to continue in that direction than not. This would prove that prices do not, in fact, move entirely randomly; that over a certain period of time, one might successfully bet that a price would keep moving in a particular direction – something that traders try to exploit in the real world, and which is known as 'momentum trading'.[16] This phenomenon indicates that market prices do not, in fact, move randomly – there are short-lived but real patterns in stock prices that reflect human hopes and fears (all such patterns are meant to be illusory – many are.)

Then there were some much longer-term effects, which were also entirely psychological in the sense that they seemed to demonstrate that investors (that is to say, 'the market') had a memory of events that was affecting their 'rational' assessment of value – something, again, that was supposed to be impossible. Economists looked at companies that had in the past been affected by some dramatic effect that had pushed their share price significantly higher or lower. The researchers showed that portfolios of 'loser' companies tended to outperform the market over the next three years while the 'winner' companies tended to underperform against the market.[17] This would suggest that the market, rather than fully reflecting prices at any moment in time, had a memory – and, quite frankly, was being a little 'sentimental' about prices: 'That company's share price took a real hammering a few years back,' the market seemed to be saying, 'so I reckon it's price is still on the low side.' Or, 'That stock went through the roof a while ago; no way is it still worth that kind of money!' The efficient-market theory could cope with that line of reasoning if it was, indeed, quickly bringing the price to its correct 'inherent value', but the fact that significant numbers of companies in this situation were under- or over-performing the market over a long period of time demonstrated that something else was going on: 'market sentiment' would seem to be real.

Then there was the fact that markets were not affected by thousands of entirely individual agents: significant amounts of trading were done by money managers, with huge sums of investors' money at their disposal. And these managers had a slightly different agenda from the individual punter: they wanted not only to make money, but to be seen to be making money. More than that, whereas the classic arbitrageur would make money by being contrarian – by spotting that a certain price was wrong, and exploiting that wrong valuation in a way that would tend to bring the price back to its correct value – money managers had a vested interest in 'going with the crowd'. The worst thing for a money manager was to be down more than the market. If the whole market was down, it was pretty easy to write the letter to investors that begins, 'This has been a particularly difficult quarter....' The letter that they do not want to have to write is the one that begins, 'This has been a particularly strong quarter for the markets in general. Sadly...'

This resulted in another well-documented example of irrational behaviour exhibited by money managers, which was sufficiently well-recognised to have acquired its own name: 'window dressing'. In 1991, a study of 769 pension funds demonstrated that there was a real tendency for money managers to sell poorly performing stocks near the end of each quarter, and particularly at the end of the year – which just happen to be the times when pension funds look most closely at the performance of their money managers, who don't want to be seen to be holding badly-performing stocks. This behaviour was entirely rational, seen from the perspective of a money manager who would like to hang on to his or her job, but it is not behaviour that follows the rational dictates of the efficient-market theory.

The phenomenon had been identified by the great British economist John Maynard Keynes back in the 1930s: he knew that the successful investor had to spot what the market had missed, otherwise he or she would simply achieve the same results as the market as a whole. As a result, 'it is in the essence of his behaviour,' wrote Keynes, 'that he should be eccentric, unconventional and rash in the eyes of average opinion'. This would not go down well with the committee charged with monitoring the long-term performance of the managers. As a result, said Keynes, money managers' behaviour would never be 'rational' in the desired sense.[18] There are a couple of other, seemingly simplistic, arguments, framed by the economists and efficient-market sceptics, Sanford Grossman and Joseph Stiglitz. Both of these questions remind me of the little boy in the fairy tale who calls out, 'But the emperor's got no clothes!' The first is this: If the efficiency of the market means that all of the available information is reflected in the price of any asset, and that the price of that asset is, as a result, correct, why does anybody trade?[19] If we are all agreed that this price is the correct price, what reason could anyone have (in the absence of any new information) to sell today and buy tomorrow?

The second killer question is this: If the market price reflects all available information, then why do people spend money gathering more, 'private' information?[20] The strong version of the efficient-market hypothesis insists that any information known by anyone anywhere must be reflected in the price (otherwise that person would make a killing by exploiting that information). But people do, in fact, spend a great deal of money acquiring information that they believe will help them make money on the stock market. And the efficient-market hypothesis itself argues that they wouldn't do that if it was a waste of money.... It's one of those delightful *reductio ad absurdum* arguments that can fatally undermine the most elegant of theories.

Irrational Exuberance

Alan Greenspan, chairman of the United States Federal Reserve from 1987 to 2006, argued in June 1999 that 'bubbles generally are perceptible only after the fact. To spot a bubble in advance requires a judgment that hundreds of thousands of investors have it all wrong. Betting against markets is usually precarious at best'.[21]

This statement, in the language of 'efficient markets', means something like this: 'It may very well look to you, or even to me, that markets are currently undergoing a "bubble" in prices, but for us to make that judgement would call into question the current valuation of the market itself, which would be foolish.' Yet Greenspan himself inadvertently created the modern definition of a stock market bubble: 'irrational exuberance'. His point, presumably, was that since stock market prices are dictated by the essentially rational decisions of myriads of investors, the only possible explanation for an overvaluation of stock market prices would be a mood of unjustified optimism. This is supposed to have been proven to be impossible by the efficient-market theorists: if any speculator sensed that there was indeed a mood of irrational exuberance, then they would sell shares and bring prices back to reality.

Intriguingly, when Greenspan uttered these words, in an after-dinner speech titled, 'The Challenge of Central Banking in a Democratic Society', given to the American Enterprise Institute in 1996, the stock market in Tokyo, which was still open, fell by 3% before he had even finished speaking, followed by similar falls in the Hong Kong, Frankfurt, London and New York markets as they opened for business.[22] If you were an advocate of the efficient-market theory, you could try to argue that this 'new information' introduced by the chairman of the Federal Reserve (as in, 'Oh no, Greenspan says we are in a period of irrational exuberance!') would cause this mini stock market crash as the market absorbed that information and adjusted itself to a new level. But if you were a truly committed efficient-marketer, you would have to confess that this opinion ('we are being irrationally exuberant') was not real information and could not affect the market, since the market had already come to its own opinion about the 'correct' price of shares. But if you were an efficient-market sceptic, as I am, you might think that investors thought, 'Greenspan thinks the market is overvalued. He knows his stuff. Time to sell!'

There is an intriguing psychological experiment that throws considerable doubt on Alan Greenspan's statement regarding the basic principle of the efficient-market hypothesis – that 'hundreds of thousands of investors [can't be] wrong.' This statement relies on the notion of 'the wisdom of crowds' – the idea that one person's valuation of the appropriate price of an asset may well be wrong, but that the pooled opinions of large numbers of people will inevitably be right. Unfortunately, a very simple experiment showed that the reverse is actually true *once those opinions are in the public arena.* Here's how the experiment worked:

> The researchers gathered 144 Swiss college students, sat them in isolated cubicles, and then asked them to answer various questions, such as the number of new immigrants living in Zurich. In many instances, the crowd proved correct. When asked about those immigrants, for instance, the median guess of the students was 10,000. The answer was 10,067.
>
> The scientists then gave their subjects access to the guesses of the other members of the group. As a result, they were able to adjust their subsequent estimates based on the feedback of the crowd. The results were depressing. All of a sudden, the range of guesses dramatically narrowed; people were mindlessly imitating each other. Instead of cancelling out their errors, they ended up magnifying their biases, which is why each round led to worse guesses. Although these subjects were far more confident that they were right – it's reassuring to know what other people think – this confidence was misplaced.[23]

This would suggest that 'the market' is more likely to *amplify* the prejudices of all the 'hundreds of thousands of investors' rather than to offer a distillation of their wisdom. Whoops!

Very soon after Greenspan said in 1999 that it was impossible to tell when a market was experiencing a bubble, the bubble that stock markets were in fact experiencing – the so-called 'tech bubble' or 'dot-com bubble' – burst in 2000, bringing an end to the decade-long surge in share prices. Despite all of the highly intelligent theorising of modern economists, and despite Alan Greenspan's conviction that it would be foolish to make a call against the market by admitting that stock prices did seem to be overvalued (that, as Greenspan had himself admitted, there was a degree of 'irrational exuberance' in the market), investors were, once again, blindsided. Fortunes were lost and companies evaporated into thin air.

Short Memories

It would seem that economists in recent years have lost sight of the difference between 'efficiency' and 'correctness' or, if you like, that they have forgotten that their theories are based on a number of fundamental assumptions about the behaviour of both humans and markets in their attempts to build models of what is happening within markets.

A fundamental assumption is that human beings make rational decisions, based on the information available to them. Sadly, of course, this is not so. People sometimes behave like sheep, and do what everyone else is doing for no good reason. People also believe, irrationally, that the future may be very different from the past: that some new development, like companies doing business via the internet, would produce far greater levels of corporate profitability than the world had seen before.

People also, as psychologists are currently demonstrating, make decisions based on a rapid assessment of the situation, and are easily misled by various factors of which we are barely, if at all, conscious. Our perception of the 'correct' price for any item, for example, is greatly influenced by a price that has been recently suggested to us, and not by some objective assessment of 'real' value. The asking price for a house or a car, for example, creates a psychological 'anchor' that we find it hard to break away from.[24] The price at which we bought a company share makes us deeply unwilling to consider that a lower price is in fact the correct price. The very fact that some clearer-thinking people are able to 'short' markets that they correctly perceive to be overvalued shows how the collective sentiment of large numbers of buyers and sellers can, in fact, lead to market prices that are over- or under-valued for significant periods of time.

Economists also made a number of assumptions about the market itself, which were necessary for their calculations about its 'efficient' functioning (and which do not, in fact, apply in the real world): all goods were essentially the same (all cars, all houses, all mobile phones); all workers were, similarly, the same; capital markets were perfect (anyone could borrow as much as they liked at competitive rates); and everyone could insure themselves against every possible risk.[25]

These assumptions are similar to the kind of assumptions made in the natural sciences, where predictive theories can be shown to work under a certain set of prescribed conditions. One of the problems seems to have been that economists became so entranced by the beauty of the extreme 'efficient-market hypothesis' that they forgot that there were qualifications to apply and conditions to be met. The market, they said, was the most efficient means of establishing the correct price of any asset, and therefore the market could be relied on to allocate resources in the most efficient way possible. People could make rational decisions about where to invest their money based entirely on the value of the market. As a result – and this is the really dangerous bit – markets should not be regulated in any way, because to interfere with the market would be to distort it.

This belief was vigorously promulgated by its proponents and began to influence government policy. Regulation of any sort was an attack on the perfection of the market. 'Deregulation' became the watchword of politicians. Ironically, some economists have argued that the quarter century from 1945 to 1971 was a period of global financial stability (the only banking crisis anywhere in the world in this period was Brazil in 1962) precisely because of the regulations put in place at the end of World War II, when the memory of the Great Depression that had preceded the war was still fresh in people's minds.[26]

The principle of deregulation – which is more like an article of faith for dedicated proponents of the efficient-market theory – led directly, as we shall see, to the current global financial crisis. Blindsided again – this time by an economic theory that held that the markets are not only efficient but *rational*. As Ron Weasley's father, Arthur Weasley, says in J.K. Rowling's *Harry Potter and the Chamber of Secrets*, when warning his children of the dangers of everyday things such as magically enchanted diaries: 'Never trust anything that can think if you can't see where it keeps its brain.' Markets work very well, but they are not rational.

3 THE SCIENCE OF DESIRE

Much of this book is concerned with the seemingly irrational behaviour of people in various situations. One of the best times to observe this is when we buy things, when we behave as *consumers*. And there is one group of people in particular that is extremely interested in the irrational behaviour of consumers: the marketing and advertising industry.

The job of advertising, and of salesmanship, has traditionally been to exploit our desires, tastes and concerns – and good luck to them both. Nobody makes any purchase, large or small – a car, a bar of soap, a house, an electrical appliance – on the basis of some strict cost-benefit analysis, thank goodness. We like one thing more than the other, but cannot explain why. We want to assert our social standing and to mark our place in society – or, conversely, we want to show that we are devil-may-care bohemians unconcerned about what society says of our behaviour and our purchases. We buy a great many things for reasons we are completely unable to articulate. We turn our nose up at other, perfectly good items or services, for similarly inchoate reasons. Our buying habits are not the result of logical deductive processes carried out under the bright light of rational examination. As a result, salesmanship and advertising have had to rely on a fairly basic and rather haphazard (if often extremely successful) appeal to our emotions. And that is how we should want it to stay.

The Id, the Ego and the Ad

In the late nineteenth and early twentieth centuries, however, human beings began, for the first time, to consider their behaviour as resulting from processes going on within that elusive item, their minds. Scientists in the fledgling science of psychology began to carry out experiments on animals, and later on humans, that suggested that some forms of behaviour could be trained, or 'conditioned'. Psychotherapists – people who tried to help those who found that their own behaviour distressing (or that of others) and wanted to change that behaviour – began to develop new theories about what might be going on inside our minds to produce such behaviour. One such therapist was Sigmund Freud, who developed a theory of mind that would explain his patients' behaviour and, he hoped, lead the way to a cure.

Though Freud seems today to be a quintessentially nineteenth-century figure – he had developed his theories on the repressed underlying emotional (or sexual) causes of 'psychosomatic' illnesses and neuroses in Vienna in the 1890s – one of his most influential books, *The Ego and the Id,* was not published until 1923. One of his key ideas was the notion that much of our behaviour is driven by 'unconscious' wishes – buried and sometimes repressed desires we seem unaware of – the emotional energy from which occasionally surfaces in our behaviour in ways that our conscious minds cannot not control or even explain.

Freud's methodology was not scientific – far from it. He created a narrative, probably best described as a metaphor, that attempted to explain our observable behaviour in terms of unobservable events happening within our minds. Because we seemed to be unaware of the mental impulses that were assumed to drive our behaviour (some 'normal', some surprising), Freud theorised that the mind was split into different parts, not all of which were available to our consciousness. From this was born the concept of the 'unconscious' and of Freud's subdivisions of the human mind into the id, the ego and the super-ego.

For the sake of simplicity, let us call the id our unreasoning, pleasure-seeking desires and drives, the ego our everyday experience, and the Super-ego our critical faculty or conscience. The poor old ego has to cope with the selfish demands of the id and, in its embarrassment (since most of what the id wants is not really socially acceptable) is forced into a number of contortions, such as denial, intellectualisation, sublimation, or simply repression. The ego also has to cope with the demands of that most prissy of nannies, the super-ego – whose main function seems to be to make the ego feel guilty about what it has just done (presumably at the promptings of the id), like making a pass at a waitress or eating the last portion of cream cake. Despite the fact that this fascinating construct bears almost no relation to what is really going on in our minds, Freudian psychoanalytic theory does offer a genuinely marvellous metaphor that delivers real insights into the human condition. The advertising men of the day came to love it.

The unholy alliance of the new science of psychology and the craft of psychoanalysis led to a revelation for the world of advertising and marketing. 'Ah ha!' they thought. 'We now know what our consumers *really* want. We understand the irrational forces that drive them. And we understand the rather ineffectual attempts of the rational self to suppress those desires. We can now devise messages whose words and images will reach out to those unconscious desires and overwhelm consumers' attempts to resist them.'

Manufacturers began to believe that, for the first time in history, they had gained the upper hand: that they would be able to manipulate consumers, via advertising in the new mass media of newspapers, magazines, radio and television, into buying what the manufacturers wanted them to buy. And, as we shall see, for this unacceptable attempt to impose their will on the general public by underhand means, the advertisers were quite rightly punished. For the first time, a merchant had dared to believe that he was able not merely to influence but to control the behaviour of his customers. Unsurprisingly, the merchants' customers (pretty much all of America) complained that they felt that they were being manipulated and abused. The American public began to fear that advertising men were using techniques that would create unconscious urges that would drive consumers to make certain choices and to buy various manufactured goods; that they were being manipulated in ways that were beyond the control of their conscious minds. The 'consumerist' movement was born, and trust between seller and buyer was in danger of being broken forever.

Selling a Cure

Advertising has a long and honourable history. Well, reasonably honourable. Since trade began, people with something to sell have, in more or less sophisticated ways, tried to let other people know that their goods are available for sale. Since trade is the engine that created the modern world, this is a good thing.

Human nature being what it is, however, some traders have, on occasion, sold goods that are not quite all that they are cracked up to be. A horse that is a little longer in the tooth than claimed; a loaf of bread whitened with alum or bulked up with sawdust; beer given its distinctive bitter flavour not from hops but from poisonous additives such as strychnine.

In particular, there has always been a steady supply of potions and elixirs that promise to relieve the woes and ills that afflict us. In the eighteenth century these potions mostly claimed to cure that most common of afflictions, the sexually transmitted disease. In the nineteenth century, thanks to scientific progress, a marvellous new generation of elixirs promised to cure... everything! They were hawked around America and sold to crowds attracted by the promise of spectacular 'Wild West' shows, and were proclaimed to draw on the ancient wisdom of the Native Americans. The most famous of these, Stanley's Snake Oil

Liniment was said to contain the oil of rattlesnakes; in fact it was based on a far less glamorous (but, happily, inert) mineral oil. The 'snake oil salesman' thus entered the language.

As advertising moved into the twentieth century, however, and became big business, things changed. Whereas the snake oil salesman could sell his liniment and move on to the next show, unlikely to be pursued by unhappy clients not cured of their lumbago or restored of their hair, as manufacturers in the twentieth century began to spend increasingly large amounts of money persuading citizens across the country to buy their products, they discovered that in a national marketplace there was no place to hide. You can sell a customer one shoddy product, but he will not come back for more. The millions of dollars invested in establishing brands of detergents, foodstuffs, cars and various appliances were now contingent, more than ever before, on the trust of consumers.

A Broken Trust

However, by the 1950s, when American consumerism was flourishing, consumers were gripped by a fear that this emerging trust had been broken.

The new science of psychology and the practice of psychoanalysis, though both in their infancy, had disturbing things to say about the forces that drive us. We were not, it seemed, the rational beings that a few millennia of human progress had led us to believe we were. Our behaviour, said the psychoanalysts, was driven by emotional states that we had repressed, some of which had their origin in our forgotten early childhood. What we 'decided' to do was far less under our conscious control than we fondly believed. It followed that our deepest fears and desires might be manipulated by unscrupulous marketers and their advertising agencies.

Even more alarmingly, behavioural psychologists were arguing that our behaviour could be 'conditioned' to respond to seemingly innocuous triggers. Ivan Pavlov, the Russian scientist, had introduced the concept of the 'conditioned response' in 1901, after his experiments on the gastric functions of dogs. Dogs, like humans, produce saliva in response to food – the sight or smell of food makes us salivate as the body assumes that it is about to need to set about the work of eating and digesting. Pavlov called this an 'unconditioned response'. But then he noticed that the dogs began to salivate not at the sight of real food but at the sight of the lab technician who habitually fed them. Pavlov experimented with other signals, like ringing a bell when food was given. He found that dogs would quickly come to salivate at the sound of the bell. A stimulus with no intrinsic connection with food and eating – the ringing of a bell – now automatically produced a physiological response. Pavlov had discovered the 'conditioned response.'

Pavlov's findings found their way into the public consciousness. Could it be that all behaviour – even the most apparently complex human behaviour – was simply a combination of instinctive responses and learned (or 'conditioned') responses? Could humans, like Pavlov's dogs, be trained to salivate at the sound of the bell, even though no food was in sight? Except that we would be conditioned not to salivate but to buy, to consume? As early as 1921, the advertising agency J. Walter Thompson had employed the psychologist John B. Watson to assist them in the business of creating advertisements. Watson, founder of the school of 'behaviourism', had been greatly influenced by Pavlov. Consumers thus had good reason, it seems, to fear that they were being manipulated by sinister commercial forces, in ways that were beyond their control.

Consumption Engineering

The economic forces at play at that point in history were unprecedented. As America began to produce more and more manufactured goods, so it was essential that people should consume them in order to maintain this engine of astonishing economic growth. A copywriter called Earnest Calkins realised that it was necessary to speed up people's rate of consumption – things that had previously been expected to last for years, or even decades, must now be seen as in need of replacement far more frequently. As Calkins wrote in an article in an advertising trade magazine, *Printer's Ink*: 'Consumption engineering must see to it that we use up the kind of goods we now merely use.' Alarmingly, Calkins went on to say that, 'Consumption engineering does not stop until we can consume all that we can make.'[1]

The idea of *planned obsolescence* hence came into currency. Goods were made less well than they could potentially be made, so that they would wear out more quickly and need replacement. Where planned obsolescence as not on option, marketing men went for psychological obsolescence: an item would need replacing not because it had stopped functioning but because it was seen to be outmoded. Something as potentially long-lasting as a kitchen range, for example, must now be replaced because it was the wrong colour or wrong brand. Considerations of style and fashion, previously the concerns of a relatively small elite of the richest people in society – and even then applicable to a relatively small list of items, such as clothing and hairstyles, furniture and interior design, architecture – were now to be applied, by means of assiduous marketing, to as wide a range of goods as possible. No consumer should be allowed to be happy with anything less than the most recent, stylish and technologically advanced version of *anything*.

To this end, the idea of 'conditioning' the American public to create demand for a huge range of new products seemed ideal – to the manufacturers at least. One firm proponent was Clyde Miller, who believed that advertisers should seek 'trigger' words and images that would provoke the desired response. Once these responses were in place, believed Miller, people's behaviour could be influenced en masse. To create the conditioning would take time, and it would be necessary to start work on the receptive minds of young children. In his book, *The Process of Persuasion* (1946), Miller blithely conjured a vision of the future that he seemed to feel was both achievable and – more chillingly – desirable:

> It takes time, yes, but if you expect to be in business for any length of time, think of what it can mean to your firm in profits if you can condition a million or 10 million children who will grow into adults trained to buy your products as soldiers are trained to advance when they hear the trigger words 'forward march'.[2]

No wonder that the consumers of the 1950s and 1960s became a little hysterical in their concerns about the forces apparently massed against them.

Fortunately, the madder scientists amongst the collection of consultants advising the advertising moguls turned out to be just that – mad scientists. The vast majority of psychologists who lent their skills to the process of marketing were humane people who have helped to create the appeals to our fancies that typify the modern consumer-driven market. Most importantly, modern corporations were quick to realise that their relationship with consumers was exactly that: a human relationship, a two-way process.

The Technique of Mass Persuasion

One can see what anxieties the combinations of these various philosophies and new scientific ideas might have had on the public mind in the early twentieth century. On one hand their behaviour was apparently the result of various 'conditioning' events, and could be scientifically predicted and controlled exactly as if they were mere billiard balls bouncing around the great baize table of life. On the other hand they were prey to strange, Freudian unconscious forces – deeply repressed urges. Added to this feeling of unease was the very real concern about the techniques of 'brainwashing' that had been experienced by American prisoners of war at the hands of their Communist captors during the Korean War. If tough American soldiers could be coerced and manipulated into denying the benefits of democracy, capitalism and free-market economics and, apparently, into embracing Communism, what might the marketing men and their pet psychologists be able to do with the minds of the American consumer?

In 1957, the American journalist and author, Vance Packard, published a book that was to be a runaway success, selling over a million copies: *The Hidden Persuaders*. The cover line of the first edition was, 'What makes us buy, believe – and even vote – the way we do; an introduction in [sic] the new world of Symbol Manipulation and Motivational Research.' The cover line for the 1961 Penguin edition was even more forthright: 'An introduction to the techniques of mass persuasion through the unconscious.' People were duly alarmed.

Fortunately for all of us, consumers proved harder to manipulate than the psychologists and marketing men had hoped. Even John B. Watson, the 'father of behaviourism' and another firm believer in the power of the conditioned response, discovered during his employment as consultant psychologist at J. Walter Thompson that his years of experience as an experimental psychologist were of little use. He devised some extremely effective consumer tests that have become standard practice in market research – such as the first-ever 'blind test', which demonstrated that the top four leading brands of cigarette all tasted exactly the same to consumers when removed from the visual context of their packaging. But he had to confess, after many years in the advertising business, that his effectiveness in helping the agency to create successful advertisements was more of an art than a science; more a matter of 'instinctive judgement'.[3]

The Id Goes Shopping

'Symbol Manipulation' and 'Motivational Research' – those terrifying sciences conjured up on the cover of the first edition of *The Hidden Persuaders* – were, in real life, relatively simple insights backed up by rudimentary psychology.

A good example of symbol manipulation would be this: for a long time, despite all appeals to reason and to efficiency, a bigger car was seen as a better car. As a result, insignificant details – like the sound of a car door closing – took on significant psychological significance. The general manager of Chevrolet boasted in 1957 that his new models had a great 'door slam noise'. 'We've got the finest door slam this year we've ever had – a big car sound!' Another commercial featured a Texan actor (who would instantly be identified as one of the relatively new breed of Texas oil millionaires) shouting, 'I ain't never seen one that big before!' The subtext is not hard to read: Texans (from 'the Big Country') have lots of money and they like things big and flashy. This particular very rich Texan 'ain't never seen one that big before!'[4] Ergo, this car is BIG.[5] You have been symbolically manipulated. But nothing much to worry about there.

Motivational research is a lot more interesting. The Institute of Motivational Research was founded in 1946 by Dr Ernest Dichter, a Freudian psychologist born half a century after Freud. He became the indispensable advisor for many of America's largest advertisers and their brands, including Proctor & Gamble's Ivory Soap, the Chrysler Corporation's Plymouth range of cars and the B.F. Goodrich tyre company, whose tyres had been fitted to the first car to cross America in 1903 (a brand-new touring car from the Winton Motor Carriage Company – open-topped, of course, and still reminiscent, in its design, of a horse-drawn carriage). B.F. Goodrich later supplied tyres for the Columbia Space Shuttle in 1977.

Dichter's psychological theories concerning marketing and advertising are, in general, as amusing today as they seemed sinister to American readers of *The Hidden Persuaders* in the late 1950s and early 1960s. Critics of Freud have facetiously described his theories as being founded on the same principles as that of domestic plumbing: various things (typically the energy of frustrated sexual desires) are always being 'dammed up' until they build up a sufficient 'head of pressure' to force an appearance in some other part of the psyche – thus the thwarted energy of unrequited lusts, for example, forces its way to the surface in the unexpected guise of artistic creativity and 'explains' the mysterious creative force.

Dichter turned this hydraulic metaphor into a more suitable model for a capitalist consumer society. A study by Professor David Bennett of the University of Melbourne on the development of market research in the twentieth century argues that these Freudian forces were best described not as a head of water (or steam), but as an accumulation of unspent capital. A reviewer from the university's journal summarised Bennett's paper:

> Freud had explained repressed sexual desire as a form of unused capital. To Dichter, consumer spending, like sexual pleasure, was an expenditure of capital through unconscious desires. Dichter's aim was to release inhibitions and encourage the id to go shopping.[6]

It should be the stuff of parody, but Dichter was deadly serious, as were the advertisers who paid his hefty consultancy fees. The accumulated capital of consumers' unconscious desires could be released through cleverly targeted marketing messages. The id (the uncontrolled pleasure principle lurking in all of us) could be sent out to 'go shopping' and the super-ego (that tedious old nanny figure that is the keeper of our conscience and is always urging restraint) could go hang. The ego, in the meantime – the bit of ourselves that we might, if distantly, recognise – is charged with reconciling the unprincipled demands of the id with the moral grandstanding of the super-ego, whilst trying to ensure that nothing really bad happens. In order to perform this balancing act, the ego resorts to a wide variety of stratagems, all of which could result in us ending up on the psychiatrist's couch: things like denial, displacement, fantasy, projection, repression and sublimation. No wonder we are all such nervous wrecks. And no wonder Dichter's 'motivational research' sounded so alarming. What could these people not persuade consumers to do, armed with such sophisticated knowledge of the inner workings (or plumbing, or dammed up capital) of our minds?

Insights and Insults

In reality, the feared insights of motivational research proved to be no more than quite interesting, really, though a few of them were also snortingly laughable. Some of them represented the kind of marketing insight into people's real motivations that can transform a product's marketing, but they were a long way short of the cynical manipulation of the American public's unconscious minds that Vance Packard described in *The Hidden Persuaders.* As every good salesperson knows, in order to sell something successfully to somebody else, you need to understand (or at least have a good inkling of) what they want, and why they want it. And a really good salesperson will also know that what a person *says* they want or need something for may have absolutely nothing to do with the real reason.

Motivational research was especially good at uncovering mistakes that advertisers were making. Dichter's client, the tyre manufacturer B.F. Goodrich, for example, had been telling customers to 'fit their tyres and forget them', because they were so reliable. The problem, decided Dichter, was that consumers really did forget about their tyres, and were only made aware of them again at the worst possible moment – when they had a puncture. The first time they noticed the brand was when they saw it written on the wall of the tyre they were trying to fix on the roadside in the rain. Dichter's recommendation: keep reminding people to be grateful for the sterling work their tyres were doing for them.

Another advertiser made a more obvious mistake. They were so proud of the durability of their luggage that they showed a commercial of the luggage falling from a plane and surviving the fall. Unfortunately, the advertisement tended to make people think about things falling out of airplanes, which they found unsettling. The researchers felt that they could also discern some consumer resentment about the fact that their luggage might survive a plane crash, while they would not.

Many of the other realisations of the time have entered marketing legend and are part of everyday modern marketing practice. The makers of instant cake mixes produced a mix that required only the addition of water in order to bake a delicious cake; milk and eggs were present in the mix in dried form. Just add water! Consumers felt, however, that they were not doing enough work; that they had been cheated of the effort that is needed to do such a homely thing as bake a cake. So, more successful mixes required the cake maker to add milk and eggs.

Motivational research was very strong on the need for marketers to assuage guilt and to give consumers permission to indulge themselves. One clever idea was to produce chocolate and candy bars made up of bite-size chunks: you are, after all, only going to eat one little bite.... Manufacturers also noticed that if they presented a product as being too 'improving' – low calorie products to help one lose weight, for example – then there was the real risk that consumers would begin to associate the product with unpleasant experiences, like dieting, or that they would decide that the product couldn't taste nice, or it wouldn't be so good for them. One low-calorie rye bread wafer began to focus more on taste and promise, using words such as 'delight' and 'delicious'. Brewers had fallen into the same trap. In survey after survey, men told researchers that they wanted a lower-calorie beer, a drier beer. What men *really* thought was that such beers would taste awful, though they supposed (when asked) that it would be better for them. But they didn't really want this 'good for you' beer. Beer drinking is supposed to be fun. It's an indulgence, not a penance. The researchers decided that a low-calorie beer was a contradiction in terms, an unsellable product. The brewers of Blatz beer embraced this philosophy with impressive wholeheartedness when they adopted their new slogan: 'Made by people who like beer for people who like to drink beer – and lots of it!'[7] That's the spirit.

Motivational researchers also unearthed what were believed to be unfortunate residual associations brought about by advertisements that had been insufficiently thought through. A fridge manufacturer, proud of their new automatically defrosting fridge, ran an advertisement showing their fridge with the door wide open: look, no frost! What consumers apparently felt was not awe but irritation. What kind of person leaves a fridge door wide open like that? And an advertisement for a washing machine that freed up so much of the family's time that they were able to go back to bed showed the entire family – mom, dad and the kids – all tucked up in the same bed. Consumers concluded subconsciously that if the family hadn't spent so much money on the washing machine, they'd be able to afford more beds.

Philip Morris used to make great play of the fact that their brand of cigarettes caused less irritation. They began to doubt the wisdom of this approach when the diligent researchers asked consumers to complete the sentence, 'When I think of Philip Morris, I think of...' and some consumers wrote in the word, 'Irritation.'

Dichter's most famous success was the long-running and hugely successful 'Put a Tiger in Your Tank' slogan for Esso. People don't want petrol, as such, reasoned Dichter, they want power for their automobiles. A tiger is 'unconsciously' perceived as a symbol of power (back to symbol manipulation again). So, *Put a Tiger in Your Tank!* It certainly worked, though maybe because people just liked driving around with a pretend nylon tiger's tail hanging out of their petrol cap, as if they really did have a tiger in their tank. They got the tiger tail free with the petrol. (*That*, you have to admit, is a really clever merchandising idea. Some people unfortunately put the tail tight in the tank, not looped around the petrol cap as was intended, and blocked their petrol intake. But you can't please everyone.)

Playing to Our Emotions

Packard's *Hidden Persuaders* – a far more well-balanced and measured (if sensational) book than the rather hysterical reaction of the advertising industry at the time would suggest – raises a number of genuine concerns that, far from having gone away, have given rise to increasing and genuine unease. We may have moved on from the concern that we can be manipulated by Professor Miller's deeply disturbing vision of a generation of pre-programmed children responding like automatons to 'triggers' that had been painstakingly implanted in their subconscious. This, happily, is mere science fiction (the more disturbing consideration is not whether this was ever feasible but why any right-minded person would think that it was an acceptable practice if it *was* feasible.) But, in many ways, Packard was absolutely right (though he was wrong about the reasons why he was right). Packard thought that this kind of advertising and marketing was a step backwards from the enlightenment ideal of intelligent people making rational choices based on the evidence that is laid before them:

> All this probing and manipulation has its constructive and amusing aspects but also, I think it is fair to say, it has seriously anti-humanistic implications. Much of it seems to represent regress rather than progress for man in his long struggle to become a rational and self-guiding being. Something new, indeed, seems to be entering the pattern of American life with the growing power of our persuaders.[8]

On this front, I believe, Packard is wrong: the notion that we are engaged in a historical process of emerging from our irrational past into a kind of hyper-rational future is misguided. We are complex, emotional, human animals, not computers, and we always will be. People who want to influence us will therefore, quite rightly, play on our emotions, on the things that motivate us without our necessarily understanding quite why they do (because we are not as clever as we think we are, and because our decisions are not 'rational'). But Packard was quite right to say that this is what makes 'persuaders' potentially dangerous. Especially when the full panoply of persuasive techniques is used to sell that most difficult of products: the political candidate.

Selling Politicians to the People

In 1952, Dwight 'Ike' Eisenhower, the World War II general and erstwhile Supreme Allied Commander of the Allied Expeditionary Force in Europe, decided to run as presidential candidate for the USA's Republican Party. America had had a president from the Democratic Party for the past 20 years (Truman for the previous eight, and Roosevelt for 12 before that). The Democratic candidate for the presidency, Adlai Stevenson, was a much younger man: Eisenhower was 62, Stevenson a decade younger. Eisenhower was not in the best of health.

Three wealthy Republican supporters asked the iconic Madison Avenue advertising man, Rosser Reeves, of the Ted Bates Company, to find a slogan for Eisenhower that would match the Democratic Party's compelling line, 'You never had it so good'. Reeves was a master of the hard sell and the inventor of the concept of the 'Unique Selling Propositon' (USP), that is, the one outstanding benefit of any product on which that product's advertising should focus. He believed that the USP should be repeated at every opportunity and should never vary. This was the man who wrote the line 'Melt in your hand, not in your mouth' for M&Ms, and 'The big difference in Anacin makes a big difference in the way you feel' – a sales line for the aspirin-based headache remedy that was drummed mercilessly into American consumers to the point of irritation – but which resulted in a tripling of sales. Reeves told the Republican Party that it needed more than a slogan: it needed a campaign. If the Republicans could raise the money, Reeves would write an advertising campaign based on radio advertising and – controversially – on the use of the relatively new medium of television.

In the 1940s the Ted Bates agency had developed a 'copy laboratory' to test the impact of advertising on random samples of the general public. They had used all of the recently developed techniques of Motivational Research: focus groups, depth interviews, projective techniques ('If this product were a car, what kind of car would it be?' 'Which of these photographs of people's faces would you associate with a user of this brand?'). The agency was ready to use the insights of a decade of psychological research into consumer behaviour and to deploy them in order to 'sell' a candidate for the office of the president of the United States of America.

Eisenhower had to be persuaded that the radical use of such short, simple messages to convey political views was sufficiently 'dignified' in an age that still expected candidates to make relatively long speeches, in person, from the hustings. After the election, Rosser Reeves reported the following conversation that he had had with Eisenhower in order to convince him of the idea.

'Well, General, do you think that it is all right for a candidate to make a thirty-minute speech on television or radio?'

'Oh, yes,' said the General.

'Well, would it be dignified to make a fifteen-minute speech?'

'Oh, yes,' said Eisenhower.

'Well, would it be in order, perhaps, to make a five-minute speech?'

'Yes,' said Eisenhower, 'I am quite sure a five-minute speech would be in order.'

'If we cut that speech to *one minute*. Is there anything wrong with that?'

At this point the General threw in his towel, grinned, and said, 'OK, let's go ahead.'[9]

'Eisenhower Answers America'

Reeves set out to recruit ordinary Americans to appear in his TV commercials, 'people from different sections of the country – real people, with wonderful native accents'.[10] They were filmed asking questions written on cue cards to match the answers that Eisenhower had already recorded – answers also written by Reeves himself. The campaign theme was 'Eisenhower Answers America'.

In the commercials, one middle-aged housewife holds out a small bag of groceries. 'I paid twenty-four dollars for these groceries. Look, for so little....' 'A few years ago,' responds Eisenhower, 'those same groceries cost you ten dollars. Now twenty-four. Next year thirty. That's what will happen, unless we have change.'

A young mother with two young children says, 'You know what things cost today. High prices are just driving me crazy.' 'Yes,' replies Eisenhower, 'my Mamie [his wife] gets on to me about the high cost of living. It's another reason why I say, "It's time for a change. Time to get back to an honest dollar and an honest dollar's worth."'

Rosser Reeves had found his USP: rising inflation. But he did introduce some other themes. Another 'ordinary American' complains that her children 'hear so much about government graft, they think everyone is dishonest.' Eisenhower replies, 'Too many politicians have sold their ideals of honesty down the Potomac.'[11]

In the commercials, Eisenhower was carefully stage-managed to present a relaxed yet vigorous image – something that Eisenhower might have struggled to achieve on the hustings. As Reeves said, 'We did a tremendous amount of work and worry on how to "package" the General ... We changed the lights. We threw away the glasses. We put him in different clothes. We made him look vigorous and dynamic – which he actually is.'[12]

These commercials flooded the 12 states that Ted Bates analysts had identified as being crucial to victory over the Democratic candidate, Adlai Stevenson. A million and a half dollars worth of television and radio spots 'poured, like a tidal wave, into these critical areas.'[13] In the words of John E. Hollitz, author of an article entitled 'Eisenhower and the Admen: The Television "Spot" Campaign of 1952':

> … millions of Americans in dozens of cities … were 'deluged' with these short advertisements which featured Dwight D. Eisenhower responding to the questions of individuals he had never met in words written for him by an advertising man. It is not too much to say that the country was 'saturated' with the spots; for example, in New York City alone, the spots were programmed at the rate of 140 or 150 a day.[14]

Eisenhower won by a landslide. Because it was a landslide, it was impossible to say how large a part the advertising campaign had played in the result, but the Democratic Party were furious. They tried to get the campaign stopped on the basis that it represented a 'monopoly of the airwaves', but the Federal Communications Commission ruled that no laws had been violated. Rosser Reeves himself said, disingenuously, that it was 'important that all the people know what the candidates stand for',[15] despite the fact that the advertisements did not tell anyone anything about Eisenhower's policies. 'The cost of living is so high!' 'Yes indeed – my wife says the same thing.' 'My children hear that all politicians are corrupt.' 'Oh dear, yes – you might say that.' It's not exactly a political platform.

The Consumer Society

Welcome to the modern world. Are we blindsided by advertising that, after much careful research, plays cleverly on our emotions? I think not. A simple can of Coca-Cola (other colas are available!) has had so much carefully crafted marketing devoted to it that we see it not as a simple can of cola but as a distillation of all the emotional messages that the Coca-Cola Company have devoted to their brand over many long years. It is perfectly arguable that our lives are the richer for it. We could insist that all of our colas were presented in blank cans, and labelled Cola 1, Cola 2 and so on. We would then be less liable to be emotionally swayed into buying our favourite (and more expensive) brand of cola, but we would also (strangely but demonstrably) get less pleasure out of the contents of each can. Wine that is lovingly presented in a fine glass doesn't merely seem to taste better, it does taste better: that is, we experience the taste as being more pleasurable than the taste of another wine that is less well presented. In a blind test in plastic cups, the two wines would taste the same. Our senses have been fooled. Who is the richer for that? The seller of fine wineglasses, perhaps, but also we, the consumers.

We are grownups after all, and we have decided, in general, to put up with a degree of emotional manipulation in return for greater choice and richer experiences. Nevertheless, we have also decided, in quite recent times, that it makes no sense to allow the full range of persuasive techniques available to advertisers in order to persuade us to smoke, or to drink alcohol. We are similarly wary of advertising that is aimed at children. We are beginning to wonder about the advertising of foods that are bad for our health. These restrictions, when they are agreed on, are in most countries enforced by means of self-regulation, voluntarily agreed between governments and manufacturers and their advertising agents. Some people may feel that this is an unreasonable restriction on their human rights and that we should be free to choose whatever we like, while others may feel that governments should impose more legislative restrictions. The point is that Vance Packard was not wrong about the power of cleverly targeted, emotionally laden messages to influence our behaviour. What Packard says in his conclusion to *The Hidden Persuaders* is intelligent and still relevant to society today:

> This larger moral problem of working out a spiritually tolerable relationship between a free people and an economy capable of greater and greater productivity may take decades to resolve. Meanwhile we can address ourselves to the more specific problem of dealing with those more devious and aggressive manipulators who would play on our irrationalities and weaknesses in order to channel our behaviour.

It's not the manufacturers and advertisers that I worry about, however. If they fall foul of consumers, then they quickly lose our good will – and the fact that they have invested so much in creating a relationship with us through advertising means that this loss is financially very painful for them. The dialogue created between manufacturer and consumer by means of advertising and other marketing communications is, ironically, a reasonably good guarantee of advertisers' good behaviour. And who really minds being sold a cleaning product or a toiletry or a biscuit that was not, on reflection, entirely essential? What would remain of the consumer society, with its many pleasures and benefits, if we took such a puritanical view of our hidden persuaders?

With politicians, though, it's a different matter.

4 NEW LAMPS FOR OLD

At the beginning of the twentieth century, Franz Reichelt, an Austrian-born tailor who had become a French citizen, tried to devise a 'parachute suit' that he hoped would help to save the lives of early aviators if (or when) their flying machines got into trouble. The suit was a kind of voluminous cloak that, in principle, would open in mid-air and allow the falling aviator to glide safely to the ground, like Batman. Monsieur Reichelt insisted on demonstrating the effectiveness of the suit by jumping from the first platform of the Eiffel Tower (about 57 metres above the ground). Sadly his suit failed to billow out in the way that it was supposed to, and Reichelt was killed. He was foolish to make the jump when his 'unmanned' tests had been inconclusive – but he was not merely mad: the silk parachute had been proven to work more than a century before, in 1797, when another Frenchman, André-Jacques Garnerin, successfully released himself from a hot-air balloon at the alarming height of about 900 metres and drifted safely to earth in a basket carried by a silk parachute. Some of Reichelt's own early experiments using mannequins with folded silk 'wings' had appeared successful.

Reichelt is a good, though poignant, example of what makes mankind such a successful species. We love to innovate. We look at the world around us and think, 'If only we had a so-and-so, then we could do such-and-such' (as in, 'If only we had wings, we could fly' or, 'If only we had a parachute suit, we could float safely to earth from a falling flying machine'). We are constantly on the lookout for ways of enhancing our quality of life: a sharper flint hand axe; a faster central processing unit; a pollution-free source of energy.

To be more precise, some of us are constantly doing this: innovators, experimenters, inventors, risk-takers, entrepreneurs. People who, unlike the majority of us, are not content to accept that it is impossible to do certain things, or that the world is simply as it is. These people condemn themselves to a lifetime of frequent failure, enlivened, if they are lucky, by the occasional success. The rest of us snigger at the failures and help ourselves, shamelessly, to the benefits brought about by the successes.

A recent failed innovation, and a personal favourite of mine (in principle, not in practice), was the petrol-powered rollerblade, which began to make an (illegal) appearance in Europe and America in 2007. The skates were driven by a 25 cc petrol engine attached to the rear of the right-hand rollerblade, which could propel the adventurous skater forward, without effort, at speeds of up to 20 mph (32 km/h), which must have been a lot of fun. The skates had a handheld throttle to control the speed, but no brakes: the only way of stopping was by means of a cut-out device, which killed the engine, but left skaters slowly running off speed, rather than actually stopping. Attempts to come to a more immediate halt tended to end badly. The plastic petrol tank attached to the skates was another slight hazard. Scaremongering headlines in the national press, such as 'Illegal and Heading Here: "Killer" Petrol-driven Rollerblades',[1] did not help to establish this exciting innovation as a popular form of recreational transport.

Innovations may succeed or fail, but at the heart of the innovation itself is an entirely laudable underlying principle: their inventors thought that they would be useful, or at least amusing and diverting. They may have turned out to be wrong for various reasons (perhaps several reasons, in the case of the man or woman who invented petrol-powered rollerblades), but the inventors' intentions were honourable.

There is another entirely different sort of innovation, which is based on the idea that a completely new way of doing things will transform our lives; not a new product, or a way of growing more food, or a more efficient distribution network, or a better means of communicating at a distance – but instead some fundamental new approach to the world of commerce that will make all of our previous efforts to better ourselves the old-fashioned way (mainly involving hard work) look foolish. These innovations nearly always involve new ways of making money, and they also usually belong in the same category as devices that make you physically fit without the need to exercise, or ways of losing weight that do not involve eating less food. We are, nevertheless, often swept away in our excitement at the potential of these new ways of improving our lives.

The problem, I would argue, is that we are easily blindsided by innovation that promises to solve our problems via *intangibles*. It's a bit like magic. We have no idea how it works, but some clever people assure us that it does work, and that it will make us all very rich, or less poor. At which point we throw our cautious scepticism out of the window and embrace the new wonder concept that will change our lives.

So when businesses declare that a revolution in the way we do business is happening, and that all of the old rules about value no longer apply (which explains why the stock market valuation of their wonderful new company bears no relation to its apparent real value based on the old-fashioned way of thinking), we and a large number of supposedly well-informed analysts and commentators tend to believe this. This is exactly what happened at the end of the twentieth century, during the emergence of the so-called 'new economy', with a USA energy corporation called Enron.

New Driver

The driving force of the new economy was, of course, the internet. Nobody quite knew what the internet might do to the economy, but it was very believable that this revolutionary new medium would change the business world in some quite fundamental way.

The central notion behind the new economy was that increases in efficiency, driven by computerisation and the instantaneous exchange of information made possible by the internet, would drive an increase in productivity. This would be a sane and rational reason to believe in the new economy, and there was some evidence to suggest that it was happening, though what looked like a surge in US productivity in the late 1990s soon settled down, and some of the increase in productivity was seen to be happening within the IT industry itself, rather than representing the effect of information technology on 'old economy' businesses.

Putting discussions about productivity to one side, there were other, less well-founded beliefs as to what the new economy would bring about. Some of them were a little mystical: now that this new, intangible medium, the internet, was finding its way into every corner of human life so, it seems, we began to believe that everything might become 'virtual'; that the old-fashioned, heavy 'stuff' of our previous lives could now be risen above; that in the new world people would make money simply via the sheer brilliance of their ideas. No doubt somebody would have to dig coal and explore for gas, but the *clever* money was to be made in dealing with the intangibles of this stuff: its inherent value. Gas in itself, for example, is not interesting, according to this theory. Gas is dull. Worse than dull, it is hard work. What could be really interesting about gas would be to make a lot of money dealing with the stuff without having to do all of the hard work of finding, extracting and transporting it.

One of the first people to see the world in this way was Jeffrey Skilling, a young rising star with the management consultancy firm, McKinsey & Company. Skilling had become a partner at McKinsey in the unusually short time of five years, and a director in 10 years. He was in charge of worldwide energy practice, and based in Houston, Texas, the capital of America's oil and natural gas industry. Not surprisingly, Skilling found himself doing some consultancy work for an up-and-coming gas company called Enron.

Banking on Gas

Skilling was normally described as not just bright, but 'incandescently brilliant'. At his Harvard Business School MBA admissions interview, he was asked whether he considered himself smart. 'I'm fucking smart,' replied Skilling – which I think we can take as a 'yes'. He graduated as a Baker Scholar, a distinction awarded to the top 5% of a class, and went straight to work for McKinsey & Company.[2]

Skilling's epiphanic idea was this: that Enron should become a 'gas bank'. Enron would enter into contracts with gas suppliers to buy gas, and enter into contracts with gas consumers to sell gas. It would make money from the difference between the price at which it bought and the price at which it sold, in exactly the way that banks make money on the difference, or 'spread', between the rate that they offer to depositors and the rate that they charge borrowers.

Skilling also saw that the existence of these contracts meant that the contracts themselves could be traded, just as other commodities were traded, and that this could be used to reduce risk by means of futures contracts: if you are contracted to supply gas in the future at a certain price, you can remove or reduce the danger of prices rising or falling dramatically by contracting with another party to buy their gas at a fixed price at some future point.

Skilling made the presentation of his gas bank idea to a group of top Enron executives in 1987. The presentation lasted less than half an hour, and it consisted of one PowerPoint slide only – which was very Jeff Skilling but a little surprising to most of the gathered executives, who had settled in for something with rather more background and detail.[3] But Skilling had made his point. In 1990, he was offered a job as the head of a new division of Enron called Enron Finance, and put in charge of taking the gas industry by the scruff of the neck and dragging it, kicking and screaming if necessary, into the world of free markets and unfettered trading.

His initial salary represented considerably less than he had been earning at McKinsey, but his package included a 'phantom equity' bonus. Phantom equity allows companies to reward executives on the basis of profitability and rising share prices, without initially giving them real equity in the company – though the phantom equity may be paid in stock, rather than cash, thus beginning to build a real equity stake for the successful executive. If Skilling's vision for Enron Finance could be made a reality, he stood to make a lot more money than he could at McKinsey, even as a director. Skilling, a gambler by nature, seized the opportunity.

It wasn't a simple matter to create the market that Skilling had envisaged. It was easy enough to find customers who would place long-term orders for a steady supply of gas at a reliable price; the problem was finding producers who were prepared to enter into long-term contracts to *sell* gas at a fixed price. As far as they were concerned, they had the gas and the market could pay them whatever the gas was worth day to day: why should they risk losing future money by contracting to sell gas at a price that turned out to be too low? This quite natural reluctance nearly killed Skilling's gas bank concept in its infancy. But he found a solution.

The gas producers, it turned out, were finding it hard to raise the finance that they needed for exploration and development. In stepped Enron, offering to make large upfront payments in return for a commitment from the producers to supply gas at agreed prices. As Skilling said, 'If you offered to buy gas at a fixed price for 20 years, they would throw you out. But if you offered to hand the producer US$400 million to develop reserves, he saw you as a partner.'[4]

The gas bank was in business. Skilling's new division, Enron Finance, set about arranging finance deals with gas producers to guarantee a supply of gas, and looking for customers who would contract for a long-term supply of gas.

In 1992, the company struck a momentous deal. It persuaded Sithe Energies, who were building a 1,000-megawatt electricity plant, to use natural gas instead of coal and to choose Enron as their supplier. The deal involved the supply of 195 million cubic feet (5.52 million cubic metres) of gas every day for 20 years, and was worth something in the region of US$4 billion over the term of the contract.[5]

As the scale of the gas bank's operations grew, so Enron's traders – the people in between the suppliers and the customers – had more to play with. They knew about the deals involved in creating the supply of gas and they were discovering the prices that customers were prepared to pay for a commitment to buy gas across different timeframes. They began to set up intermediary deals to hedge the risks that both sides of the equation represented, using the whole paraphernalia of commodities trading – puts, calls, swaps, forwards, options and doubtless other arcane devices that I have never heard of and certainly do not understand. Enron always maintained that its trading book was 'matched' – that every deal in which it was taking a 'long' position (based on the assumption that prices would rise) was matched by a different deal in which it had taken a 'short' position (based on the assumption that prices would fall).

In this way, Enron almost single-handedly created natural gas trading. In 1990, the New York Mercantile Exchange began trading in natural gas futures for the first time, though only for gas delivered to a key 'hub' in Louisiana. By 1993, other major energy companies such as Dynegy and El Paso had followed Enron's lead, setting up their own gas trading desks.[6]

'The Death Knell of Every Traditional Integrated Firm'

In 1999, Enron launched their online trading facility, EnronOnline (EOL), 'an internet-based global transaction system which allows Enron's customers to view real-time prices from Enron's traders and transact instantly online'.[7]

EOL became famous in business studies because it had been developed by 'stealth'. A gas trader called Louise Kitchen realised that the internet was a far more efficient medium for trading than the desperately old-fashioned method of actually ringing people up and asking if they wanted to do a deal. She was encouraged to develop this idea by a team of colleagues (a large team – about 350) who were prepared to devote their spare time to the project.

Money was, of course, spent ('just [sic] US$20 million in back office upgrades'[8] according to an article in *The Economist*), which was never budgeted for or signed off by top management in the usual way. But financial controls at Enron were so lax that it was never a problem to find a budget for anything that seemed like a good idea. Legend has it that the stealth concept was not presented to Skilling until just before it went live. Skilling was initially underwhelmed, imagining it to be a kind of energy equivalent of eBay, bringing together buyers and sellers. He was more impressed when he understood that the model was not for Enron to be an intermediary: the company would be the principal in every trade that was done via EOL.

This gave Enron even more of what it craved – information – which gave it huge power as a trading operation. It had by this time begun to acquire a body of knowledge about the natural gas market that no other trading desk could match. It is said that EnronOnline led to Enron being involved in over 50% of all of the gas trades in the United States. Experienced traders questioned the wisdom of making sensitive information about pricing so transparent and so widely available, and they seem to have been right; Enron's trading margins were squeezed by EOL. That loss was said to have been offset by the greatly reduced transaction costs provided by trading online. Other parties were more concerned that Enron, the principal in every trade via EOL, would use the information it gained to manipulate the market. These parties, as events would soon demonstrate, were very right in their concerns.

The core argument in favour of the online trading system was that it transformed the sheer volume of trades that Enron was doing: after the launch of EOL, trading volumes grew by 60% year on year, compared with the 30% growth they had enjoyed in the year before the launch.[9] As the BBC reported, two years after its launch, EOL was averaging 6,000 transactions a day, worth an average US$2.5 billion. And it wasn't just gas trades:

> 2,100 different financial products were on offer to traders, across four continents in 15 different currencies. The site is offering products as varied as Dutch aluminium, Japanese weather derivatives, US lumber, European plastics and Argentine natural gas.
>
> ...There is no commission and no subscription fee, an offer which led some analysts to forecast the extinction of traditional brokerages.[10]

No wonder people thought that Enron was taking over the world.

In many ways, EOL can be said to define the intangible mystery at the heart of Enron. Nobody was sure that EOL was making money, taken in isolation, but it was facilitating massive volumes of trades, in every one of which Enron was the principal, and it was beginning to extend way beyond gas and energy trades into every conceivable market. Here surely was the ultimate proof of Skilling's fundamental strategy: Enron would move into any market – broadband, steel, wood pulp, water – and acquire enough assets to ensure that it could deliver on its contractual obligations. As the market developed in size and liquidity, so those assets could be sold off, leaving Enron to make money from trading alone. As the previously cited *Economist* article said:

> One [Enron] manager says that the firm's goal is 'the commoditisation of everything'. [...] Mr Skilling himself describes his vision of the future as one of 'dis-integration'. He thinks the advance of deregulation, the rise of free markets, and the dramatic decline in the cost of intermediation, all sound the death knell for the traditional integrated firm – be it in energy, telecommunications, or indeed anything else.[11]

'The commoditisation of everything.' 'The death knell of every traditional integrated firm.' Now that is *very* Jeff Skilling. And he was quite serious. As he saw it, by creating access to any commodity via a highly efficient market run by an expert intermediary (Enron), Skilling's model would simply do away with the reason why companies used to want to control their own assets. In the old days companies controlled every aspect of their business, from manufacture to marketing to distribution. But if a perfect market existed in various aspects of the process, then the cost advantage of controlling the whole process might vanish. If there is a perfect market available in trucking, why own your own trucks? Simply go online and book your trucking slot. If you want to get your goods to market, why go to all the trouble of finding customers and supplying them? Just sell your goods to the market intermediary (Enron) and they will find a customer for you.

Virtual Integration

Skilling believed that the sheer efficiency of the Enron-style intermediary market meant that it would no longer make sense for companies to 'vertically integrate' (meaning, to control as much as possible of every element of their business, from raw materials right through to the sale of the finished product to individual customers). Take wood pulp, for example, one of the many markets that Enron believed it could move into, now that it had conquered the gas market. The old-fashioned way to get into wood pulp was to own a forest. At the beginning, Enron would need to own forests too, to ensure that it could deliver the product to its first customers.

But once Enron established itself as a seller of timber, as it had done with natural gas, it could then begin to bring buyers together not only with Enron's own product, but with other suppliers' products too. Wood pulp manufacturers would turn to Enron for marginal supplies of timber, and find that the efficiency of the Enron market allowed them to buy timber at very competitive prices — possibly even at better prices than they could manufacture the stuff for themselves. At that point, who needs a forest? Wood pulp manufacturers would sell off their forests, bank the proceeds, and make a far more efficient living buying wood pulp from the market. It ties up less capital, and you are more certain of delivery: if a vital part of the supply chain of a vertically integrated business fails, then the business doesn't have a product. But if they are buying from an Enron market, the diversity of their portfolio means that they have access to the product via many different routes. As Skilling said in an interview with *BusinessWeek*:

> The fundamental advantage of a virtually integrated system versus a physically integrated system is you need less capital to provide the same reliability.... Delivery is a non-systematic risk. If a pipeline blows up or a compressor goes down or a wire breaks, the bigger your portfolio, the greater your ability to wire around that. So, if for example, I'm just starting in the gas merchant business and I'm selling gas from central Kansas to Kansas City, if the pipeline blows up, I'm out of business. For Enron, if that pipeline blows up, I'll back haul out of New York, or I'll bring Canadian gas in and spin it through some storage facilities. If you can diversify your infrastructure, you can reduce non-systematic risk, which says there's a ... very strong tangible network effect. [...] But you've got to be big, you've got to get that initial market share, or you're toast.[12]

Also, Skilling believed, the efficiency of the Enron market meant that it was now cheaper to use the market than to carry the internal 'interaction' costs of running various bits of the process within one organisation. Organisations would be far slimmer, far more agile: they would be 'temporarily assembled' to supply a particular need. 'There's only been a couple of times in history when these costs of interaction have radically changed', said Skilling. 'One was the railroads, and then the telephone and the telegraph. We're going through another right now. The costs of interaction are collapsing because of the internet, and as those costs collapse, I think the economics of temporarily assembled organisations will beat the economics of the old vertically integrated organisation.'[13]

This, then, was Skilling's remarkable vision: Enron would move into many different markets, initially acquiring sufficient assets to become a player in the market. And then it would establish, understand and control a market to the extent that it no longer needed those original assets, and could sell them off. It would make its money (lots of it) by trading in the market that it had created, using sophisticated financial derivatives to balance risk. At this point, the old vertically integrated companies should begin to shed their assets too, and specialise in whatever niches genuinely reflected their core business. There would be no need for cumbersome infrastructure. If you want some wood pulp, buy it from the market for wood pulp. If you want to make wood pulp, buy some timber from the timber market to make wood pulp. If you want to own forests, own forests. But there is no longer any point in doing all three things – owning the forests, making the wood pulp and looking for individual customers for your wood pulp: just sell your product to Enron via EnronOnline and Enron would sell the product on to somebody else.

One Side of Every Trade – Is That Too Much to Ask?

There are at least a couple of flaws in this argument. The first, slightly philosophical, but I think fatal, flaw, is that Skilling's vision of the new market contained the seeds of its own destruction: taken to its logical conclusion it leads not to a hyper-efficient market, but to a monopoly.

Skilling was adamant that Enron should be 'asset-light': it would own assets only for as long as it took to establish itself in a market, and then it would get rid of those assets. But what happens if everybody takes the same approach? What if every organisation follows Enron into the new world, as Enron recommends that they should, selling their own assets and relying on contracts to supply their needs? Companies would logically begin to leave the market that they currently supply, and look to the market to supply what they previously made.

To give an example, if you own a forest in order to supply timber to make your own wood pulp, you would hope to be able to run your business in such a way that your own timber was available to you more cheaply than anyone else's. But supposing the market could sell you timber for a lower cost per unit than your own cost of maintaining the forests and harvesting the timber, because somebody, somewhere, had lower costs and more efficient processes than you? According to Skilling's theory, everyone whose timber was more expensive than the market price would be sensible to get out of the business of forestry and, instead, buy timber from the market, releasing all of that capital needlessly tied up in forests. This, taken to its logical conclusions, would eventually leave only one supplier of timber left in the world: the most efficient supplier, who produces the cheapest product. And once there is only one timber supplier left, they would have a monopoly, the market would disappear and prices, one imagines, would go up.

Now let's consider another implication of this new and exciting situation, where one player (Enron) comes to dominate a market to such an extent that it is able to do all of the clever things that Enron proposed: offering long-term deals at competitive prices, laying off the risk of these contracts via clever derivatives and all that jazz. EnronOnline (EOL) was seen as the model by which this idea could achieve perfection: EOL would be the principal in every transaction, thereby acquiring unprecedented levels of information about the market. The transparency of this system would drive costs down, but Enron would be rewarded by an increased volume in transactions.

In the *BusinessWeek* interview quoted above, Skilling went on to explain why Enron were 'the good guys' by creating new, efficient free markets. 'We're taking on the entrenched monopolies,' he said.

> In every business we've been in, we're the good guys. That's why they don't like us. Customers love us, but the incumbents don't like us. We're bringing the benefits of choice and free markets to the world. You have no idea how frustrating it was in the early days of gas. They had built all the rules to protect their monopolies.[14]

Sceptics, as we have seen, worried whether Enron's increasing involvement in and knowledge of the market would allow it to manipulate outcomes. It was actually worse than that.

We have seen that Enron may at one point have been involved in more than 50% of all trades in natural gas in the US. Hypothetically, that share could have crept ever closer to the 100% mark. Bear in mind that EOL is the *principal* in these deals: it actually bought the gas from one party before selling it on to another party. As EOL approached the point at which it was involved in every natural gas transaction, so it approached the point in which, technically speaking, EOL owned *all* of the natural gas. This is what EOL explicitly wanted.

The effective head of Enron's trading operation was a former army captain called Greg Whalley, who would later be appointed president and chief operating officer of Enron after Jeff Skilling's resignation. It was on Whalley's trading floor that EOL was created and Whalley could see where EOL might take him and his traders. 'All I'm asking for is one side of every trade,' said Whalley. 'Is that too much to ask?'[15] Imagine a moment in time at which the bustling trading floor of EOL is stilled – or switched off. 'Stop the picture there,' Greg Whalley might have said. 'We are now on the buying side of every natural gas transaction in the US. Now stop selling gas to anyone ... and look: we own all of the gas.' A total monopoly has been achieved once again.

Better Than the Market?

There is a second, much more practical, flaw to the Skilling philosophy. If you own your own forest in order to make your own wood pulp, then your source of supply is as secure as it gets. You will have timber for wood pulp today, next year and in ten years' time. Skilling argued that Enron's markets were just as reliable: you could contract with Enron to supply timber in ten years' time at a guaranteed price. The sophistication of Enron's risk-spreading would guarantee that Enron could afford to fulfil the contract, even on such a long timeframe.

It must be remembered that the Enron vision is not the same as the 'efficient market' vision. Enron was not saying that markets would always supply everything as efficiently as possible at the best possible price. That's what a public market does, such as the stock market. Enron's argument was that for the markets in which they were major players, their unique knowledge of that market and their ability to control future pricing by means of sophisticated derivatives meant that, in the words of Professor William Bratton of the George Washington University Law School, 'Enron claimed to provide a level of intelligence higher than that of a market place, traditionally conceived.' He quotes Enron's own year 2000 annual report, which carried the headline, 'In Volatile Markets, Everything Changes But Us':

> When customers do business with Enron, they get our commitment to reliably deliver their product at a predictable price, regardless of market

> condition. This commitment is possible because of Enron's unrivalled access to markets and liquidity. [...] We offer a multitude of predictable pricing options. Market access and information allow Enron to deliver comprehensive logistical solutions that work in volatile markets or markets undergoing fundamental changes, such as energy or broadband.

As Bratton concluded, 'Enron, in short, aspired to be *better* than a market.'[16]

As these supposedly new and brilliant ideas are explored further, so it becomes clear that Enron and EOL were, in effect, parasites of the market – or, to put it more kindly, they were offering a service that might be useful (a guaranteed supply of some commodity at a fixed price) but which could never be 'better than' (surprise!) or replace that market.

The ideal is eminently meaningful – if there is a readily available and flexible market in haulage, for example, then why own trucks? But in the real world, there will always be companies for whom it makes sense to rent haulage and companies for whom it makes sense to own a fleet of trucks and drivers, not least because these companies do not want to be at the mercy of the market in truck rental. Despite Enron's assurances that their ability to guarantee prices over the long-term meant that companies could divest themselves of unnecessary assets and join the Enron 'asset-light' revolution, many companies were always likely to want to retain control over key elements of their business. In the Enronian version of the system, as we have seen, Enron controls the market and there is no point in anyone looking anywhere else for that particular commodity. This, of course, is a monopoly; but, in this case, a monopoly by a supposed market intermediary.

Enron, not surprisingly, were quite happy with that concept, but seem to have to missed the obvious point that, in the real world, this outcome (monopoly by a market intermediary) would not actually come about. Competitors would quickly enter the intermediary market. One of Enron's competitors in the energy market, Dynegy, for example, made it their business plan to copy whatever Enron was doing. Within months of the launch of EOL, Dynegy had launched a similar online trading platform, Dynegy Direct. The particular joy of markets is that a good idea, a unique new product or service, will be quickly copied and improved; cannibalised and undercut. The idea that Enron would be able to dominate this brave new world of market intermediaries, should their vision be realisable, was an obvious illusion, as was the idea that every company, everywhere, would abandon the degree of control over their destiny that was offered by the old-fashioned model of vertical integration and would instead whole-heartedly embrace Jeff Skilling's model of 'virtually integrated' systems, controlled and managed (but of course!) by Enron.

There is a final flaw in the concept of creating a market that can guarantee to deliver anything at any time at a fixed cost. Nobody – not even Enron – can possibly hedge every risk in such a way that they can overcome every turn of the market. If that were possible, then Enron would indeed have found the Philosopher's Stone. All of their customers would be protected from the vagaries of the market because Enron would be able, for a modest premium, to guarantee future prices regardless of the future state of the market. If Enron could do that, then they would indeed be better than the market.

In practice, when prices boom or crash, Enron might be able to deliver its promised contract because of its clever derivative deals, serve their clients and stay in business. But somebody, somewhere, will be left with the mirror image of the deal that has protected Enron's promised price: the disaster that balances the success. In the ideal world, the counterparty smiles ruefully, pays up and hopes that their next bet is more successful. In practice, somebody, somewhere, is not just going to lose their shirt; they are going to go bust and fail either to settle the invoice or to deliver the goods. Enron seemed to believe that it is possible to hedge every bet. It isn't.

Funnily enough, they weren't even very good at hedging their own bets.

An Environment Ripe for Abuse

It is perfectly feasible for a well-managed company to run a trading floor in a way that works hard to keep risk to a minimum – but that sort of approach to trading was not in Skilling's blood, nor could it have lasted long in the fiercely competitive, survival-of-the-fittest, dog-eat-dog atmosphere that Skilling worked hard to create at Enron. Following the huge success of his gas bank idea and the successful establishment of a natural gas trading market in North America, with Enron as a major and extremely profitable player, Skilling was given greater levels of responsibility within Enron, and made chief operating officer in 1997. He began, increasingly, to fashion Enron in his own image. Individual brilliance was prized above everything else. Failure to be brilliant led swiftly and brutally to the exit; success was extravagantly rewarded; people were set against each other in a fight for survival.

A *BusinessWeek* article entitled, 'At Enron, The Environment was Ripe for Abuse', argues that this so-called 'entrepreneurial culture', which was supposed to be one of the company's great assets, created an atmosphere where it was almost inevitable that corners would be cut and that ethical issues would be ignored. 'Skilling's recipe for changing the company was right out of the New Economy playbook,' the article claimed:

> Layers of management were wiped out. Hundreds of outsiders were recruited and encouraged to bring new thinking to a tradition-bound business. The company abolished seniority-based salaries in favor of more highly leveraged compensation that offered huge cash bonuses and stock option grants to top performers. Young people, many just out of undergraduate or MBA programs, were handed extraordinary authority, able to make US$5 million decisions without higher approval.[17]

The trouble was, the article continues, and as you may have figured out for yourself, that without any systems of control from senior and experienced management, this was an extremely risky strategy.

On the same theme, Bethany McLean and Peter Elkind, authors of *The Smartest Guys in the Room: The Amazing Rise and Scandalous Fall of Enron,* wrote this about the working environment Skilling created in his deal-driven division:

> No company can prosper over the long term if every employee is a free agent, motivated solely by greed, no matter how smart he is.... There is a reason companies value team players, just as there's a reason that people who get along with others tend to do well in corporate life. The reason is simple: you can't build a company on brilliance alone. You need people who can come up with ideas, and you also need people who can implement those ideas and are well compensated for doing so. The pure meritocracy Skilling thought he was installing was, in fact, a deeply dysfunctional workplace.... The very qualities Skilling prized – the opportunity for creativity to run wild, the mixture of brains and hubris, the absence of grey hair and structure – all turned Enron Finance into a chaotic, destructive, free-for-all. Over time, as that culture infected the entire company, Enron began to rot from within.[18]

Very soon, it seems, and under intense pressure to deliver the kind of earnings that could not possibly be delivered via the 'matched book, earnings by commission only' model, a company that became increasingly dominated by highly motivated (and highly bonused) traders and dealmakers began not to manage risk, but to speculate. This was entirely at odds with what Skilling continued to say about the company in public.

After the collapse of Enron, Skilling was convicted on various charges of securities fraud, making false statements to auditors, insider trading and conspiracy, and is currently serving a 24-year prison sentence in Colorado. As the documentation from the United States Court of Appeals noted:

> ... the evidence overwhelmingly proved that Skilling and his co-conspirators falsely portrayed Wholesale [the division that included Enron's trading operations] to the investing public as a low-risk company that made sustainable profits by delivering gas and electric power to customers (i.e., a 'logistics company'), even though they knew that Wholesale actually made most of its profits from its highly volatile trading operations.[19]

A Cool New Kind of Company

Enron was presenting itself to the world as a new kind of company. In fact, Enron was an unhappy marriage of an ironically asset-hungry energy production company (Enron International, who invested not very successfully in a selection of energy-producing plants around the world) and the famously 'asset-light' revolution that started life as Skilling's Enron Finance.

Whereas Enron International was a troubled but nevertheless recognisable division, the rest of Enron was not, in fact, a revolutionary company; it was actually a good old-fashioned trading operation. Nothing wrong with that, but everybody understands that trading operations are inherently risky. More to the point, trading operations do not – cannot – post steadily rising earnings and guarantee to do so for the foreseeable future. The sleight of hand highlighted in the Court of Appeals judgement was Enron's public conflation of its 'Wholesale' division, which was an out-and-out trading division, and its 'retail' division, Enron Energy Services (EES), which supplied gas and electricity to both corporations and consumers.

EES, based on Skilling's big idea of a gas bank (or electricity bank or broadband bank...) was explicitly meant to hedge all the trades they undertook so that their promised contract to deliver any particular commodity over a period of time was counterbalanced by a deal that took the opposite market position. In fact EES was not running a 'balanced book': they were making a number of unhedged bets that went horribly wrong. In 2000, for example, the division effectively placed a very large speculative bet that the price of electricity would fall. Unfortunately, electricity prices went through the roof and EES lost a fortune.

By early 2001 it was estimated (no one could be quite sure) that the retail division was about US$500 million in the red.[20] It wasn't just the bet on electricity prices. EES had guessed wrongly about the amount of energy its clients would need. EES had also grossly underestimated its exposure to credit risk: when the California energy crisis hit, one of Enron's clients, Pacific Gas & Electric, went bust, owing Enron hundreds of millions of dollars.

And, finally, EES was a grisly example of plain, old-fashioned sloppy management. Teams of accountants, parachuted into EES to try to stop the rot, found trays full of unopened envelopes containing cheques from utility companies, payable to EES, and amounting to some US$10 million. At the same time, Enron was running up late payment fees for electricity supply to its own buildings because nobody could get their act together to pay the bills on time.[21]

And so the whole shiny edifice of Skilling's 'cool new kind of company' began to tarnish. But actual holes in the structure would not appear for a while yet, mainly because Enron began to use some incredibly complex sleights of accountancy to prevent those holes from breaking into public view.

In the meantime, Skilling continued to insist that Enron was primarily a logistics company, not a trading company. The losses EES incurred were never declared or made obvious to the financial community or to shareholders; they were cancelled out by the huge profits Wholesale was making from the soaring price of electricity (unlike EES, Wholesale had bet the right way on electricity prices). The one thing that Skilling could never admit was that EES was an out-of-control failure: if that became public knowledge, then Skilling's brilliant vision of a gas bank (or its equivalent in other commodities) – making its money on the spread of prices commodities bought and sold, hedging its bets via derivatives in order to guarantee long-term contracted prices and enabling a new kind of asset-light company – was shot to pieces. The temporary success of a trading operation in a bull market and the illusion of an outstanding corporate performance was by now all that was underpinning Enron's stellar performance on the stock market: the company's shares peaked in August 2000, priced around US$90, at the astonishing price-to-earnings ratio of 60:1.[22]

Jeff Skilling could have gone down in history as the man who created a market for trading natural gas, which revolutionised an industry where previous heavy-handed and ill-thought-through government legislation had resulted in gas exploration companies with no incentive to explore for gas (because the regulated wellhead price was too low) and schools and factories in America's Midwest unable to get enough gas to heat their buildings (because gas-producing states were disincentivised from sending gas across state borders). Instead, he will be remembered as one of the chief architects of an epic corporate failure.

The Unthinkable Happens

Enron was the darling of Wall Street for several years in the late 1990s. In the early years, from 1990 to 1998, its stock performed only slightly better than the Standard & Poor's 500 – the index of the stock prices of America's large, publicly owned companies that trade on the two main exchanges, the New York Stock Exchange and the NASDAQ. But in 1999, Enron's stock rose by 56% while the S&P 500 rose by 20%, and in 2000 it rose a further 87% when the S&P fell by 10%. By 31 December 2000, Enron had a stock valuation of US$75.2 billion, even when its book value was only US$11.5 billion.[23]

And then the unthinkable happened: a major, supposedly blue-chip American corporation simply imploded. Employees lost not only their jobs but also their pensions: Enron had matched employee's pension contributions, not with cash, but with shares:

employees had more than 60% of their pension funds invested in Enron stock. To make matters worse, employees were 'locked out' from being able to sell these shares during a vital period when share prices began to slide. Not long before this critical moment, key Enron executives – the only people who could have known the precarious state of Enron's real finances – had sold vast numbers of their own shares.

The chief executive, Kenneth Lay, cashed in US$103 million in shares between early 1999 and mid 2001, a mere few months before the company filed for bankruptcy. Lou Pai, former chief executive of one Enron division, cashed in US$353 million. The company's Finance Director, Andy Fastow, cashed in US$30 million (having already made a great deal more in fees paid by Enron for his services in setting up the extremely dubious financial entities that Enron used to hide the true state of its finances). Jeff Skilling, who was given the role of chief executive of Enron by Kenneth Lay in 2000 but resigned in August 2001 after less than one year in the role, sold 1.1 million shares worth US$66.9 million over the same the period.[24]

Handsomely Rewarded for Losing Billions

When Enron became the world's largest bankruptcy, it is estimated to have been carrying US$38 billion in debt, both on, and infamously off, its balance sheet.[25] In the course of its corporate life, Enron's various businesses are estimated to have lost US$10 billion.[26] That is to say, the company took a huge amount of capital, employed a great many talented individuals and used up a large amount of effort and industry, and the net result was to dissipate US$10 billion.

None of the executives who earned such vast sums of money from Enron were the founders of the company – not even its chairman, Kenneth Lay, who joined a company called Houston Natural Gas as its CEO, and later became the CEO of a new company called Enron that was created by a merger of Houston

Natural Gas and a larger energy exploration to gas pipelines company called InterNorth. Neither Lay nor any other Enron executives had risked their shirts building up a company from scratch with their own capital; they were not the company's owners (prior to being handed large slices of the company in the form of shareholdings) but rather its executives – employed by the company to be the servants of that company. These executives then ran a rather shambolic, dysfunctional and loss-making operation for several years, but they reported earnings that made the shares of the company one of the hottest tickets on Wall Street.

They disguised their real losses and their poor earnings by some complex 'off balance sheet' financial skulduggery that buried the losses and, more remarkably, also generated phantom earnings. At about the time that it became clear that their systematic misrepresentation of the company's financial situation would not fool even the most dim-witted financial analyst for much longer, these executives dipped their buckets into a well filled by the share purchases of millions of ordinary, hardworking people, and made many millions of dollars by selling shares that they had good reason to believe would soon be worthless. At the same time, they exhorted employees to buy shares, continued to pay employee's pension contributions in shares, not cash, and, at a vital point, prevented employees from selling those shares when doubts emerged about their future value.

The collapse of Enron was headline news around the world: a major American corporation had simply vanished. As the news began to leak, reports talked of 'the biggest corporate failure in US history'.[27] Big corporations are not supposed to simply disappear in a puff of smoke. They are obliged by law to submit annual accounts, and those accounts must be audited by firms of accountants whose moral integrity is unquestioned. A few weeks after the announcement of the looming bankruptcy of Enron, BBC News reports were saying this:

> At the end of February this year, accounting giant Arthur Andersen gave its official seal of approval to Enron's annual report. Although hedged about with much legal jargon, the auditors' statement was clear: the energy firm's accounts presented 'fairly, in all material aspects, the financial position of Enron Corp and subsidiaries'. Nine months later, Enron admitted that its accounts for that year, and for the three previous years, had been more or less fictional.[28]

Accounting Held to Account

Nobody emerges from the Enron debacle with any credit; the one party who should, perhaps, shoulder most of the moral blame is Enron's auditors, the prestigious firm of Arthur Andersen.

Andersen's Enron client team allowed themselves to be so distracted by the huge fees they were earning from their 'client' that they lost sight of the responsibilities of their role as 'auditor'. They signed off sets of accounts that they knew to be a misrepresentation of the economic realities of Enron's finances, and by doing so, gave a gloss of respectability to the whole fraudulent affair. It was their stamp of approval, more than anything else, that allowed other participants – and the lowliest shareholder – to say, with some justification, 'Well, the accounts were signed off by Andersen, so they must be OK.'

Andersen, with great irony, were finally convicted, not for fraud, but for obstruction of justice: when Enron first went into meltdown, the Enron client team at Andersen began to systematically shred vital documents recording the details of their transactions with the energy giant. Once convicted for obstruction of justice, Andersen as a 'convicted felon' was no longer allowed by law to audit companies. This leading firm, one of the 'Big Five' accountancy practices in the United States, was effectively out of business.

We will never know whether the courts would have judged Andersen's involvement in signing off Enron's accounts to have been fraudulent. Ironically, the firm's conviction was reversed on appeal to the Supreme Court on the basis that the trial judge's instructions to the jury had been too vague to allow them to decide whether there had, indeed, been an obstruction of justice. But it was too late. Arthur Andersen's reputation had been ruined. The firm had also been the auditor of WorldCom, the telecoms company that had gone bankrupt only six months after Enron, for an even larger amount of money, having been guilty of the same kind of manipulation of its accounts in order to disguise its real financial position. The reputation of corporate America was in tatters.

Was the world blindsided? It certainly was. Are we, even today, sufficiently outraged? I am not sure that we are. Can we be certain that another, similar den of thieves will never steal the public's money on such a scale? Dream on.

The Slippery Slope

Really major debacles like the collapse of Enron do not happen overnight; no one bad decision, failed project or market collapse is sufficient to cause a disaster of this scale. It's very easy to go bust, but to go so explosively bust takes a certain amount of preparation – the outside world needs to have been misled in a deeply systematic way to allow a crisis of such proportions to appear, as it were, out of the blue. And it is equally rare for this kind of deception to begin suddenly. Senior executives tend not to wake up one day and decide not to tell the truth any more but instead to tell a series of elaborate lies that conceal the real state of affairs. There is always a slippery slope.

Yet, even when this near fatal point is reached, as executives take their first tentative steps onto the gentle incline, there is supposed to be a team at the top of any large organisation whose job it is to spot slippery slopes. They are called the board of governors and its chairman. The chairman and sometime CEO of Enron was, of course (and unfortunately for the company), Kenneth Lay – a man who would not consider that he might be on a slippery slope even if he was flat on his back and hurtling downhill at great speed.

Lay was extremely interested in the trappings and wealth of senior executive positions. His compensation package in 1999 was worth over US$42 million. By early 2000, he held 5.4 million shares of Enron stock, worth at that time about US$380 million. He took great pleasure in choosing the customised fittings of the US$45-million G-5 corporate jet that he ordered, just around the time when the state of California was suffering from a series of power blackouts as a result of electricity shortages that many people blamed on Enron's manipulation of the electricity market. Lay, as ever, managed to rise above this apparent crisis and focus on the important task at hand: the selection of the correct fabrics for the interior decoration of the G-5.[29]

It is not so much that Lay had a useful knack of rising above the fray, of distancing himself from the hurly-burly of frontline activity in order to maintain a useful mental distance. It was, rather, that Lay had never entered the fray and disliked the hurly-burly. Lay just wanted somebody else to take care of business, so that he could go about the very tolerable chore of being CEO and chairman. He seems to have had a scant idea of what actually went on at Enron and was, fatally, extremely bad at spotting the necessary talents that might have allowed him to select key executives who would genuinely be able to take care of business for him.

Ken Lay is ranked third in CNBC Portfolio's 'Worst American CEOs of All Time'. He fails to make the number one slot only because two other chief executives have subsequently led their corporations to even greater disaster: Angelo Mozilo, CEO of Countrywide Financial, the man most blamed for the subprime mortgage crisis; and Dick Fuld, the man at the helm of the once mighty global financial services firm, Lehman Brothers, who filed for the United States' largest-ever bankruptcy. CNBC is pretty scathing about Lay:

> When it comes to bad CEOs, Lay was the complete package: He was not only dishonest but disastrously inept as a manager as well. Lay, who founded Enron and turned it into a US$70 billion energy company, was uninterested in the day-to-day tasks of running the business. Consequently, he gave free rein to untrustworthy subordinates.... He also signed off on a maze of convoluted transactions that formed the basis of a massive accounting fraud that would wipe out investors and bring down the corporation. Lay was convicted of securities fraud in 2006. If he hadn't died soon afterward, he would have faced as many as 30 years in prison.[30]

Why Were We So Blindsided by Enron?

There are several reasons we were so blindsided by the Enron scandal. They do not make for very reassuring reading, but here we go.

Wishful Thinking

We allowed ourselves to be blindsided by complexity and innovation. We persuaded ourselves that, although we didn't actually understand how the thing worked, a lot of very clever people assured us that it did work and so it must be true. Another way of putting this would be to say that we indulged in wishful thinking, and allowed ourselves to be persuaded by plausible stories without thinking too hard about them.

In order for analysts to persuade themselves, for example, that Enron was worth its sky-high valuation, they would need to know that the company had some other assets, other than its balance sheet and its earnings, that would justify the remarkable 60-times earnings valuation that was given to Enron shares in late 2000. There can be a good reason to believe that a corporation had some immensely valuable 'intangible assets': some incredibly clever system or infrastructure that would explain why its shares should be worth such a high multiple of their earnings. Intangible assets might be a thriving research and development division delivering exceptional numbers of new patents, or an exceptional investment in training and staff development.

In Enron's case it was presumably believed to be the extreme version of Skilling's 'cool' gas bank concept, in which Enron became the market intermediary of choice for... everything! On this analysis Enron, the pioneer of virtual integration, had discovered an amazing new way of doing business that would produce unheard of levels of profitability – the new, 'magical' kind of innovation by which we are regularly blindsided. Skilling, after all, had compared his vision for the future of business to be a revolution – like the coming of the railways, or the telephone.

Unfortunately, Enron's 'magical' new ways of working did not represent the kind of intangible assets that would justify its hugely over-valued share price. As Baruch Lev of New York University's Stern School of Business wrote in 2002:

> The best evidence that Enron lacked substantial intangibles is that its demise made hardly a ripple in the energy trading market.... Intangibles, by definition, are unique factors of production that cannot be quickly imitated by competitors. The fact that Enron's competitors quickly stepped in to fill the gap is inconsistent with the existence of intangibles conferring on their owners sustained competitive advantages. So the answer to the question posed at the opening of this note – where have Enron's intangibles gone? – is a simple one: Nowhere. Enron did not have substantial intangibles, that is, if hype, glib, and earnings manipulation do not count as intangibles.[31]

Greed and Selfishness

When we find a good thing, we don't ask too many questions about how it can be so good. If, after all, everybody else is making money, then why shouldn't we? This point of view was most cogently expressed by the character Yossarian in Joseph Heller's best-selling 1961 anti-war (and anti-bureaucracy) novel, *Catch-22*:

> Yossarian: From now on I'm thinking only of me.
> Major Danby: But, Yossarian, suppose everyone felt that way?
> Yossarian: Then I'd certainly be a damned fool to feel any other way, wouldn't I?

In the case of key Enron executives, there was greed and selfishness of the most offensive sort: the kind of greed that assumes that the sole function of great corporations is to make a very few individuals extremely rich; that sees the delivery of products that represent good value to customers as a secondary consideration; and that treats shareholders as suckers whose only role is to dutifully buy the much-hyped stock at whatever inflated price the management team have managed to justify by dubious means. This kind of selfish greed also sees the whole structure of modern business – so essential for the creation of wealth and the bettering of the lives of large numbers of citizens – as a game to be played by those clever enough to get their hands on the levers of power, and with only one aim: the creation of great wealth for a select few.

For Enron's suppliers – its large roster of heavyweight investment banks in particular – the greed was of a far more understandable, and therefore more disturbing, kind. Enron was spending colossal amounts of money on fees for banking, legal and accountancy services. You either joined the race and fought for a slice of that money or you took a principled stand and lost out. But for what principles, exactly? Enron was deemed by the financial establishment to be trading legally; more than that, it was the darling of Wall Street and the financial media. *Fortune* magazine named Enron the 'Most Innovative Company' for six consecutive years. There is a kind of amorality in business at this kind of level. As one banker says, 'In investment banking, the ethic is: "Can this deal get done?" If it can and you're not likely to get sued, then it's a good deal.'[32]

If this is a common business 'principle' (or lack of one), we should stop wringing our hands and staring around with wide-eyed amazement when scandals like the Enron collapse occur. We should simply acknowledge that some businesses will, on occasions, follow courses of action that are based on greed and dishonesty, rather than any more honourable motivation. The world of business is a pretty rough place, even at the most basic level, and has always been so: people have had to take care not to be cheated in the marketplace for millennia. Regulators and fair-trading officers do their best to prevent abuses, and the whole system continues to function fairly well, despite regular abuses.

But if this slightly bleak analysis is correct, then we should stop being blindsided so frequently by events that we should, rather, come to expect. When companies present impartial or confusing accounts and start to use complicated if technically legal devices to hide money off balance sheet, then we should expect the worst. We should ignore partial stock market analysts who tell us that this company's stock is good value and should be expected to climb further; we should sell our stocks and refuse to buy any more until we understand how that business is operating.

But, of course, we won't do that. If the figures *could* be portrayed as believable and if high-flying analysts tell us that we *should* believe them and that the stock is likely to increase in value, then we know that we can make money by doing precisely that. Even if we feel that a day of reckoning is coming, we (because we are so clever) will be able to make more profit and get out before the bad times arrive.

And so we are as complicit as the bankers who do deals that they know to be dodgy because they don't want to lose out on the fee. We are all greedy. We are all, perhaps, dishonest at some level. We need to look the world more squarely in the eye and, most importantly, we need to give our regulators a sterner brief and bigger sticks. Otherwise we are doomed to be blindsided time and again, to find ourselves staring at the wreckage and wondering how this can possibly have happened.

Trust

We have an inbuilt tendency to trust people, but especially people in authority. We are social, hierarchical animals. For many people, the chief executive officer of a major corporation is about as far up the hierarchy as you can get. Sadly, and most unfortunately, we find it hard to imagine that people who enjoy vast wealth, move in the highest circles of society and regularly appear on our television screens being shown great deference by journalists, interviewers and all around them, are barefaced liars.

When Enron was at the top of the heap of corporate America, its top executives were amongst the most powerful and feted people in the country. They were the mighty to which the legitimate spoils of free market capitalism had now fallen. In the more aggressively capitalist societies, the successful corporate executive is at the top of the social ladder. These guys and girls have made it, and made it big. Their astonishing rewards in salary and stock options are a badge of honour. When these great achievers tell us everything is fine, we tend to believe them, especially if they claim to have found a new way of doing business that explains how they have achieved their remarkable results. Skilling was always viciously damning of people – especially employees – who 'didn't get it'. He was the smartest guy in the room.

People outside of Enron, even smart people, looked at Enron's remarkable stock performance and, if they had any doubts, were afraid to express them because maybe they just 'didn't get it'. We all hate to look foolish. It takes a brave person to face up to the people at the peak of corporate American life and say, 'This is all nonsense'. The very people who should be saying this, of course, are highly-paid stock market analysts; sadly, because they are paid by brokers who make money from successful stocks, it is in nobody's interests to talk down a stock whose rise is making everybody rich. The only people who will give you a warning signal are the hedge fund operators who are busy shorting a stock that they believe is overvalued. Unfortunately, they don't go around shouting about it.

I Want My Share

This is a kind of cross between greed and herd mentality. If everybody is making money by investing in Enron then (a) can they all be wrong? and (b) why am I not getting my share of this?

This probably made sense when we were hunter-gatherers: if everybody else is helping themselves to some resource – a crop of berries, perhaps, or a shoal of fish – then it might be life-threatening not to get your share. We still find it hard to resist the urge to join in. Human beings, as social animals, are as prone to the herd instinct as any other large mammal. We tend to do what everybody else is doing, normally for good reasons (Can everybody else be making a mistake?), but occasionally for bad reasons (Yes, they can). When we see somebody else making a large amount of money from something that we could do ourselves – like buying shares in a successful company – then the urge to do likewise is almost irresistible, even if we are far from certain that whatever is making all of this money is genuinely worth the price that is being paid.

Experts Live In Herds, Too

If everyone believes that something is true, then it might as well be true. If Enron is the hottest share on Wall Street, then it is. It is a brave analyst who says that Enron is massively overvalued and advises his clients not to buy, only to watch the share price steadily increase in value and his clients lose an opportunity to make money.

Sadly, although investment bankers and fund managers like to believe that the herd instinct belongs further down the food chain than the exalted position that they themselves occupy – that it is the common punters of the financial market who are prone to herd instincts while, they, the 'masters of the universe', rise serenely above the fray – in fact, even the 'masters of the universe' are swayed as much by the actions of their own highly paid herd as other mere mortals buying and selling their few dollars' worth of stocks and shares. The analyst who goes against the herd, who bravely asserts that Enron stocks are overvalued and that clients should immediately sell their shares in the company, looks foolish. His words are immediately proven to be wrong when Enron's shares rise once more.

But there is another more fundamental reason why lone voices are not heeded: the person who goes against the herd in this way is wrong by definition, because they are *not one of us*. They have left the club to which everybody else belongs. The same thing happens in every field of human endeavour, whether it be politics, economics, or science. People who go against the currently accepted view are not merely wrong, they are bad – treasonous even. The economist Joseph Stiglitz makes the point tellingly. As what is now known as America's subprime crisis was developing into a full-blown credit bubble, Stiglitz and other like-minded economists were busy telling anyone who would listen that this was, indeed, a bubble. Nobody listened. When, after the event, Stiglitz and his colleagues were presenting their understanding of the events leading up to the crash at a meeting of the World Economic Forum at Davos in 2008, here's what happened:

> As I and a couple of other colleagues explained how the bubble had developed and what its breaking meant, a chorus of central bankers in the front row chimed in: 'No one predicted it', they claimed. That claim was immediately challenged by the same small band that had been talking about the bubble for several years. But the central bankers were, in a sense, right; no one *with credibility in their circle* [Stiglitz's italics] challenged the prevailing view, but there was a tautology: no one challenging the prevailing view would be treated as credible. Sharing similar views was part of being socially and intellectually acceptable.[33]

Principles are Expensive

A lot of bankers sensed that all was not well with Enron, but it was not in their interest to refuse to fund the company's projects and take the rewards. If banks could be persuaded that a deal with Enron was technically legal, and they felt that their money was safe, then to make a stand on principle would be to watch a competitor take the fee and benefit from the interest payment.

To the man on the street, the Skilling-god had created a money-making machine that had enriched thousands of Americans and he would be a fool to miss out on an opportunity to enrich himself by buying his own little slice of the company. To the investment bankers and their tame 'analysts', Enron was a different kind of money-making machine: a self-fulfilling prophecy. Even if they had doubts about the fundamental reality of the business that was propping up Enron's remarkable earnings, these financial luminaries had no incentive to tell anybody about their concerns. They were in the business of advising their clients in how to make money. To use an extremely apt horse-racing analogy, they were in the business of predicting winners. If you advised your clients not to back Enron, and Enron announced another set of remarkable earnings figures which pushed their stock price higher, then you (the prophet of doom, the Cassandra) didn't look prescient and clever, you looked stupid. The only time you wouldn't look stupid is when you advised your clients to pull all of their money out of Enron just before the company went bust. If they were to advise their clients to do this any earlier, then they would cost their clients weeks (days? hours?) of money-making time.

Such is the brutal logic of making money by the minute. Advisors are no longer rewarded for sage advice about avoiding good-looking investments that may actually turn sour in the long run. The long run is for suckers. What investors increasingly want is a quick buck: 'Don't tell me about the fundamentals, just tell me if the stock is going up tomorrow.' Driven by this inexorable logic, analysts, advisors and even fund managers are forced to join the herd of their fellow analysts, advisors and fund managers and to recommend stock that will, almost certainly, go up in value in the short term, even when they know that the rise is illusory and that a crash is likely, if not inevitable. Bubbles, they reassure themselves, can only be seen with the benefit of hindsight.

When a bubble is growing, no client will thank you for advising him or her not to make money while the going is good. They only want the bad news in that critical window – a few moments before disaster, when it is time to jump off the train before it crashes. Not many analysts manage to make that call successfully. And, perverse as it may seem, even fund managers will not be criticised for a fall in the fund value caused by an event that was, after all, *unexpected.* All of their competitor funds will have fallen in value for the same reason, so they are not guilty of letting their clients down – everyone has merely been the victim of circumstances beyond their control.

These, then, may be the reasons why the world was so blindsided by the most shocking corporate collapse the world has ever seen: our old friends, greed and selfishness; our ingrained habit of trusting the people at the top of social hierarchies (though not, of course politicians – that is a different matter); our inability not to want our share of something that everybody else is helping themselves to; the fact that 'expert advisors' suffer from herd mentality along with the rest of us; the sad fact that a principled way of conducting our affairs is a very good thing until it begins to cost us money (greed and selfishness in a slightly different guise).

These are all part of what makes us human and of the ways in which society works. We recognise all of them, and would like to believe that we are conscious and wary of the effects that they may have on our decision-making and our behaviour. The fact is that, for most of the time, we do not keep these things to the front of our minds and we are not, as a result, wary. We are all capable of being swept along by an illusion that we want to believe in: the possibility that a new age has dawned, that the good times have arrived, and that we will all be rich.

5 THE GUNFIGHT AT THE OK CORRAL

Society and business are often blindsided by sudden outbreaks of violence and lawlessness. We may be aware of tensions simmering below the surface, but the final trigger that leads to violent action is often relatively trivial, and the sudden eruption of violence is always deeply shocking, damaging and hard to come to terms with. Communities are left shell-shocked, horrified by the violence that has emerged in their midst. Nations are forced to re-evaluate their shared values and sense of identity.

The 'tensions' that lead to this eruption may be political or social. When they are political, there is a greater chance for the experts and analysts to warn of a likely upheaval, and a considerable need for the powers that be to consider whether they still have a mandate to govern. When the origins are social – as with outbreaks of rioting with no obvious root cause – society is taken completely by surprise. Why has this happened to us? What does this mean? Why are people destroying their own communities?

The year 2011 began with a series of upheavals in North Africa and the Middle East: the now-famous 'Arab Spring', which saw citizens of various North African and Middle Eastern countries stage what ranged from robust demonstrations to outright revolution. The president of Tunisia fled his country; President Mubarak of Egypt resigned after 30 years as head of state. Colonel Gaddafi, Libya's ruler of more than 40 years, had been overthrown and killed following a five-month civil war. Other heads of state have stepped down, or promised to step down at the end of their current terms. If any political pundits, at least in the West, saw this coming, then they kept very quiet about it in their forecasts for the year ahead as the first decade of the twenty-first century came to an end.

In the summer of the same year, London and other major cities in Great Britain were rocked by outbursts of violence, arson and looting: the capital, which had just recently provided the glorious backdrop to the royal wedding of Prince William, Duke of Cambridge, and his bride Kate Middleton, was now ablaze. Its own citizens, some of whom had presumably taken part in the good-natured celebration of the marriage of the nation's future king, were now putting the city to the torch, threatening the lives of fellow citizens, and indulging in a frenzy of organised looting. The people of Great Britain, I can assure you from personal experience, were completely blindsided.

People Power

There is no shortage of historical precedents for all of these events. The New York riots of 1987 – so similar in many respects to the London riots of 2011 – were triggered by nothing more remarkable than an electricity blackout. The lights of New York went out, and large numbers of people decided to loot, pillage and set fire to buildings in their neighbourhoods.

The fall of various Eastern European Communist regimes in 1989 provides an exact parallel with the Arab Spring of 2011. Dissatisfaction with ruling regimes had been widespread for some time. When public demonstrations began, they were triggered by events that seemed to have little significance. On occasion, there was an eruption of violence – as with the overthrow of the hateful President Ceausescu of Romania – but, more often, the people suddenly shrugged off the constraints of their rulers without fuss or threat. They'd had enough, and they could no longer be cowed or controlled. When this happens, it is presumably a terrifying spectacle for those who have tried to cling to power for too long and for the wrong reasons.

The Arab Spring has provided the cheerful spectacle of several bewildered autocrats struggling to come to terms with the fact they are certainly no longer loved nor, more interestingly, feared. There are few more joyous spectacles, few sights so uplifting to witness, as a people, apparently without leadership or organisation, suddenly and calmly making it known that enough is enough and there will be changes – right now, right here, regardless of the often terrifying powers of the state's security forces. One moment the secret police and the armed guards on the street are all-powerful and intimidating; the next moment they are disappearing into the shadows, hoping that their role as instruments of government oppression will be forgotten.

When Tyrants Fall

In 1989, the people of Romania took to the streets in a wave of protest against the regime of Nicolae Ceausescu, one of the bloodier and more unpleasant rulers of countries within the Soviet-dominated Eastern Bloc. As shops ran out of bread, eggs, flour and butter as a result of the regime's inept economic policies, Ceausescu appeared on state-controlled television in shops apparently full of food (much of it made from polystyrene), in order to demonstrate the great feast of plenty that his regime had brought to the Romanian people.

As anti-government demonstrations suddenly began, Ceausescu addressed a mass meeting in Bucharest's Palace Square (now called Revolution Square). The meeting would be broadcast to the nation as a 'meeting of support': a spontaneous demonstration of the people of Bucharest's love of their great leader. Ceausescu began one of his typical speeches (extremely long, deadly dull and full of meaningless Marxist-Leninist slogans) in praise of the achievements of his regime. The crowd was not in the mood; he was booed and heckled – a previously unthinkable thing in a country controlled by a brutal state police force, the Securitate. Ceausescu faltered in his speech. He raised his hand for silence, but was ignored. The moment was broadcast to the nation by state television: the moment when a dictator realised that he had lost control. Ceausescu scurried back to the safety of his state building. Television transmission was interrupted, but it was too late. The self-styled 'great leader' was no longer a figure of fear.

The next day, Ceausescu and his wife were forced to escape by helicopter from the roof of the Central Committee building in Bucharest, avoiding by a few minutes the demonstrators racing through the building in search of him. The demonstrators reached the roof in time to see the helicopter gathering speed to take the Ceausescus away from the capital in search of a safe haven. The helicopter was ordered to land by the regular army, which had defected to the popular cause and closed off Romanian airspace in fear of incursions by Soviet aircraft seeking to support the old regime.

On Christmas Day 1989, four days after his rather unsuccessful speech in Palace Square, Ceausescu and his wife were handed over to the army by the police to whom they had surrendered, and sentenced to death by a hastily assembled military court for crimes including genocide (the Romanian secret police are held responsible for the disappearance and death of thousands of Romanian citizens). They were taken out and shot.

Walls Come Tumbling Down

Elsewhere within the Soviet Bloc in 1989, regime collapse had been happening equally spontaneously but far less violently, as civil disobedience spread through Poland, Hungary, Czechoslovakia and Bulgaria.

In East Germany, the German Democratic Republic imploded quietly, and the Berlin Wall fell without a shot being fired.

Increasing numbers of refugees had begun to flee the country by various means, especially via Hungary, which was by now only nominally a Communist state and was on the verge its own transition to democratic government. Hungary opened its borders and allowed East German refugees in Hungary (normally described by the East German state as 'tourists') to cross the Hungarian border into Austria. East Germany began to relax its border controls to allow a controlled exit of disaffected citizens and intended to do this also via certain checkpoints in the Berlin Wall, allowing people to move from East to West Berlin.

In a botched press announcement, an East German official confirmed incorrectly that the new regulations were to take effect 'immediately' (in fact, the regulations were meant to take effect the following afternoon, to give border guards time to make arrangements for an orderly movement). The general tone of his uncertain answers to questions from the press conveyed the impression that people were free to leave East Germany, effective immediately. People took to the streets, and what happened next at one location, the infamous Checkpoint Charlie, was reported by BBC reporter Gavin Hewitt:

> On the street, people, couples, groups were tumbling out of apartment buildings. Many were young, their faces alive, daring to believe. We headed through the dimly lit streets towards Checkpoint Charlie, one of the crossing points to West Berlin.
>
> Suddenly, it seemed, we were no longer individuals but a crowd, drawn close by an unspoken hope. As we neared the checkpoint we slowed. From the West German side we could hear cheering, the sounds of a party, of celebration. In that moment, defined by a distant sound, some around me knew their world had changed and they embraced, their tears running on to the shoulders of friends.
>
> Ahead of us were East German guards, edgy and uncertain, standing back in the shadows. Beyond them, on the other side of Checkpoint Charlie was a bear, a dancing bear. Someone placed an East German border guard's cap on its head and the crowd laughed and drank from bottles.

> Then a middle-aged couple walked past me towards the crossing and just kept walking. Two ordinary anonymous people. The crowd fell silent and watched this slow agonising walk into history. The guards did not stop them. They just checked out. On the West German side there was a roar and the couple were swallowed up in celebration.[1]

The border guards, uncertain of their orders, had lost the will to open fire on their own people, though they had done so often enough in the past: at least 136 people are thought to have been killed attempting to cross the Wall into West Berlin.[2]

There seems to come a crucial tipping point at which what was previously law and order falls apart and a new consensus emerges. A moment when ruthless armed guards facing a cowed people suddenly become nervous armed guards facing a resolute people. There was, apparently, no hostility shown towards the previously feared guards. People simply began, humiliatingly, to ignore them.

Rights, Rents and Total Democracy

When groups of people find themselves in situations where they are beyond the reach of the law – when they embark on a dangerous journey together across the ocean or the desert, or find themselves looking for some precious resource in the wilderness along with several of their equally hopeful, greedy and selfish fellow men and women – what tends to break out is not anarchy but a surprising degree of law and order. A kind of total democracy arises, as people come together, draw up the rules by which they want to abide, and administer their own justice where necessary. What, in general, does *not* happen is that people – like some collection of vicious pirates – fight and squabble amongst themselves until only one man is left standing, and he finds that he can no longer sail the ship without the crew that he has helped to annihilate. Humans are not that stupid. Our success as a species comes from our instinct to cooperate with each other.

The 'taming of the West' in late-nineteenth-century North America is often taken as a classic example of the imposition of law and order on a lawless society. What is ironic is that the West had, by and large, already been tamed, by the remarkably peaceful and cooperative – and no less heroic – efforts of the earliest pioneers.

The early wagon trains heading west from such towns as Independence, Missouri, on the Oregon and California trails, knew very well that they were leaving the protection of the law. Many wagon trains drew up governmental-style constitutions to spell out the rights and obligations of wagon-train members, and the forfeits and punishments that transgressors would face. They also, on occasion, formed themselves into joint-stock or partnership companies, coming together to buy the necessary equipment for the journey, disbanding at journey's end and selling off the assets, to be divided among the investors. One such company's constitution began with the stirring words: 'We the undersigned hereby agree to form ourselves into a company for our mutual benefit and protection in emigrating to California & we pledge ourselves to protect each other in person and property in all justifiable cases and also to conform to the constitution and the bye laws.'[3]

Under the terms of such constitutions, justice on the trail could be stern and swift, as one account relates:

> A brutal murder ... aroused strong reactions from the emigrants.... Lafayette Tate brutally stabbed a man by the name of Miller, the leader of a section of the train.... The murderer started off at an attempt to escape, but he was shortly apprehended by a group of 15 men. Tate maintained that there was no law upon the plains and his trial should be held in organised territory. His claims were ignored and a judge, defence, and prosecuting attorneys and a jury were quickly selected from the trains in the neighbourhood. Justice moved rapidly and that midnight, the murderer was hanged for his crime, much to the relief of many of the emigrants. It was a relief to be assured that justice existed

> on the trail and that travellers were protected from those elements of the migration whose behaviour was dangerous to life.[4]

In an entirely similar way, life in the mining camps that were springing up in the West (the sort of camp that gave birth to the famous Wild West town of Tombstone, which we will see more of in a moment) were not subject to the sort of anarchic violence that is often portrayed as holding sway when people leave the bounds of society, driven by selfish greed to seek their fortunes without concern for their fellow fortune hunters. Driven by greed we may well be, but humans are cooperative and intelligent animals. We know that if the spoils go to the mighty, then life for the majority becomes extremely unpleasant.

As Terry L. Anderson and Peter J. Hill argue lucidly in their book, *The Not So Wild, Wild West: Property Rights on the Frontier*, the early pioneers demonstrated an instinctive grasp of the pivotal importance of property rights for the successful (and peaceful) development of new resources – or what Anderson and Hill, as economists, would call 'rents' (defined as 'the value of a unique asset that cannot be reproduced'). Rents are not the same as profits, which can be competed away, because they stem from a unique asset, not from a process. In the absence of property rights, a free-for-all would inevitably ensue, and the spoils would go to the most formidable. Pioneers had the sense to see that this was in nobody's interest (other than that of the mightiest).

Ironically, the widespread availability and affordability of the new 'six-shooter' pistol helped greatly to level the playing field: when nearly everyone is armed, or might be armed, the scope for opportunistic armed robbery is reduced. This, of course, is the argument used in favour of the continuing right of American citizens to bear arms, which seems to have been extended to the right of every alienated teenager with low self-esteem and a grudge against his high school teachers and classmates to amass an arsenal of high-powered automatic weapons which would be the envy of a special forces operative.

As it was, life in even the earliest of the camps springing up around successful 'strikes' was remarkably free from violent dispute. As Anderson and Hill write:

> When conflicts arose among miners in a camp, a meeting was called, and a contract drawn up that specified how property rights would be defined and enforced. The contract specified the boundaries of the district, the size of the allowed claims, and the methods by which claims would be enforced. It also provided for the registration of claims, usually with one of the more respected miners in the camp. A typical claim would be not more than 100 square feet per miner; leaving tools on the site (which were rarely stolen) was proof that the claim was being worked – though a claim could be forfeited if no work was carried out for a period of more than five days, except in cases of injury or illness. As was the case with the wagon trains, justice was dispensed rapidly and democratically: 'local' decisions about claims or the management of a camp's affairs were settled by the members of each camp, but for serious offences – robbery or murder – anyone attending a tribunal had the right to be heard. A cry would go up around the hills to draw the miners together to pass judgement and to agree punishment: typically eviction from the camp, a whipping or, in the case of murder, hanging.[5]

Law and Fair Play

These recent examples of 'total democracy' functioned remarkably well, but they reflect the relative simplicity and homogeneity of the societies from which they emerged: groups of like-minded people, outside the framework of any system of law enforcement, engaged in the same activity, with every incentive to cooperate with each other and thrash out ways of recognising individual rights and obligations and of deterring those predatory people who tried to gain an unfair share, or to help himself to the fruits of another man's labour.

As the early communities of miners, ranchers, trappers and shop holders began to acquire more of the trappings of civilisation

– shops, banks, saloons, stables, stagecoaches and photographic galleries – so the scope for anti-social behaviour and the need for organised law enforcement grew. It is one thing to respect a neighbour's property in a new community where each individual is reliant on the other's support and cooperation, but the accumulation of wealth and its tempting presence – in banks on the main street, on vulnerable stagecoaches and trains, and in people's pockets and hand luggage – led to increasing numbers of robberies, all involving the use of firearms, that began to threaten the still-precarious new community's development.

And so 'The Law' emerges, complete with a more overt set of rules and proscriptions, enforced, most significantly, by professional lawmen who take over the role of law enforcer. Members of the community are no longer required to enforce the law themselves: the selfishness of the individual is circumscribed and curtailed by laws and punishments, and a kind of settled order – a fledgling society – emerges. Selfishness and bad behaviour never go away, of course, but at this point the selfish ones are not, as they would have been in the early days, on the journey, or in the mining camps, in danger of destroying the whole endeavour. Now they are merely predators, looking for a free lunch at the expense of a settled society. They are expensive and dangerous, but they are unlikely to prove fatal to society as a whole.

A little further down the line, however, as societies become more sophisticated, so a different risk appears: the group no longer holds together; the members of society are no longer clear as to who is 'us' and who is 'them'; different sectors of society have different goals and agendas; the people who were previously society's leaders no longer speak for everyone in society. At this stage in a society's development, breakdowns in law and order come suddenly and unexpectedly.

The danger may come from outside or from within. Some civilisations, like ancient Rome, weaken at the centre and begin to fray at the edges. Others lose touch with their citizens and are suddenly attacked from within. Typically, in the latter case, there is a political agenda: the state has an ideology to which large numbers of its citizens no longer adhere. Monarchs are overthrown and replaced by republics; capitalism is replaced by Communism; autocracy is replaced by democracy.

But, throughout history, we have also seen another kind of phenomenon: the riot. Riots that are politically motivated don't really count – if you will allow me the distinction: these have an agenda, an outcome that the rioters would like to see brought about. A proper riot is, in contrast, essentially meaningless. It is simply an outbreak of violence between two different groups, 'us' and 'them', like a football riot. There have been lots of good examples.

Oxford, 1355

In 1355, the mother of all 'town and gown' disputes broke out in the university city of Oxford, England: the St Scholastica Day riot. Two students were drinking (why is one not surprised?) at a tavern and were unhappy about the quality of the wine that they had been served. They threw the wine over the landlord and knocked him about.

Town bailiffs asked the students to make amends and they refused. The mayor of Oxford asked the chancellor of the university to arrest the students (who, like all members of the university, were outside of the mayor's jurisdiction) but the chancellor refused. The students rallied and may have assaulted the mayor; the chancellor fled the town and the next day the students closed the city gates, set fire to buildings and assaulted townspeople. The people of Oxford fought back, firing on students with longbows. Finally, 2,000 locals are said to have descended on the university, shouting, 'Slay, slay, havoc, havoc, smite fast and give good knocks...' (which is a robust, if not catchy, rallying cry) and set about the students.[6] As many as 63 students and perhaps 30 townspeople died, and many more were injured.

Why did this minor incident flare up into a major event? Because 'the people of Oxford' and 'the university' no longer shared a common objective, nor even a common jurisdiction.

New York City, 1977

In more recent times, another riot raises more familiar, modern issues. In New York in 1977, thunderstorms led to lightning strikes on substations and transmission lines that triggered a series of events within the electricity supply system that led to the blackout of much of New York City. As the *New York Times* reported in a recent retrospective: 'In little more than 24 hours – the blackout lasted from 9.34 p.m. on July 13 to 10.39 p.m. on July 14 – 1,000 fires were reported, 1,600 stores were damaged in looting and rioting and 3,700 people were arrested. Neighbourhoods from East Harlem to Bushwick were devastated. The authorities later estimated that the total cost of the blackout exceeded US$300 million.'[7] The riots made the cover of *Time Magazine* on 25 July 1977, and the leading article described 'a night of terror':

> Roving bands of determined men, women and even little children wrenched steel shutters and grilles from storefronts with crowbars, shattered plate-glass windows, scooped up everything they could carry, and destroyed what they could not. First they went for clothing, TV sets, jewellery, liquor; when that was cleaned out, they picked up food, furniture and drugs.... The arsonists were as busy as the looters. Firemen fought 1,037 blazes, six times the normal number, and received nearly 1,700 false alarms. They were set either to divert the attention of the cops or just for the fun of it. When the firemen showed up, their sirens screaming, the crowds pelted them with rocks and bottles. Of the fires, 65 were considered serious, including a store fire in Brooklyn at which 22 firemen were hurt. Another blaze began in a looted factory warehouse in Brooklyn, then leaped across the street to destroy four tenements and finally spread to two other houses. In all, 59 firemen were injured fighting the fires.[8]

London's Burning, 2011

Thirty-four years later, in August 2011, and to the astonishment of its citizens, it was London's turn to burn. Only three months earlier, on 29 April 2011, the world had watched Prince William, second in line to the throne of the United Kingdom and the Commonwealth, marry his university sweetheart, Catherine Middleton. Catherine (Kate) was technically described as a 'commoner', meaning that none of her recent ancestors have been aristocrats, and her immediate forebears include labourers and mineworkers. The heir to the throne was marrying a girl with working-class origins, Britain laid on a day of pageantry that dug deep into the country's rich history and ancient traditions, and the world watched in fascination. Some one million people are thought to have descended on London on the day of the wedding. They stood patiently for hours in order to get a glimpse of the happy couple and the rest of the royal family. There was no trouble. This, surely, was a nation at ease with itself.

Three months later, the nation's TV screens were filled with very different images of London: gangs of hooded youths throwing missiles at the police and setting fire to cars and buildings. The trigger had been a peaceful demonstration in Tottenham, north London, by family and friends of a young man shot dead by police in disputed circumstances. When rioting broke out later that night, it was widely assumed to be the usual expression of anti-police sentiment by groups of disaffected young people. The country watched in horror as copycat riots broke out across the capital and then in other major cities.

The rioters' main preoccupation, as in New York in 1977, was with looting and indiscriminate arson. Shops and buildings burned through the night as areas of London came to resemble a war zone: newspaper headlines recalled 'the Blitz' – the bombing of London by Nazi Germany in the early phase of World War II. But these fires were caused not by enemy bombs but by fellow citizens who seemed to take delight in the destruction of their own communities.

For a few days, looting became a way of life: shops large and small were targeted, with many family businesses ransacked. In some locations, the looting became institutionalised: residents in the South London district of Clapham reported groups of 'well-dressed women in expensive cars' turning up in the wake of the rioters to help themselves to stolen goods in a systematic way. A fourteen-year-old youth told London's *Evening Standard* newspaper: 'Now we feel we can get away with it because we see it on TV.'[9]

Police recorded over 3,000 crimes during five days of looting in the capital. On the assumption that between five and ten people were involved in each incident, this would mean that between 15,000 and 30,000 people decided to be outlaws that week in London alone.

The Gunfight at the OK Corral

When anarchy breaks out on peaceful streets – when residents cower in upstairs bedrooms while gangs smash down their front doors and ransack their houses, or when diners are menaced and terrorised in restaurants and thugs steal phones and wallets and pull the wedding rings from women's fingers – it is easy to think that society is collapsing and that we have gone back to a kind of Wild West. Back to the wild frontier towns of America where the rule of law was slowly and painfully established by heroic town marshals and their deputies, facing down gangs of rowdy cowboys and, from time to time, being drawn inevitably into a 'showdown' – the classic Western confrontation between the forces of law and order and the forces of anarchy, in which, in a very American way, the matter is resolved by gunfire.

On 26 October 1881, there was a brief but bloody shoot-out in the American frontier town of Tombstone, Arizona – a small town that had sprung up out of nothing a mere two years earlier, when a prospector struck a rich vein of silver ore in the nearby hills. By 1881, the boomtown created by the rush to stake out mining claims was home to 1,000 people. Tombstone could boast many of the facilities of a modern town, including hotels, saloons, various stores and a photograph gallery (where residents could have images of themselves recorded for posterity, dressed in their finest clothes, proving that life in Tombstone was just as sophisticated as in any swanky town back east), a gun shop, a sheriff's office and, of course, a corral, offering stabling, hay barns and a blacksmith for the horses and mules that were the region's only mode of transport. This particular corral was called the OK Corral.

The shoot-out in Tombstone didn't actually happen in the OK Corral, but in a nearby vacant lot, next to Fly's Photograph Gallery. The antagonists were the forces of law and order and a group of cowboys – the term, in that region, at that time, carried more of the implication of a clan of cattle rustlers and stagecoach robbers than it did of the law-abiding employees of a cattle ranch. The original term used at the time was more typically 'Cow Boy' or 'Cow-Boy', as in the newspaper headline: 'A Desperate Fight Between Officers of the Law and Cow-Boys – The Killed and Wounded!'[10]

Exactly what happened at the OK Corral is still disputed and much raked over by historians. 'Cowboys' tended to make a living by rustling cattle from Mexico and selling them on in American territory, or by robbing Mexican smugglers coming into the United States to buy alcohol and tobacco, which were more lightly taxed in the United States. Many, however, also ran legitimate or semi-legitimate ranching businesses. They behaved themselves (within reason) in Tombstone itself and were good customers of the saloons and stores; many were well liked.

When the Mexican authorities reduced its taxes on alcohol and tobacco and began to crackdown on American banditry – asking also for US government support – American outlaws increasingly turned on homegrown targets, such as the vulnerable stagecoaches. The shoot-out in Tombstone was between two such cowboy families – the McLaurys and the Clantons – and the forces of law and order: city marshal Virgil Earp, his brothers and deputy sheriffs, Wyatt and Morgan Earp, and Doc Holliday, who was in fact a one-time dentist, gambler and drinker, but who was recommended by the fact that he had saved Wyatt Earp's life in an earlier saloon bar shoot-out with 'desperadoes' when Wyatt was city marshal of Dodge City, Kansas.

Doc Holliday was fast on the draw; in the coming fight, however, he used the short double-barrelled shotgun or 'coach gun' favoured by stagecoach guards. He may, or may not, have switched to a pistol later in the fight. The following is Wyatt Earp's own account of the fight, given as part of his testimony to the hearing in which it was decided that the lawmen did not have to face trial for the unlawful killing of the victims of the gunfight.

> When I saw Billy and Frank draw their pistols I drew my pistol. Billy Clanton levelled his pistol at me but I did not aim at him. I knew that Frank McLaury had the reputation of being a good shot and a dangerous man, and I aimed at Frank McLaury. The two first shots which were fired were fired by Billy Clanton and myself; he shot at me, and I shot at Frank McLaury. I do not know which shot was first; we fired almost together. The fight then became general.... My first shot struck Frank McLaury in the belly. He staggered off on the sidewalk but first fired one shot at me.[11]

In the space of less than 30 seconds, Doc Holliday shot the other McLaury brother, Tom, in the side with his shotgun. Morgan Earp was hit in the left shoulder blade, possibly when he had turned to face a shot that seemed to come from behind. The shot ricocheted through his body, just missing the spine and emerging through the left shoulder. The spent bullet stayed inside Morgan's shirt. Morgan fell to the ground but, impressively, raised himself to a sitting position and kept firing. Frank McLaury, wounded at the outset by Wyatt Earp, fired off a shot at Holliday that grazed the ex-dentist's side. Frank was then hit by several further shots, and died in the street. With Tom McLaury also dying from Holliday's shotgun wound and two of the cowboys having fled, Billy Clanton was last to fall, with a shot to the chest. He died later in a nearby house to which he had been carried.

The gunfight has been portrayed in several films as an emblematic encounter between the forces of law and order and those of lawless, if rather romantic, anarchy. The drama of the occasion, and the very American belief in the decisive use of firearms to resolve complex issues, has made it the perfect symbol for the 'taming of the West'. The bad guys (robbers, rustlers, outlaws) were defeated by the good guys (the upholders of settled values and due process; the protectors of business and property rights). The symbolism is very real, though the reality was murkier. Several people claimed that not all of the cowboys had been armed; the Clanton and McLaury families argued at the hearing that the Earps and Doc Holliday had set out to pick a fight following a number of previous confrontations, and that the shootings were effectively illegal executions. This rather draws a veil over the fact that the 'previous confrontations' by the Earps and others had involved trying to bring members of the Clanton and McLaury families to justice for various offences, ranging from stealing mules belonging to the US Army to robbing stagecoaches, and on the occasion of one stagecoach hold-up, of the murder of the driver and a passenger.

The sheriff of Tombstone, John Behan, himself a man of dubious reputation, and something of an ally of the cowboy faction, said that he had attempted to disarm the cowboys to prevent trouble, and had advised the Earps to do the same, but that they seemed to be set on fighting. On the Earp family's side, it was argued that their previous arrest of friends and accomplices of the cowboys had led to threats against the Earps from the McLaury family.

Whatever the truth of the matter, two months after the

gunfight at the OK Corral, the cowboy clans launched revenge attacks. Virgil Earp was shot and wounded in the first revenge shooting. Hit in the leg and arm by three shotgun blasts fired from a vacant building as he left the Oriental Saloon to return to his rooms, Virgil had staggered across the street and fallen into Wyatt's arms. Doctors removed nearly six inches of bone from his shattered arm, leaving it floppy and useless for the rest of his life.

Wyatt went looking for Ike Clanton, a hothead who had been responsible for stirring up the animosity that led to the gunfight at the OK Corral, but who had come to the confrontation unarmed and run off after a brief tussle with Wyatt (who, to his great credit, had shoved Ike aside rather than shooting him). Ike surrendered to Sheriff Behan and stood trial for Virgil's attempted murder, but provided alibis from several friends to prove that he was somewhere else on the night of the shooting. Ike was acquitted. Wyatt sent a message asking Ike to meet him one-to-one for a final showdown, but Ike wisely refused.

Wyatt's brother Morgan was killed in a billiards room a few months after the shooting of Virgil Earp, by a shot fired through the glass window of the saloon door. Wyatt, worried for Morgan's safety in the febrile atmosphere of the feud, had gone with him to make sure he was safe. Having failed in this task, he was obliged to watch his brother die on the floor of the billiards room. Morgan asked Wyatt and Doc Holliday to make sure that his legs were straight and his boots removed before he died, so that he didn't look like some cowboy gunned down in a brawl.

The Earp Vendetta Ride

Wyatt blamed himself for not having killed the cowboys who were stalking the Earp family. Amazingly, there was to be another attempt on Virgil's life. After his shooting, Virgil went back to the family home in California to recuperate. Wyatt and Doc Holliday went with him, having heard rumours that Ike Clanton and others were planning to ambush Virgil on the train. The rumours were true. As the train was waiting to leave Tucson, Wyatt spotted two men with rifles lying on top of a flatcar in a siding. Wyatt left the train, crept up on the gunmen and surprised them. One was indeed Ike Clanton; the other was a cowboy called Frank Stilwell. Ike ran off, which was his usual response to trouble, but Wyatt caught up with Stilwell and shot him dead in what looked suspiciously like cold-blooded revenge.

Wyatt didn't make any particular attempt to portray the killing any differently. In an interview with the Denver Republican on 14 May 1893, Wyatt made it pretty clear what he thought of Stilwell, and how and why he shot him:

> I went straight for Stilwell. He killed my brother. What a coward he was! He couldn't shoot when I came up to him, but just stood there, helpless and trembling. As I rushed to him he put out his hands and clutched at my shotgun. I let go both barrels, and he fell dead and mangled at my feet. I started for Ike Clanton then, but he disappeared behind a moving train of cars.[12]

Wyatt Earp and Doc Holliday then led a posse in the famous 'Earp Vendetta Ride', hunting down the people they believed were responsible for the shootings and killing at least four (and possibly as many as 15), with very dubious legality.

Wyatt never did catch up with Ike Clinton, though: Ike was killed several years later by a detective who was pursuing Ike and his brother Phineas on charges of cattle rustling. During the Vendetta Ride, the Earp posse had itself being chased very ineffectually by another posse, headed by John Behan, in an attempt to arrest Wyatt for the killing of Frank Stilwell in Tucson, Arizona. Behan and his posse never did catch up with Earp.

With public and government support for the vendetta fading, Wyatt left Arizona for Colorado, hoping that Arizona would issue a pardon for his actions, and that he could return to Tombstone as Sheriff. The pardon never came, and Wyatt headed west again, to California. Late in life, he became an advisor to the new Hollywood studios who were making silent films about the 'Wild West', amongst other topics of historical interest. In the studios he met a young would-be actor called Marion Morrison, who later changed his name to John Wayne, and who always said that it was his conversations with Wyatt Earp that formed the foundation of his on-screen portrayals of the hard men who dealt out such rough justice in Wild West.

Law and Peace

We tend to forget the law that the wagon-train pioneers and the early miners brought peacefully to the 'Wild West', and focus instead on the heroic exploits of a brave but violent man such as Wyatt Earp. In times of lawlessness, we feel threatened. We seek the comfort of harsh retribution. Wyatt Earp took on the bad guys and overcame them, with fatal violence. This is the morality (or its absence) of life in the wilderness: when groups of people are attacked by predators, they fight back. This, presumably, lies at the heart of why modern America is surprisingly comfortable with the lionisation of Earp and similar frontier lawmen: without their harsh justice, the predators, the 'Cow Boys', might have destroyed the communities that were struggling to take hold in the inhospitable territories of America's Wild West.

But if society was constantly and genuinely threatened by such outbreaks of predatory lawlessness, human civilisation would have collapsed irrevocably a long time ago: we would exist as scattered bands of people, constantly threatened by predatory outsiders. The fact that, for several millennia now, such scattered bands have come together to form great civilisations proves that we are able – and apparently keen – to form greater social units; to overcome the hostility that exists between different groups.

In the same way, society would fail to cohere if it was constantly and genuinely threatened by outbreaks of rioting and opportunistic law-breaking. We have come a long way from being groups of people united in a common purpose, such as the American Pioneers on their wagon trains. Any complex society will have within it disaffected groups who will seize the opportunity for mindless violence and some profitable looting – justifying this after the event as a reasonable expression of their dissatisfactions. Such riots, disturbing and even deadly as they can be, will not inflict lasting damage on a healthy society.

On those rare occasions when what is at first derided as mindless violence is, in fact, an expression of a deeply-felt dissatisfaction with a country's ruling elite then, quite frankly, anything can happen – but the general populace usually win.

Us and Them

People, it turns out, are 'automatically social'. Our brains seem to be wired for empathy, for sociability. This empathy even manifests itself physically: the muscles in our face adjust slightly to mirror the expression of emotion in another person's face; we show signs of neural activity suggesting pain when we witness other people's pain. Alarmingly, we are much better at demonstrating this kind of 'automatic sociability' with members of our own group. Studies have shown that Caucasians, for example, show a stronger 'neural signature' of pain when they witness the pain of another Caucasian than when they see, for example, a Chinese person in pain. The same thing happens in the reverse scenario.[13] This is uncomfortably familiar: history has shown that we are very prone to seeing other groups of people as not only 'not the same us' but even as 'less human than us'. The good news is that our conscious minds – our frontal lobes in the terms of neuroscience – can quickly inhibit this automatic response. The bad news is that, in times of heightened tension, it does not always manage to do this.

This constant, complex social interaction is at the heart of the human experience. We are remarkably good at empathy, at forming instinctive bonds with others that allow us to share their joys and sorrows, and so happily form groups with shared goals and objectives. We will give up some of our freedom of action and sacrifice some of our benefits for the good of the group. We are, equally, very prone to seeing other groups as being different; we fail completely to empathise with them, and we have no concerns about the pain that we inflict on them if they conflict with our interests.

The constant tension between these two states of affairs pretty much explains the course of human history. We should not be surprised when conflicts of interest erupt into sudden and unexpected violence, but we are. If we were able, in every case, to see these things coming, then we would be able, in principle, to take steps to avoid them – and we would have arrived at something approaching our dreams for the perfect society and the ideal state. In the meantime, we – the governed and the governors – should brace ourselves for more occasions on which we are completely blindsided; when rulers are suddenly toppled by a completely unexpected upwelling of popular dissent, and when apparently settled communities find violence exploding on previously peaceful streets.

6 WEAPONS OF MASS FINANCIAL DESTRUCTION

Imagine, for a moment, that you run a business that depends on a steady supply of some particular raw material: cotton, perhaps, or olive oil, or copper. Now imagine that there are worrying signs about its future availability – perhaps this year has seen shortages, and next year is expected to be worse; perhaps a competitor has moved into your market and is buying up large quantities of the vital raw material; perhaps you simply have a hunch that next year's prices may increase so much that it will put your business in danger.

In these circumstances, it would be entirely natural for you to enter a contract with a supplier who is prepared to do a deal to supply your cotton, olive oil or copper next year, or at some other date in the future, at a price to be agreed now. Your supply is now guaranteed and the seller has the benefit of knowing that they have already sold some or even all of their future goods. All that remains is to agree on the price – which involves some intelligent guesswork for both parties. You have entered into a 'forward contract'.

What we call 'futures' or 'futures contracts' are simply a more sophisticated, regimented and tradable version of such simple forward contracts. Futures are traded on an exchange, and, to help ensure that neither party defaults at the point of delivery, the exchange takes a deposit, called a margin, from both parties. Every day, the exchange notes the difference between the agreed price of the future and that day's actual price, and moves money from one party's margin to another. The exchange turns futures trading into a daily affair, rather than a one-off transaction, and reduces the risk that, at the future day of reckoning, one party may refuse to pay or the other refuse to deliver.

Anything Except Onions

A great many commodities are traded on futures exchanges and, in principle, literally anything can be traded in this way between interested parties. As the Commodity Futures Modernization Act of 2000 states:

> The term 'commodity' means wheat, cotton, rice, corn, oats, barley, rye, flaxseed, grain sorghums, mill feeds, butter, eggs, *Solanum tuberosum* (Irish potatoes), wool, wool tops, fats and oils (including lard, tallow, cottonseed oil, peanut oil, soybean oil, and all other fats and oils), cottonseed meal, cottonseed, peanuts, soybeans, soybean meal, livestock, livestock products, frozen concentrated orange juice, and all other goods and articles, except onions, as provided in Public Law 85-839 (7 USC 13-1) and all services, rights and interests, in which contracts for future delivery are presently or in the future dealt with.

So: anything that you can think of, any article, goods, service, right, or interest, can be traded as a future – *except onions.* The Chicago Mercantile Exchange had launched onion futures in the late 1940s, partly in an attempt to replace the revenues that it had lost when the introduction of federal subsidies on dairy produce removed the need for a market in butter futures: the 'Merc' had started life in 1898 as the Chicago Butter and Egg Board.[1] Farmers decided that the futures market in onions was responsible for a crash in onion prices, and lobbied a Michigan congressman called Gerald Ford to persuade Washington to ban the market in onions futures, which it did. The ban was not overturned in the Commodity Futures Modernization Act of 2000.

What was overturned in the 2000 Act was the regulation of certain kinds of derivatives. 'Derivatives' are contracts that derive their value from an underlying asset – a futures contract is a kind of derivative. What the Act of 2000 declared was that most so-called 'over the counter' derivatives – contracts set up between 'sophisticated parties' such as banks and investment groups – would not be regulated in the same way as futures. This piece of deregulation was seen as a great step forward in allowing the development of sophisticated financial products that were supposed to reduce risk.

The absence of a futures market in onions, for example, is thought to have played a part in the recent volatility of onion prices, which quadrupled in price between 2006 and 2007 when bad weather reduced harvests, then crashed by 96% in 2008 as a result of over-production, and then rapidly bounced back, tripling in value.[2]

Futures are supposed to smooth our financial path by allowing traders to 'hedge' – to offset the risk of something happening by taking a position that effectively insures against that event: you lose money if the event does happen, but the clever 'derivative' that you have bought pays you back most or all of what you have lost. By declaring that over-the-counter derivatives need not be regulated in the same way that the futures market is regulated, the Commodity Futures Modernization Act allowed consenting parties to set up contracts without all of the dull paraphernalia of the exchange: all of that reassuring stuff about keeping a daily track of how those derivatives are currently valued to ensure that neither party defaults when the day of reckoning arrives, for example.

Some people blame this piece of deregulation for the latest financial crisis. As financial journalist Alan Kohler wrote in Australia's *Business Spectator* magazine: 'This bill, by the way, was

11,000 pages long, was never debated by Congress and was signed into law by President Clinton a week after it was passed. It lies at the root of America's failure to regulate the debt derivatives that are now threatening the global economy.'

Transition and Trauma

At the start of the twenty-first century, the United States was sucking in money from foreign investment at an alarming rate. As ever in these situations, this was rationalised in a way that made it seem non-threatening. Successful economies with high rates of savings, such as Germany and Japan, had a surplus of capital seeking safe but attractive investment opportunities, as did emerging economies, like those of China and other Asian countries. America was the most sophisticated and successful economy in the world – of course capital was flowing into the country! The fact that the economies of Latin America and other developing markets had been badly damaged by huge inflows of foreign capital in the 1960s and 1970s was ignored; the United States was different. In 2006, for example, the US current account deficit stood at 6.5% of GDP – or US$800 billion. This was not a problem, it was agreed, because increasingly complex international financial integration was allowing countries to sustain higher levels of debt with the certainty of benign outcomes. The US financial sector grew rapidly while its main players (and beneficiaries) believed – as Carmen Reinhart and Kenneth Rogoff show in their book, *This Time Is Different* – that 'financial innovation was a key platform that allowed the United States to borrow much larger quantities of money from abroad than might otherwise have been possible'.[3]

Record levels of foreign investment were financing the United States' burgeoning current-account deficit, but government, and regulatory bodies, persuaded themselves that the success of the financial sector in developing products of increasingly bewildering complexity was part of the solution – that these, in effect, were the magical devices that were allowing the American economy to absorb huge amounts of foreign capital and to continue to grow serenely, without any bad side effects.

What was actually happening was that the United States was in the middle of a very difficult and probably traumatic transition from being a manufacturing-based economy to becoming a service-based economy. The manufacturing jobs, which used to sustain millions of Americans, had gone: the mixed blessings of globalisation ensured that these jobs had migrated to countries where the costs of large-scale manufacture were lower than in the United States.

As a result, large numbers of Americans were worse off than they used to be. Or they should have been. But in fact, rather than having to adjust to these newly straightened circumstances, Americans were able to sustain their previous lifestyle by borrowing money on an unprecedented scale, fuelled by a boom in house prices, which was in turn fuelled by the money flooding into the country. People didn't even have to move homes in order to join in — they used the rising values of their houses as a kind of ATM from which to withdraw cash to fuel other spending by remortgaging. The money enabled purchases that would otherwise have been unaffordable and, in some cases, it provided injections of capital that sustained a whole lifestyle that could, and indeed should, have been no longer affordable. In one year, these remortgages released capital in people's homes to the value of US$975 billion, or more than 7% of GDP.[4]

Why Did No One See It Coming?

A significant slice of the US economy was based on the nominal value of the nation's housing, and was at risk if those apparently ever-increasing nominal values were ever to fall. In the meantime, fuelled by cheap credit and by a money-making machine that took the nation's burgeoning debt and turned that debt itself (remarkable as this may seem) into further financial products that could be sold to investors, house prices in North America began to rise steeply and, it seemed, inexorably.

This is, of course, an entirely familiar phenomenon, which has been witnessed in nearly every advanced economy to varying degrees: most booms are accompanied by an associated housing-price bubble. What was entirely new about America's housing bubble was that 'financial sophistication', the very thing that was supposed to be preventing this obvious credit bubble from damaging the US economy, was not only worsening the effects of the bubble itself – the 'repackaging' of debt and its selling-on to other investors meant that mortgage lenders had almost unlimited funds to lend to increasingly unsuitable borrowers – but was also ensuring that the final crash would be of horrific proportions and would affect every corner of the globe.

Along the way to what should have been a relatively run-of-the-mill crash, the money men had created some financial instruments that were not merely 'sophisticated', but arguably insane, as we are about to discover. These instruments (created certainly for private gain, and possibly in the mistaken belief that financiers were insuring themselves against the possible effects of their other dubious money-making schemes) were unprecedented and unregulated – a bad combination. They were also successfully marketed around the globe, infecting the whole financial system and creating the conditions that would lead to the ensuing credit crunch.

It was Queen Elizabeth II who, speaking for all of us, asked the obvious question of a group of economists at the London School of Economics: 'That's awful. Why did no one see it coming?'[5]

The answer, ma'am, is that we were all blindsided, partly by the familiar mixture of greed and stupidity, but in this case with a truly incendiary admixture of what might be mere intellectual arrogance ('For well-informed and intelligent investors, these sophisticated derivatives are invaluable tools for spreading the risk of a complex portfolio…') but which looks suspiciously like a moral failure ('Do these suckers have any idea what we just sold them? Well – what the hell!'). Or maybe the explanation is pure stupidity, after all, because the banks bought their own toxic products as well ('Hey – maybe we should buy a couple of these things ourselves, just in case!').

Infinity... and Beyond

What Wall Street created was a financial product – a derivative – that was not actually linked to the real value of anything. It looked like a kind of bond, and it behaved like a kind of bond, but it was actually just a bet, or a series of bets. And because it was just a bet, supply was unlimited: you could sell as many of these as you could find willing buyers, of which there were many around the world.

What the willing buyers didn't seem to realise was that these apparent bonds were actually a bet against Armageddon: a bet that financial meltdown was not about to begin. Unfortunately, and because of the actions of the people who were selling these bets against Armageddon, financial meltdown was just around the corner and that 'bet' was just about to cost these punters the Earth. Unfortunately, the money that the 'punters' were playing with was yours and mine: the savings and pensions of people around the word.

The basis for the belief that financial sophistication could avoid the disastrous business cycles of the past (such as the Great Depression, for example) was largely theoretical, but it had the backing of some extremely heavyweight mathematics crunched by some very heavyweight economists in the post-Depression era, as memories of that harsh reality began to fade and economists began to persuade themselves that the booms and busts of the past could be avoided by sheer cleverness.[6]

In the 1950s, an economist called Kenneth Arrow had suggested that it would be possible to override such uncertainty if it were possible to buy securities that covered every possible version of the future: if, in effect, it were possible to hedge every bet. It's a charming idea, which is disproved by even the most cursory examination of reality. Nevertheless, in the 1970s, a student of Kenneth Arrow called Stephen Ross believed that he had developed financial instruments that would enable Arrow's vision. With derivatives, Ross believed, you could create a financial instrument that would indeed cope with any version of the future. As he wrote, in 1976, 'although there are only a finite number of marketed capital assets, shares of stocks, bonds... there is a virtual infinity of options or "derivative" assets that [these] may create.'[7]

With a 'virtual infinity' of such complex bets and side bets to call upon, any financial position, it was believed, could be hedged. It was these magical 'derivatives' that were being so assiduously developed and sold by an increasingly deregulated finance market in the US at the end of the twentieth century that were supposed to protect the American economy from what would otherwise have seemed like a simple case of over-heating. In fact, some of these derivatives were largely responsible for the current global financial crisis. Instead of reducing risk, they ensured that risk was spread around the global financial system in ways that are still not understood – except in the sense that it is still quite possible that the ticking time bombs that these derivatives represent have still not actually exploded, and that we have still not seen the worst effects of the financial disaster. Derivatives, as investment guru Warren Buffet warned apocalyptically and prophetically in 2003, are potentially 'financial weapons of mass destruction'.[8]

One of the early areas of 'increasing financial sophistication' in the United States was the 'securitisation' of mortgages: the selling on of mortgage debt to other investors. The lender is no longer tied to the mortgage for its lifetime and has therefore freed up his capital – a previously illiquid asset has become liquid.

You will notice that something else has happened in this

transaction. Traditionally, the institution that issued a home loan kept the risk on their own books: it was their money, and they wanted to get it back one day and therefore had a vested interest in lending money only to people who seemed to be likely to be able to pay it back. When you securitise your loans, you pass on the risk to another investor who buys the cash flow represented by your debtors (that is to say, the investor gets an income in the form of an agreed interest rate in return for his capital), thereby giving you another load of capital that you can now lend to other people. It is a highly dangerous way of destroying the normal relationship between lender and borrower. It led to dreadful excesses in the selling of loans to people who couldn't afford them. And then it got worse.

Subprimes, Teasers and Balloons

As we enter the murky waters of America's subprime mortgage disaster, you will notice that words no longer mean what they traditionally mean. Our first exhibit is the word 'subprime'. Since time immemorial lenders have been selective about their borrowers: they like to lend money to people who are likely to pay it back. Let's call those people 'prime' borrowers (though, so far as I know, nobody has ever called them that). Now you have the general picture: 'subprime' borrowers are those people who are not likely to pay back the loan. Sadly, and in fact cruelly, the home loan market in America in the 1990s began to make extremely attractive-sounding offers to people who should never have been enticed to take on a loan that they could never hope to repay.

The early subprime mortgages were at least fixed-rate mortgages: the borrower knew what they should repay each month for the term of the mortgage. But deals got considerably more enticing.

The 'teaser' deal became commonplace: an early low interest rate for the first few years that was replaced with a higher floating rate thereafter. The common practice (indeed the expectation) in these cases was that the borrowers would make their repayments in the early, affordable teaser-rate years and, as their house inevitably increased in value, would remortgage at a more advantageous rate before the higher interest rate kicked in, based on the greater equity in their properties. Falling house prices and shrinking equity were not considered.

Many of the mortgages sold to Americans in the 1990s look like clear examples of what an old-fashioned regulator might call 'mis-selling'. Consider the 'no docs' or 'liar' mortgages that became commonplace. These mortgages did not ask for any proof of earnings from borrowers. Many borrowers duly obliged, and did not supply any evidence of their earnings. One school of thought therefore put the blame on these mendacious applicants: they avoided declaring their (lack of) earnings, and were therefore morally culpable for the mess they soon got into. Another school of thought blamed the sellers of these mortgages for offering them in the first place.

Abuses of this kind escalated until truly surreal mortgage deals were being offered to relatively poor Americans eager to get a foot on the property ladder. Customers were advanced more than 100% of the value of their home, often with a 'non-recourse' mortgage, which meant that the borrower would not be chased for any losses that resulted if the value of their house were ever (but this is, of course, unthinkable) to fall. If one day the borrowers could no longer keep up the repayments, they could simply hand over the keys to the lender and walk away. When house prices are steadily rising, this looks like a one-way bet: the bigger the loan you take out, the bigger the house you can buy and the more profit you can make from a rising market, while bigger loans also mean higher fees for the happy lenders. Everyone wins! Except, of course, when the market crashes, the borrower is left homeless and without assets and the lender is left owning a large amount of overvalued property that they can't sell.

Mortgage Madness

The non-recourse mortgage looks positively sane, however, in comparison with some other mortgage products that were being touted on the market. The 'balloon' mortgage, for example, had previously typically been used as a short-term instrument for the commercial property market. The repayments on this kind of mortgage do not repay the loan over the term of the mortgage – seven years, for example – and at the end of that period, a very large payment (known as a 'balloon payment' because it is very large) is needed if you want to keep the property. Otherwise, the borrower has to refinance, which was what buyers were fully expected to do, since everyone was certain that house prices would continue to rise indefinitely and a refinance deal on more advantageous terms would be easy to find. It would also generate another set of fees for the lenders.

Some mortgages were offered where the agreed repayments were not even sufficient to meet the *interest* payment in full: the unpaid interest was simply rolled up into the capital forever and a day – until the borrower defaulted. But this wasn't going to happen because the value of the borrowers' houses would increase and they would, in fact, be better off, not poorer.[9] It was amazing.

Another 15-year fixed-rate loan was simply blatantly mis-sold. Imagine, said the sales material, that you were paying this loan back over a more typical 30 years. Then your interest rate would only be an effective rate of 7%. Um, yes. But the loan was actually being offered for a 15-year term, so the real rate of interest was more like 12.5%. This, as one of the few subprime cynics noted at the time, looked suspiciously like fraud.[10]

'Silent second' mortgages were routine: that is to say, an additional loan based on the value of one's property, which one could spend on luxuries or – in some cases – on simply getting by each month. The second mortgages were only 'silent' in the sense that the holder of the first mortgage didn't know about them, and was therefore unaware that his or her borrower was now far more financially stretched than when the original loan was offered, and was all the more likely to default on their original mortgage.

Originate and Sell

As a result of all of this unsound lending, house prices boomed. Between 1999 and 2005, house prices in the US rose by 42%, and the house price-to-income ratio rose from 3.72% to 5.29%, the highest level since records began, in 1991.[11]

The level of lending, as we noted earlier, was driven far beyond what would normally be possible by the fact that lenders were not reliant on their own capital. In what I think we are now allowed to call the 'good old days' of mortgage lending, funds dried up when lenders had used up all of their available capital. This had the happy effect of causing the lenders to ration their precious capital by careful lending. But now lenders had a new option: to pass on their debt to other investors (in these particular circumstances at this particular time in the US, this meant mainly to overseas investors) by means of securitisation.

The extent to which securitisation – the packaging up and selling on of mortgage debt in the form of bonds – was crucial to the developing problem is illustrated by the fact that the first group of companies to enter the subprime market were also the first to go bust. They sold much of the mortgage debt that they had acquired on to the bond market, but not all: this was a mistake. As Michael Lewis writes in *The Big Short,* his account of the financial events leading to the credit crunch:

> The original cast of subprime financiers had been sunk by the small fraction of the loans they made that they had kept on their books. The market might have learned a simple lesson: don't make loans to people who can't repay them. Instead, it learned a complicated one: you can keep making these loans, just don't keep them on your books. Make the loans, then sell them on to the ... big Wall Street investment banks, which will in turn package them into bonds and sell them to investors.[12]

Everyone came to love this model. It was called 'originate and sell'. Finance houses had every incentive to sell mortgages to people who probably couldn't afford to make the necessary repayments, because they would not be saddled with the bad debt: they could pass it on to Wall Street, which would package it up into a bond and sell it on.

It should be stated at this point that this is not *necessarily* a cynical economic notion. People on low incomes want to own their own houses and should be able to do so if at all possible. If financiers who are lending money to less well-off people can raise more cash by selling on their debt in the form of bonds, this enables them to make more loans and, potentially, drives down the cost to the borrower. As Columbia Business School professor, Joseph Stiglitz, says in his book, *Freefall: Free Markets and the Sinking of the Global Economy*, this money machine could have been used to create good mortgages: mortgages with low transaction costs and low fixed interest rates that people knew they could afford in the long term. Perhaps also, in cases where borrowers' incomes were erratic, mortgages that came packaged up with insurance to ensure that repayments could be maintained during a period of unemployment.

> Had the designers of these mortgages focused on the ends – what we actually wanted from our mortgage market – rather than on how to maximise *their* revenues, then they might have devised products that would have *permanently* increased homeownership.... Instead their efforts produced a whole range of complicated mortgages that made them a lot of money in the short term and led to a slight temporary increase in home ownership, but at great cost to society as a whole.[13] [Stiglitz's italics]

This is recurring theme of Stiglitz's: that leaving the provision of some essential services for a healthy society – such as the provision of good mortgage products that will enable and encourage wide home ownership – to an almost unregulated free market is not actually 'efficient'. There are strong incentives for various players to make a great deal of money for themselves while creating situations that do a great deal of damage to society as a whole. When extrapolated to include the financial system as a whole, one of the clear and deeply unsavoury aspects of the current financial crisis is that large numbers of dealmakers have made huge amounts of money creating and selling ever-riskier products. They misunderstood the risk involved, but it is not they who have been asked to pay the colossal price of the bailout, which includes, in the United States alone, a US$700 billion bailout of banks in the shape of the Troubled Asset Relief Program (TARP), funded by the taxpayer.

Not surprisingly, the American public was outraged to find that a substantial proportion of these bailout funds was used to pay huge bonuses to the bankers who had brought their own financial institutions down and done great damage to the world economy along the way. More than US$33 billion of taxpayers' money was paid out as bonuses by nine of the banks that were being bailed out by the government, including payments of more than US$1 million dollars to nearly 5,000 individuals.[14]

However, apparently, if you don't pay bankers their bonuses, regardless of how inept and disastrous their actions, they get very upset and may even leave the company and seek their fortunes elsewhere. While you and I might think that having to say goodbye to the employees who have bankrupted the organisation might be something that one could live with, there is, remarkably, a worldwide shortage of people who are prepared to undertake such highly paid work; we are told that it would be impossible to find new bankers to replace the previous failures, since the organisation would now have a reputation for not paying massive bonuses to people who have just made the worst banking decisions in history.... It may take a while for those of us who are not bankers to come to understand the logic of this position.

The Financial Instruments Formerly Known as 'Bonds'

As you will have gathered by now, the policy of 'originate and sell' – the packaging up of mortgages into bonds to be sold to other investors – did not result in the efficient creation of good mortgages; it resulted in the creation of an increasing number of very bad mortgage products, sold to people who would inevitably default on their repayments unless the perpetual-motion machine of ever-rising house prices continued without end.

But it took more cleverness than this to create a global crisis of the magnitude of the one in which we are still embroiled. There was a whole new level of cleverness; and then there was a final level of cleverness that looks suspiciously like madness. It's all about bonds, which used to be quite simple, useful things but which have recently become immensely complicated things that no longer bear any resemblance to what we should perhaps now call 'the financial instruments formerly known as "bonds"'.

Bonds have an honourable history. The classic bond is a way for corporations to raise capital, in order to grow and to develop. You, or I, or a financial institution, lend the corporation some money, we get paid interest on our loan, and the corporation owes us the money back when the bond matures. The more creditworthy the company, of course, the more likely it is that we will get back our money when the bond matures, and so the rates of interest that we get for lending our money are more modest. You can get a better return if you are prepared to lend money to more risky concerns; the popular term for these riskier bonds is 'junk bonds'. You get a higher interest rate, but you run a much higher risk that the company involved may go bust, in which case you don't get your money back.

Bonds are also issued, of course, by nation states as a way of raising money to finance national debt. These bonds are usually seen as the safest of all bonds but, as recent international events have shown, the same principle applies: when lenders are less certain that they will get their money back, the interest rate goes up.

Rating Risk

There are credit-rating organisations that are responsible for classifying the level of risk that any bond may represent (for example, in the United States, Standard & Poor's and Moody's). Ratings follow a pattern of AAA (the best) declining through AA, A to BBB (all of these are 'investment grade' bonds) and continuing through BB and all the way down to D, which means that the borrower is already in arrears, at which point the cautious investor might consider putting his money elsewhere. This reassuring system of classifying levels of risk is, surprisingly, at the very heart of what went wrong with the American subprime market.

A bond is backed by an asset: if you are lending to a corporation, then it is the general financial health of that corporation that you need to consider: its assets, income, outgoings and other commitments. Funnily enough, one of the assets that an organisation might have is that it is owed money (in its role as creditor). Many organisations exist in order to make money available to other individuals or corporate entities, for example the organisations that fund credit card debt or make loans available for people to buy cars or to pay school fees (or, of course, as we have seen, to lend money in the form of mortgages to enable people to buy houses). These organisations have contractual agreements that will deliver money in the future, but their capital is tied up: the borrowers have got it, and the lender must wait for it to be returned in dribs and drabs (the companies' assets, as the experts say, are 'illiquid').

However, since these contracted loans are indeed assets, a financier might decide to buy this debt from the lender: the financier gives the lender cash for this asset and, in order to get a return on his money, issues a bond inviting people to give him money for a fixed period of time in return for the payment of interest. Now everyone, apart from the investors in the bonds, has got their capital back (minus fees), and the mortgage lender is looking for new loans to use the capital he has been given back by the financier. The financier is also looking for new places to invest the capital that he, in turn, has received from the investors in the bond. The whole arrangement drives the wheels of capitalism, but the buck stops in two key places: the ultimate flow of cash comes from the original borrowers making their monthly repayments, and the ultimate owners of the debt are the investors in the bonds. In effect, we have simply inserted a new level of ownership between the ultimate borrower and the ultimate owner of the debt.

Repackaged Bonds

One of the key reasons why bond-holders feel comfortable in buying bonds that are based not on the success of a particular corporation (like Chrysler or Microsoft), but on debts owing to the corporations who have issued credit card loans, or car purchase loans, or student loans, is that the underlying asset is made up from the repayments of very large numbers of individuals. It is, after all, extremely unlikely that *everyone* will suddenly fail to make the monthly repayments on their credit card debt or their car repayment loan (though it is a certainty that a percentage will do so). These debt-based bonds were understandable, as was the level of risk involved in owning such a bond.

Sadly, long before we get to the point where bonds based on subprime mortgages were being sold, somebody had already had the bright idea that a number of bonds could themselves be packaged up into a new entity: the snappily named 'collateralised debt obligation' (CDO). This was a clever device for supposedly spreading the risk involved in a number of different entities. This instrument bundles up a number of bonds of varying degrees of risk. The clever thing about a CDO is that it creates different levels, or 'tranches', which are sold at different levels of interest. If the cash flow of the underlying asset suffers, then the first 'senior' tranches are repaid first, followed by the lower levels. The lowest tranches run the risk of not being repaid at all, and so pay the highest levels of interest. Because the senior tranc theory, extremely likely to be repaid, these tranches a higher credit rating than the bonds that have been packa together to create the CDO.

The financial house that invented the collateralised debt obligation in 1987 was Drexel Burnham Lambert Inc., whose employee, Michael Milken, a hugely successful bond trader, became famous for developing the market in junk bonds: that is, high-yielding bonds issued by companies whose trading history does not earn the bonds an investment-grade rating. (Michael Milken was, of course, indicted for insider trading and Drexel Burnham Lambert collapsed, but this has nothing to do with the financial usefulness or otherwise of either junk bonds or CDOs.) In Milken's day, junk bonds were packaged up into CDOs and the 'senior' tranches of those CDOs would then acquire a higher credit rating than any of the individual bonds that made up the package, based on the theory that though some of the 'junk' companies might fail, they would not all fail simultaneously.

When CDOs based on collections of subprime mortgage bonds were first created, however, this was a laughable deceit. The only way in which the established principle of rating CDOs could work was if the subprime mortgage bonds were in some way substantially different. Of course, the finance houses did their best (successfully) to prove to the ratings agencies that this was the case. Some of the subprime mortgage bonds were based on housing in Florida and California, for example, and some in Oklahoma. What could be more different? A fantasy was created: the housing market might experience peaks and troughs, but it could never collapse nationwide at the same time. The government contributed to this fantasy. As *New York Times* columnist Paul Krugman wrote in 2009:

> Key policy makers failed to see the obvious. In 2004, Alan Greenspan dismissed talk of a housing bubble: 'A national severe price distortion,' he declared, was 'most unlikely'.[15]

Greenspan was apparently able to make these statements with a straight face, despite the fact US housing prices had collapsed nationwide during the Great Depression by 31%.[16] A 'national severe price distortion' had happened before and, given the obvious boom in house prices going on at the time of Greenspan's comment, was very likely to happen again.

But now, thanks to the ingenuity of Wall Street, CDOs had been created from, for example, hundreds of triple B-rated subprime mortgage bonds; but because these bonds were agreed to be different in some significant way, so the risk in the new CDO was deemed to be 'diversified', and the credit rating agencies were prepared to give the new CDOs a much higher credit rating overall than their constituent parts warranted. The senior tranches of the new subprime mortgage-based CDOs were given triple A rating by the credit rating agencies – the same rating as treasury bonds issued by the US government.

In fact, the madness of CDO credit rating was such that starting with *nothing but* triple-B mortgage bonds as the raw material, it was possible to create a CDO where 80% of the tranches had a higher rating than triple B. Some of the triple B-rated bonds had even become triple A-rated tranches of a CDO, others double A, others A – even though everything within the CDO was composed of mortgage bonds that were themselves rated triple B.[17]

There were some intriguing further refinements to this madness: the whole basis of the 'tranche' device was that the 'senior' (and best-rated) tranches are the first to be paid off as money is collected from whoever is the ultimate debtor on which the bonds, and the CDO, are based. But some clever bankers discovered that if part of a triple A-rated CDO tranche was used to divert money to a lower-rated tranche in another CDO in certain circumstances (triggered by some 'highly unlikely' event, such as the default rate of loans on which the lower-rated tranche was based reaching 50%), then the rating agencies were happy to keep the triple-A rating of the original tranche, while the rating of the lower-rated bond that now had a potential source of payment from the triple-A bond was improved.[18] CDO tranches became hopelessly interrelated in what was clearly (surely even without the benefit of hindsight) a circular arrangement: the various tranches of the CDOs were now all lifting each others' ratings off the ground by their own bootstraps.

Weird Beasts from the Wall Street Jungle

It is no wonder that so many commentators use the metaphor of alchemy to describe this nonsense. It was as if Wall Street had managed to achieve what had eluded the philosopher-chemists of the Middle Ages and beyond: they had succeeded in turning lead into gold. Investors (mainly foreign investors), not surprisingly, assumed that these new triple-A bonds were a sound investment and bought them – presumably without any awareness that every single home loan that made up every one of the mortgage-based bonds that made up the triple A-rated collateralised debt obligation was, in fact, a loan made to a borrower who was highly likely to default. When the US housing bubble burst, foreign investors were appalled at their apparent lack of judgement. They should not have been so hard on themselves: although the ratings agencies tried, after the event, to protest that their ratings were essentially guidelines rather than hard and fast assessments of risk, this is not what investors had historically believed. As Michael Lewis writes in *The Big Short*:

> Wall Street investors had long interpreted [ratings] to mean the odds of default. For instance, a bond rated triple A had less than a 1-in-10,000 chance of defaulting in its first year of existence. A bond rated double A … stood less than a 1-in-1,000 chance of default and a bond rated triple B, less than a 1-in-500 chance of default.[19]

Collateralised debt obligations may well seem mad and bad enough, but when I wrote earlier that it got worse, I was not kidding. The next stage in the madness was the *synthetic* collateralised debt obligation – but to get our heads around that, we first of all have to meet another weird beast from the Wall Street jungle, the 'credit default swap'.

Some clever money men became convinced, even before they began to investigate the murky depths of CDOs in more detail, that the housing market boom was unsustainable and that a number of mortgage-based bonds were going to be in trouble as default rates of individual homeowners began to rise. They wanted to place a bet that this would happen: they wanted to short the US housing market. They finally discovered how to do this – via the credit default swap, or CDS.

This was a device invented by J.P. Morgan Chase in the 1990s, and because we are examining a world where words do not mean what they say, you should not be surprised to learn that it is not a swap and does not involve credit in any meaningful way, though it does involve default. A credit default swap is a very simple insurance policy, which insures the holder against the eventuality of a particular bond issuer going bust and defaulting on repayment of their bonds. As commentators have pointed out, it is a slightly strange notion. If you think that a major corporation might go bust, then not buying their bonds in the first place is a pretty fail-safe way of not being exposed to that risk. There were, however, cases where major finance houses felt obliged, for example, to buy the bond issues of their major clients and would then be grateful for a bit of insurance just in case their client had overstretched itself and those bonds went belly-up at a later point in time. As was the case with so many on the new 'financial innovations', the supposedly innocent birth of the credit default swap created a strange monster that would play a large part in the looming disaster.

CDSs were not regulated. As we saw earlier, the Commodity Futures Modernization Act of 2000 ensured that products offered by banks would not be regulated in the same way as futures contracts were regulated. This surprising piece of deregulation thereby ensured that banks could devise any kind of derivative that behaved like a futures contract without them having to be subject to the same regulations. It is far from clear why this was considered to be a good idea.

One of the truly strange things about a CDS is that although it is an insurance policy, you do not have to own the thing being insured: you do not, for example, have to own a corporation's bonds in order to insure against the corporation defaulting on those bonds. This was why the people who wanted to short the US housing market became so excited by CDSs: they could buy 'insurance' against the possibility of certain subprime mortgage bonds defaulting without having to own the bonds themselves. To buy insurance on a triple A-rated tranche, for example, might cost 0.2% per year; to buy insurance on triple B-rated tranches (the ones that seemed most certain to default) might cost 2%.[20] So, for an annual payment of US$2 million, you could insure US$100 million of subprime mortgage loans.[21]

A Collection of Betting Slips

It becomes clear at this point that 'insurance' is the wrong word to describe a CDS. It is not insurance, since the people who buy the CDS don't have to own the asset they are insuring. It is better described as a bet. And if you were pretty sure that the US housing market was about to crash and that tens of thousands of borrowers were about to default on their mortgage payments, then betting that these CDOs would themselves default on their interest payments by buying an insurance policy in the form of credit default swap looked like a pretty good idea.

The hedge funds that started shorting the market in this way began by buying credit default swaps against mortgage-backed CDOs in chunks of US$5 million or US$10 million, having found it difficult at first to find banks who would set up the deals, but Wall Street soon began to show more interest. One hedge fund manager was soon asked by Goldman Sachs if he would like to increase his trades to US$100 million per deal. You may need to pause for breath here, to remind yourself that US$100 million is quite a lot of money. The hedge fund manager soon built up his portfolio of CDSs to US$750 million dollars' worth of subprime mortgage bonds.[22]

Some hedge funds played both sides of the table. They bought the riskiest tranches of mortgage-based CDOs and – allegedly – put pressure on the banks to include ever-riskier mortgage bonds in the 'toxic' tranche that they were buying. The banks may well have been happy to oblige: the CDO market was drying up, and in the heyday of the mortgage-backed CDO, top bankers had been making US$3–4 million a year from the creation and sale of CDOs. Finding a new purchaser, or 'sponsor', for the riskiest tranches of CDO helped keep the money-making machine on the road for a bit longer (and may have continued to prolong the housing boom and thus may have exacerbated the crash). These hedge funds then bought CDSs on the very CDOs that they had helped to create; the high rates of interest that they were now making from the risky tranches that they had sponsored paid for the premiums on the credit default swaps. Their toxic tranche of the CDO might have cost them, for example, US$50 million, but the insanity of the CDS enabled them to 'insure' the entire CDO, even though they didn't own the entire CDO. Having helped to create a dodgy CDO by sponsoring the riskiest tranche of that CDO, the fund managers stood to clean up if the CDO did, indeed, blow up.[23]

In 2006, the investment bank Goldman Sachs began actively to market CDSs on subprime mortgages. This, in itself, is surprising, since Goldman were now in the business of selling both subprime mortgage-based bonds and CDOs to its clients, and also selling bets that those bonds and CDOs were going to default. But here comes the truly mind-boggling next step.

A credit default swap is a bit like a mirror image of the bond that it is betting against. In the case of the original bond, money is given to the bond issuer, who pays a rate of interest to the buyer in return. If the bond issuer goes bust, the investor loses his money. In the case of the credit default swap, the buyer *pays* an insurance premium, and if the chosen bond defaults, then the CDS holder *receives* the money. There are almost identical cash flows and risk involved in both vehicles. So, obviously, Wall Street began to construct collateralised debt obligations (CDOs) out of credit default swaps (CDSs), and it sold them to investors as '*synthetic* collateralised debt obligations.' You may have to run that through your head a couple of times to work out what was going on but, having done so, you will not perhaps be surprised that these were, in turn, given triple A ratings by the agencies.

If you accept my suggestion that a CDS is essentially a bet that something will or will not happen, then a synthetic CDO, which consists entirely of CDSs, is essentially a collection of betting slips. They are not based on anything real, such as a bond: they are based on bets about bonds. They are utterly surreal. They were marketed, of course, as a kind of CDO – the relatively well-understood device based on real bonds. It seems certain that many investors had no clear idea that they were no longer 'investing', but were, in fact, gambling. The money that they were being paid was not 'interest', it was a slice of the insurance premium that other parties were paying in the expectation that some other event would happen: that certain mortgage-based CDOs, for example, might default.

Synthetic Bets, Synthetic Assets

One of the great joys of synthetic CDOs (for Wall Street) was that nobody actually had to lend large sums of money to large numbers of house buyers to create a CDO out of the bonds created from the securitisation of those loans. As Michael Lewis writes in *The Big Short*:

> The market for 'synthetics' removed any constraint on the size of risk associated with subprime mortgage lending. To make a billion-dollar bet, you no longer need to accumulate a billion dollars' worth of actual mortgage loans. All you had to do was find someone else in the market who was willing to take the other side of the bet.[24]

By now, an obvious question may well have struck you: who was taking the other side of these bets? Who was issuing this 'insurance'? To a large extent, it was the giant American multinational insurance company, American International Group, or AIG. They had been in the business of selling credit default swaps on corporate bonds. From their point of view, a CDS was an insurance policy against a very unlikely event, such as a major American corporation defaulting on its bond interest payments. It seems, surprisingly, that AIG were persuaded that mortgage-backed CDOs were as risk-free as Wall Street said they were. AIG ran up huge exposure to the housing market without appearing to notice that it was doing so: it is estimated that AIG had issued some US$450 billion of credit default swap contracts.[25]

When the US housing market finally crashed, a chain of events unfolded that brought AIG to its knees. The collapse lowered the value of AIG's own mortgage-based securities (AIG is at the time of writing suing Bank of America, alleging that the bank was guilty of a 'massive fraud' when it sold AIG more than US$28 billion of mortgage-backed securities with what AIG argue were 'inflated' credit ratings; the Bank of America have countered by arguing that AIG 'recklessly chased high yields and profits').[26]

Under new regulations introduced in the wake of the Enron scandal (see Chapter 4), AIG were obliged quickly to declare these investment losses. The losses were sufficiently large to weaken AIG's capital base, and the ratings agencies (with some irony, given the murky role played by them in the rating of the mortgage-backed securities that lay at the heart of the problem) downgraded AIG's rating from triple A to single A. The downgrading of AIG's credit rating triggered clauses in its CDS contracts, obliging it to post collateral against its exposure: if you have a multi-million dollar bet with someone, you want to be sure that they can pay if you win the bet, after all. The collateral that AIG needed was US$100 billion, which it did not have. The government stepped in and provided AIG with a secured credit facility of up to US$85 billion.

At the Heart of the Credit Crunch

This chain of events lies at the very heart of the ensuing global credit crunch. Nobody can be quite sure which financial institutions are exposed to which credit default swaps. As David Paul, president of the Fiscal Strategies Group, wrote in the *Huffington Post* in October 2008:

> After the AIG collapse, how does one institution trust its exposure to another? If CitiBank seeks a loan from J.P. Morgan, how does J.P. Morgan know whether some event might be looming that will result in a collateral call under some of the myriad derivatives contracts to which CitiBank is a party, a collateral call that in a matter of hours could bring Citibank to its knees.[27]

As Joseph Stiglitz points out in his book, *Freefall,* all of the supposedly sophisticated derivatives that were meant to reduce risk and lay off bets relied on the essential premise that neither party to the transaction goes bankrupt.[28] With such huge sums of money at stake, the possibility of this happening was actually rather high. A series of 'clever' bets that expose one party to a potential loss of *billions* of dollars obviously has the potential to bring the party on the wrong side of the bet to its knees.

Sadly – thanks to the selling of synthetic CDOs based on credit default swaps – the people holding these scary devices were not just banks, and the CDOs were not only mortgage-backed securities. Synthetic CDOs were constructed from CDSs based on what looked at the time to be a list of risk-free blue chip companies – that is to say, the investors who bought these instruments thought that their money would only be at risk if a series of almost unimaginable events happened. Writing in Australia's *Business Spectator* magazine in 2008, however, financial journalist Paul Kohler listed some of the 'reference companies' included in at least US$2 billion worth of synthetic CDOs sold to Australian charities and municipal councils: 'the three Icelandic banks, Lehman Brothers, Bear Stearns, Freddie Mac, Fannie Mae, American Insurance Group, Ambac, MBIA, Countrywide Financial, Countrywide Home Loans, PMI, General Motors, Ford and a pretty full retinue of US home builders.'[29] The list doesn't make such comfortable reading today as it must have done to investors in 2008.

Many other synthetic CDOs are still 'out there' waiting for us to find out if enough 'reference' companies in these CDOs will go bust to trigger massive losses for the investors. But the picture is even murkier than that: it's not just the investors who will lose out – the banks 'laid off' these bets with other banks, creating a tangled web of interrelated risk, the potential implications of which may never be fully understood, unless we find out the hard way in a series of global corporate collapses.

In an article titled 'A Tsunami of Hope or Terror?' in November 2008, Kohler had surmised that the bad news was that investors such as charities, councils and pension funds would lose huge amounts of money, but at least the good news was that this would potentially recapitalise the banks. In 2009, Kohler revised his opinion.

> In November [2008] I suggested that although the seven or eight defaults would be very bad for investors (the 'terror'), it would potentially recapitalise the banking system (the 'hope'), since something like half a trillion dollars would forcibly be moved from investor bank accounts onto the balance sheets of banks. Alas, it won't work like that, because most of the issuing banks laid off the entire amount in back-to-back CDS contracts and hedges with other banks and hedge funds, which in turn laid

> it off against others. So where the cash ends up when any particular synthetic CDO blows up is anybody's guess. It will be dispersed among hedge funds, banks and other investors. The losses, however, are real, and are not dispersed.[30]

Various companies are still suing various financial institutions over synthetic CDOs sold to them. The conclusion of the 'Report on the Financial Crisis', published in January 2011 by the National Commission on the Causes of the Financial and Economic Crisis in the United States, said this:

> While the vulnerabilities that created the potential for crisis were years in the making, it was the collapse of the housing bubble – fuelled by low interest rates, easy and available credit, scant regulation, and toxic mortgages – that was the spark that ignited a string of events, which led to a full-blown crisis in the fall of 2008. Trillions of dollars in risky mortgages had become embedded throughout the financial system, as mortgage-related securities were packaged, repackaged, and sold to investors around the world. When the bubble burst, hundreds of billions of dollars in losses in mortgages and mortgage-related securities shook markets as well as financial institutions that had significant exposures to those mortgages and had borrowed heavily against them. This happened not just in the United States but around the world. The losses were magnified by derivatives such as synthetic securities. [...] The crisis was the result of human action and inaction, not of Mother Nature or computer models gone haywire. The captains of finance and the public stewards of our financial system ignored warnings and failed to question, understand, and manage evolving risks within a system essential to the well-being of the American public. Theirs was a big miss, not a stumble.

The Commission split along party lines over the report's findings, with the six Democrat members endorsing the report and the four Republican members announcing in advance of its publication that they would not agree with its findings. They have obviously failed to agree on exactly what blindsided us, but the usual suspects look pretty hopeful to me: greed and stupidity

— the stupidity being, as so often happens, exacerbated by the fact that we thought that we were being incredibly clever.

Survival of the Greediest

The logic of the deregulation that led to the unfettered creation of CDSs and other exotics was based on the premise that markets will be motivated to devise new products because of greed — which is good, because it fuels innovation — but that the magical power of the market to choose which of those products it actually wants will act like an evolutionary force, selecting only those products that should survive. Wall Street created products such as subprime, mortgage-backed bonds and synthetic CDOs out of greed, but there was no meaningful 'market' that could accept or reject these in a useful timeframe or at an acceptable cost.

Let's remind ourselves what senior Goldman Sachs trader Fabrice Tourre said about the synthetic CDOs that he had created, and about the collapse of the subprime market, and about the selling of synthetic CDOs to people who did not understand them, in private emails that he did not intend for public viewing:

> More and more leverage in the system, the entire system is about to crumble any moment ... the only potential survivor the fabulous Fab ... standing in the middle of all these complex, highly levered, exotic trades he created without necessarily understanding all the implications of those monstrosities!!!
>
> When I think that I had some input into the creation of this product (which by the way is a product of pure intellectual masturbation, the type of thing which you invent telling yourself: Well, what if we created a 'thing', which has no purpose, which is absolutely conceptual and highly theoretical and which nobody knows how to price?...)
>
> According to Sparks [Daniel Sparks, a former head of the mortgages department at Goldman], that business is totally dead, and the poor little subprime borrowers will not last so long!!! ... I do not intend to wait for the complete explosion of the industry and the beginning of distressed trading, I think there might be more interesting things to do in Europe.

> Just made it to the country of your favorite clients [Belgians]!!! I managed to sell a few Abacus* bonds to widows and orphans that I ran into at the airport…[31] [*Abacus is a highly controversial Goldman Sachs synthetic CDO[32]]

Tourre is acting in the way described in Adam Smith's *Wealth of Nations*: utterly selfishly, and with contempt for the people he sells his products to (those 'ironic' widows and orphans). But we need not worry, because the actions of 'the market' will magically turn the collective actions of lots of little Fabrices into something useful for society. That looks unlikely, in this instance.

It seems that the whole world knows now that it does not want the synthetic CDOs of Fabrice Tourre and his colleagues – the 'thing which has no purpose'. But what has it cost the world to discover this? And in what sense is this a 'market' – where are the actions of many buyers and sellers weeding out the good from the bad, the wanted from the unwanted? The making and selling of synthetic CDOs were just, as Wall Street is often accused of being, the actions of a rich man's casino.

The weird financial products created and sold by Wall Street were driven by greed – of course – but there was no market mechanism that would turn this into a good for society. The bankers made a lot of money; unfortunately, there has been no accompanying benefit for society. The frantic selling of mortgage-based securities to overseas investors fuelled a US housing boom and bust, while the weird derivatives known as synthetic CDOs did not reduce risk: they took existing risk and spread it around the global financial system. We still cannot be sure of the full extent of the damage done to the world economy.

This was not the operation of a free market; this was the financial system being exploited by greedy people, at huge cost to society. The fact that public money has been used to pay bonuses to the very people who indulged in these pointless, risky but lucrative activities is a scandal that will not quickly fade.

7 DUST BOWL AND THE DIRTY THIRTIES

The easiest way to get blindsided is not to think things through: to do something that 'seemed like a good idea at the time', only to find not long afterwards that it really wasn't a good idea after all. The Great Plains of America, which used to be known, for good reason, as the 'Great American Desert', provide a classic example of this, on a very large scale. This great ecosystem, once entirely self-sustaining despite its very low rainfall, has been the victim of what are in effect a number of large-scale experiments, driven partly by people's desire to make a living wherever they can, but also by the misguided concerns and interests of various American governments.

The grasslands of the Great Plains were the wrong kind of country. When European settlers first encountered this territory, it scared them. This was a land for hunters and trappers, whereas the settlers were farmers. Successive American governments looked to turn the plains, despite their scant rainfall, into productive lands that could be settled by ranchers, farmers and their families – people who could form the bedrock of a settled community. As a result, the Great Plains were changed from being self-sustaining grasslands to being a giant experimental cattle ranch, to being an even more experimental giant agricultural project.

Those farmers on the Great Plains in the 1920s and 1930s were just trying to make a living, doing what the government had encouraged them to do: take over a patch of grassland, plough it up and plant wheat. But they were unlucky: they started farming the dry land during a period of exceptional rainfall; then the rain went back to normal, the crops died and the soil blew away. And one day the farmers woke up to find that the sky outside the farm had turned black, and that the winds had picked up the topsoil from a million or so acres of land and dumped it on farms, roads, schoolhouses and grocery stores. Animals died in the fields; people died yards from their own houses, trying to find a way back though the darkness and the choking winds to their own front door. The 'Dust Bowl' of the 1930s was an ecological disaster on an unprecedented scale.

The Great Plains have since become productive agricultural lands once again – but only because improving technologies have enabled us to extract more water from the huge Ogallala Aquifer that lies beneath the plain. There is, however, a fatal flaw in this process: the sedimentary rocks of the aquifer hold 'fossil water' that dates back at least to the last Ice Age. This water is no longer being replenished. Or rather, it is being replenished, but at an average rate of less than 25 millimetres per annum for the region as a whole, whereas in the 1980s and 1990s, for example, water was being extracted at the rate of 82 *centimetres* per annum.[1] No recent measures have, as yet, been taken that will prevent the aquifer from being drained to the last drop. One day, very soon, the aquifer will run dry and the Great Plains will return to being a prairie – if the ancient grasses can re-establish themselves. Will we wake up on that day and ask: how can this have happened?

We really do need to stop allowing ourselves to be blindsided in this particular way; otherwise we will soon find that we have run out not only of water, but also of other abundant but finite resources – like fish, or rainforests, or copper. Why are we so short sighted about unsustainable practices? What is it the makes us persist in sawing away at the branch that we are sitting on?

The Sale of the Century

It is one of the interesting accidents of history, at least in terms of the way in which nations and empires have carved up the planet and claimed various bits of it as 'theirs', that the Great Plains are American, rather than being British, but equally feasibly, Spanish or French – especially French.

In the early 1600s, a French explorer called Samuel de Champlain helped to establish French settlements in northeastern America, and began to explore the Great Lakes, looking for a route to China via the great waterways of North America. A later French explorer, René-Robert de La Salle, continued in Champlain's footsteps, both literally and metaphorically, also in search of a westward route to China that would be easier than the arduous land or sea journey eastwards. He was granted lands on the Island of Montreal, or 'Lachine' (named, it is said, in an ironic reference to de la Salle's obsession). When he and his men returned from their unsuccessful search for a westward route to China, the locals dubbed them 'Les Chinois' – the Chinese. In 1682, La Salle canoed down the Mississippi River, reaching the Gulf of Mexico. He claimed the whole of the Mississippi basin for France, and named it 'Louisiana' in honour of King Louis XIV, the 'Sun King' of late seventeenth and early eighteenth-century France.

In the middle of the eighteenth century, a territorial war between Britain and France broke out in North America, with both British and French forces supported by various Native American allies. The war, known in Britain as the French and Indian War, was to become part of a wider conflict. France, Austria and Russia had formed an alliance against Prussia, led by Frederick 'The Great'. Britain became Prussia's only ally, but the combination of British naval might and Prussian military strength and genius proved very effective. Britain was able to focus its relatively small army on the war in North America; the war in Europe ended with something of a stalemate, but France was the emphatic loser in the New World. She was forced to give up all of Louisiana east of the Mississippi to Britain, having already given the Louisiana territory west of the Mississippi to her ally, Spain. When the United States later won its independence following victory in the Revolutionary War (1775–83), they acquired these lands from Britain. In 1800, Spain, which had been at war with France following the French Revolution in 1789, made peace with the new leader of the French Republic, Napoleon Bonaparte, and handed back to France the western portion of Louisiana territory as part of a new alliance.

The Louisiana Purchase

As American settlers pushed westward across the Appalachian Mountains, this natural barrier between them and the seaboard states that they had left behind meant that the best way to ship goods back east was to float them down the Mississippi on barges and load them onto ships that could make the voyage back up the eastern coast of America. But the port of New Orleans now belonged to France.

In 1801, Robert R. Livingston, one of the founding fathers of the United States, was despatched to Paris by President Thomas Jefferson to try to negotiate the purchase of New Orleans. Spain had previously given the United States the rights to navigate the Mississippi and to store goods in New Orleans for export – with a brief exception for the period 1798–1801. Though the sale of the Louisiana Territory to France in 1800 was officially a 'secret', and New Orleans remained under nominal Spanish control in the meantime, it is clear that the Americans knew with whom they needed to do a deal.

Jefferson was uneasy that the constitution of the new United States of America did not allow the purchase of new territory, which could be seen to increase the power of the national executive at the expense of that of the individual states (a burning issue, given the American states' recent hard-won freedom from the control of the British crown and parliament), but he was even more uneasy about a foreign power being able to control the United States' interior access to the Gulf of Mexico. Jefferson wanted control of the port of New Orleans and free use of the Mississippi River.

Two years later, Jefferson sent a second diplomat, James Monroe – another founding father, who was to become the fifth president of the United States – to join Livingston in an attempt to clinch the elusive deal. To his negotiators' great surprise, just before the arrival of Monroe in France, Livingston was offered the whole of the Louisiana Territory.

The French had just lost control of the Caribbean island of Haiti. Without sugar revenues from the Caribbean, Napoleon had little interest in recreating *Nouvelle-France* again in North America. There was also the risk of the hated British moving into Louisiana from their territories in the north: Napoleon believed that an enlarged United States of America could become a friendly and powerful republican ally against Great Britain.

Monroe and Livingston took the decision to accept the offer to buy the whole of Louisiana without getting approval from Jefferson. They had been prepared to pay US$10 million for New Orleans alone; the whole of Louisiana Territory was offered to them for only US$15 million.

In October 1803, the US Congress ratified the purchase, and President Jefferson found himself at the head of a country that had doubled in size. Spain still controlled Florida and the southern areas of North America's western coast, while Great Britain still laid claim to the northwestern coast: Oregon, Idaho and Washington (or Columbia District, as it was known to its British owners prior to the settlement which ceded all territory south of the 49th parallel to the United States).

Disputes immediately began as to how far west the territory actually extended. The land was essentially unexplored, and the Spanish interpretation of 'Louisiana' was the vital port of New Orleans and a relatively small strip of land west of the Mississippi. The matter was resolved by treaty in 1819: Spain ceded Florida, but kept control of the far southwest of North America; it would be many years before the United States occupied the territory that it does today.

In the meantime, as the dispute with Spain moved towards resolution, it would be confirmed that Jefferson, as his negotiators had always believed, had just acquired for his nation some 890,000 square miles (over two million square kilometres) of new territory, stretching all the way from the Mississippi in the east to the Rocky Mountains in the west. Jefferson, a firm believer in the yeoman farmer as the bedrock of republican society, was desperate to populate the new area with pioneers who could put down roots and work the soil.

The Wrong Sort of Country

Army captain Meriwether Lewis was selected to lead an expedition up the Missouri River, which flows from the Rockies to the Mississippi, to explore the new territory and search for a river route to the Pacific coast. He and his fellow officer, William Clark, set off in the summer of 1804 and travelled up the Missouri River to its headwaters, but were disappointed to find that they still had the Rocky Mountains between them and the Pacific. The size and extent of the Rockies were unknown, and crossing the mountains was far more arduous and dangerous than imagined. Once over the Rockies, the expedition canoed down the Columbia River, which separates the modern-day states of Oregon in the south and Washington in the north, reaching the Pacific Ocean in December 1805. The Lewis and Clark expedition provided the first accurate maps of the United States' northwestern territories and detailed accounts of the local flora and fauna.

They had crossed the Great Plains and seen animals unknown in the east: coyotes, antelope, mule deer. An unfortunate prairie dog was dragged from its burrow and despatched back to President Jefferson in a box.

With the acquisition of Louisiana and Lewis and Clark's breakthrough to the Pacific, the United States, for the first time in its short history, could claim territory that stretched from coast to coast. It was a vision that was to become seen as the 'manifest destiny' of the American people: the conviction that Americans could not only expand into the west of the continent, but that it was their destiny to do so.

But there was a snag, an imperfection. When Zebulon Pike was despatched by Jefferson in 1806 to explore the areas of the new territories further south of the Lewis and Clark expedition – the territories south of the Missouri and north of Spanish-owned California and New Mexico – he discovered more of the Great Plains that Lewis and Clark had traversed on their expedition further north. He compared these vast, flat, treeless plains to the Sahara Desert in Africa. Fourteen years later, another explorer, Stephen Harriman Long, described the Great Plains as 'The Great American Desert'.

This great 'desert', which stretched from the northern territories owned by the British to Spanish territories in the south, provided a useful buffer zone for American citizens against the foreign nations on its borders. But it was, reported Long in 1820, 'a Great Desert ... unfit for cultivation and of course uninhabitable by a people depending upon agriculture for their subsistence.' There was little rainfall, no wood to make housing or supply fuel, high winds, scorching summers and hard winters. But both Pike and Jones were wrong. This was not a desert; this was a steppe, or prairie – the short-grass prairie of the western Great Plains giving way to the tall-grass prairies of the eastern areas, with their more fertile topsoil. The prairies were a rich and well-adapted ecosystem: grasses survived the extremes of temperature, the low rainfall and the frequent spells of drought, and supported a rich ecosystem, from invertebrates, reptiles and birds to small mammals and the most obvious larger species such as bison and elk, prairie dogs, antelopes and coyotes.

Wild and Untamed

For nearly a century, the Plains were treated as a hostile area – territory to be crossed, with great hardship, on the route westwards. Part of the worry nagging at the American psyche was that the Great Plains was *the wrong sort of land.* It was a land for hunters on horseback. A land for fugitives. A land where nearly-wild trappers and miners might join forces with the hunter-warriors of the Native American tribes. The inhospitable territory was fully expected to turn anyone who lived on it into an outlaw. The lands could not be civilised (since civilisation depended on agriculture), therefore the people who lived on these lands must by definition be beyond civilisation's control.

Successive American governments worried about how they might control and settle this wilderness. They encouraged the extermination of the huge herds of buffalo that had sustained the Indian tribes, and moved the Indians onto reservations. Huge ranches sprang up to raise cattle where the buffalo had once grazed, and the great 'long drives' were established, taking cattle from the open ranches of Texas to Missouri, where they could be loaded onto trains bound for Chicago or the hungry miners looking for gold in Colorado. In a bitter irony, ranchers supplied beef on contract to the US government to feed Native Americans on the new Indian reservations: driven off the land that they had used so well to sustain themselves, Native Americans were now dependent on food aid.

The cattle proved less tolerant of the vicious winters of the Great Plains than the buffalo, but it was the coming of the railways, overstocking and the fall in market prices that killed off the great ranches; the heyday of the cowboy – icon of the American

West – had come and quickly vanished, as the ranch land was sold off as farmland. The government encouraged settlement of ever more arid and precarious regions, and the Great Plains were turned over to the plough – to the 'sod buster'.

By the early twentieth century, the Great Plains seemed almost tamed by the combined influence of government and private enterprise, enabled by dramatic new technological developments such as railways, John Deere's steel plough and the tractor, and driven by the people's yearning for a piece of land to call their own. The land was ploughed and planted with wheat by the thousands of homesteaders who were encouraged to exploit the new 'dry farming' techniques promoted by the government.

Rain Follows Plough

Dry farming techniques are a reality, and an important part of the agricultural future for many of the earth's regions. It can enable the successful cultivation of crops in dry areas – typically, regions that receive less than 20 inches (50 centimetres) of rain per annum. What it cannot do is defy nature or work miracles. Some techniques were poorly understood or practised by farmers. Some beliefs were sheer nonsense. 'Rain follows plough' was the most insidious: the mistaken belief that the very act of cultivating the soil would bring rain in its wake. It was also believed that the steam from the steam engines on the new railway lines brought rain. On the cover of an influential farming book of the day, *Campbell's 1907 Soil Culture Manual* ('A Complete Guide to Scientific Agriculture as Adapted to the Semi-Arid Regions') was an illustration of a camel, with the words, 'The camel for the Sahara desert, The Campbell Method for the American Desert'. Campbell's vision was exactly the same as every US government since Thomas Jefferson:

> The great west ... is indeed the land of great possibilities. We have never more than half appreciated it in the past. It is a region which, under

> application of true scientific principles in the cultivation of the soil, is destined to be covered with countless homes of happy American families, with cities and towns prosperous and growing [...] All the grass and cereals of the best agricultural regions of the earth will be grown here in abundance.[2]

As a result of this collective will to settle the Great Plains, the complex and successful ecosystem of the region was destroyed and replaced, eventually, with a monoculture: wheat.

Wheat flourished for a couple of decades, which happened, by sheer chance, to be years of relatively high rainfall. The success of their crops made some farmers rich beyond their dreams, as the demand for wheat soared during World War I and prices were guaranteed by the US government, making wheat farming on the prairies seem like a one-way ticket to a better life. What had started as a dream of subsistence became a vision of plenty. 'Suitcase' farmers descended on the Plains, got a piece of land, ploughed it and sowed it, planning to return the following year to harvest their valuable crop.

Then the stock market and the economy crashed, and the Plains entered one of their normal periods of drought. The soil that had been upturned in an orgy of mechanised ploughing – and, increasingly, left unplanted as the price of wheat plummeted – was whipped up into the air by the great winds of the plains, forming apocalyptic dust storms. The precious topsoil that had developed over tens of thousands of years was scattered around North America, falling on New York, and in places as far away as the decks of boats in the Atlantic Ocean 200 miles (320 km) off America's eastern coast. It piled up in against the fences of the farms on the Great Plains and trickled into the rooms of the farmhouses and the lungs of the people. People caught outdoors in dust storms could go blind; livestock were maddened and choked. Swarms of grasshoppers, spiders, worms and rabbits plagued the countryside. The rich ecosystem of the Great

Plains – the place where the deer and the buffalo roamed – had become the 'Dust Bowl'.

Wrong Side Up

The US government was most responsible for the land rush that caused this disaster. Abraham Lincoln's Homestead Act of 1862 (passed by Congress during the American Civil War) had made millions of acres of government land available to settlers. The object was not to raise money for the government, but to create a nation of yeoman farmers – Jefferson's old dream of free citizens who owned the land that they worked on. This was, of course, a political issue at the time. The Southern states had recently seceded from the Union and the vision of freemen working their own land was in stark political contrast to the situation in the South, whose large estates were worked by slave labour.

Homestead land was available in 'quarter sections' (160 acres); a 'section' being the land surveyors' term for a square mile, or 640 acres. Settlers had to live on the land for five years, raise crops and build a dwelling of at least 12 × 14 feet (3.7 × 4.3 metres). On application, the land then became theirs on payment of a minor registration fee. Like any piece of social engineering, the Homestead Act, so noble and clear in principle, became muddied and abused in practice. Railroads, timber industries and other corporate speculators paid people to file claims and sign over the land, or simply submitted fraudulent claims.

In the harsher, drier territories, 160 acres was not enough to sustain a family. In 1909, the Enlarged Homestead Act doubled the land available to a 'half section' – 320 acres – in a deliberate attempt to encourage settlement of the arid western portions of the Great Plains. The government offered free train rides to settlers to come and see the new opportunities. Brochures were distributed in Europe and at the major ports of the United States. A year after the Enlarged Homestead Act, more than 100 million acres of the Great Plains had been taken up by homesteaders.

By 1914, the peak year for homestead applications after the initial applications following the first Homestead Act, farmers were already beginning to leave homesteads in the northern plains, driven out by the harsh conditions and winter temperatures of -40°F (-40°C) that froze farm animals on the spot. Settlers poured into Oklahoma and Texas, even as they were leaving Montana.[3]

It would be different in the south, they convinced themselves. The farmers ploughed over the ancient grasses of the plain. Over the course of a few decades in the early twentieth century, farmers had progressed from walking behind a plough pulled by a mule, to riding on a plough pulled by a horse, to driving a tractor (probably a Fordson, made by the Ford Motor Company) pulling a combine. The time needed to plough and harvest a crop was slashed. The Great Plains homesteaders ploughed up millions of acres of grassland, to the dismay of the ranchers and Native American Indians, who believed that the grass was the 'wrong side up'.

The weather was kind: rainfall was adequate. The price of wheat was rising. In 1910, wheat fetched 80 cents a bushel; by 1915, with World War I under way in Europe, the price had doubled. When Turkey, which was allied to Germany, closed the Dardanelles Straits – the channel linking the Black Sea and the Mediterranean Sea – Russian wheat could no longer be shipped to its traditional markets in Western Europe. The United States stepped in to feed the Allies. Farmers were encouraged to increase production and wheat prices were guaranteed at US$2 a bushel, with the cost of production at around 35 cents. After the war, rainfall was higher than average and prices stayed high. More and more land was ploughed up. Between 1925 and 1930, another 5 million acres were ploughed in the southern plains, an area twice the size of the Yellowstone National Park.[4]

Then, in 1929, wheat stocks began to pile up. Europe was now being supplied by Russia once more. In the United States, prices fell to US$1.50 a bushel. Many farmers had taken out mortgages to pay for their new equipment, so to maintain their income they planted more wheat.

On 29 October 1929, the American stock market crashed. By early 1930 the price of wheat was down to 40 cents a bushel, barely covering costs. With unemployment rising fast and banks closing all around the country, a period of drought began. Farmers ploughed up more land, this time with the desperate and circular logic that if they could raise more wheat, they could sell enough even at rock bottom prices to scrape a living. They ploughed up fresh land in the autumn, knowing that this was dangerous: the turned soil would be exposed to the high winds in winter and spring; if there was no rain, the dry soil could blow away. The suitcase farmers had already disappeared, their dreams of making easy money as part-time farmers exposed as fantasies. Millions of acres that had been ploughed but not planted were also left exposed to the elements. The bare topsoil, with no living roots to bind it to the subsoil, was waiting for a high wind to lift it into the air. And the Great Plains had plenty of high winds.

Black Sunday

Dust storms began early in 1932. At first, the weather bureau saw them as fascinating, unprecedented phenomena. They began to classify them: the worst was a storm carrying so much air-borne dust that visibility was reduced to a quarter mile; in 1932 there were 14 such storms.[5] In March and April 1933, dust storms were almost continuous as winds stayed high. At the end of April, a dust storm lifted by 40-mph (64 km/h) winds lasted for 20 hours and sand-blasted the paint off farmhouses.[6] In May 1934, a giant dust storm stretched from the Great Plains to the Atlantic. Measuring 1,800 miles (2,900 km) wide and carrying an estimated 350 million tons of dirt, it hit Chicago, Boston and New York. In Manhattan, tourists on the observatory platform of the Empire State Building could not see the ground below.[7]

In 1935 came the worst day of all, 'Black Sunday' – a day when 20 'black blizzards' hit the Great Plains at 60 miles an hour (97 km/h), killing thousands of small animals and many large animals and people. Visibility dropped to a few feet, even inside houses, where they were forced to light lamps. Many people thought that the end of the world had come. An Associated Press reporter used the words 'dust bowl' to describe the area hit by these apocalyptic storms.

The Dust Bowl destroyed the lives of thousands of well-intentioned, hard-working settlers who wanted nothing more than to carve out a free life for themselves and their children. They would have been content with subsistence – a life that provided food for their families and enough extra to buy clothing and supply their few material needs. If there was any spare money, the settlers spent it on luxuries such as a timber-framed house to replace the sod house which they had built when they first arrived on the plains – a hut made entirely from turf, bound together by the thick and interwoven roots of the prairie grasses that the settlers were intent on ploughing under. Sometimes, the wind blew away the frames of their timber houses before they were finished, and they were reduced to scouring the plains for the timber that the winds had scattered.

Sustainability

It would be unfair to blame the settlers for the devastation that their activities were about to wreak on the environment. The problem, which only a handful of people in America, or even in the world, had grasped at that time, was one of sustainability.

The prairie grass and the bison and the Indians had coexisted for centuries in an entirely sustainable ecosystem, regardless of the inevitable periods of drought or of the frequent hard winters. The wheat that the settlers had planted, on the other hand, could be destroyed in a single hailstorm and it would not survive the dry spell that arrived in the early 1930s.

Conditions were exacerbated by a poor understanding of the farming techniques needed to sustain crop farming in semi-arid conditions: crop rotation, maintaining fallow land, use of cover crops. Farming has since recovered and even thrived in what was once the Dust Bowl – but primarily through the increasing use of water from the huge underground Ogallala Aquifer. Dust Bowl farmers pumped up water from the aquifer, but primarily as drinking water for people and farm animals, and to water small kitchen gardens and fruit trees. Technological advances in efficient and affordable pumps accelerated irrigation using Ogallala water.

During the 1970s, the dramatic rise in the price of oil and natural gas led to boomtowns springing up around the oil wells of Montana, Wyoming, Dakota and Colorado. These boomtowns needed feeding, and the price of agricultural products rose accordingly. Farmers took to ploughing the soil again, but on a modern, fully-mechanised scale. Tens of thousands of acres were turned over, only for the downturn of the 1980s to blow dry dust over these new farmers' dreams.

Today, many farmers are taking the initiative, changing their farming methods and exploring dry farming techniques in more systematic and scientific ways. Nevertheless, some regions are already experiencing quite sudden declines in productivity as the water in the Ogallala Aquifer dries up. These areas are being deserted by families; those who remain in the most difficult areas are facing a decline in local services and a drop in living standards. Agricultural populations are getting older and poorer. The hard times show signs of returning. Parts of the Great Plains have, even in recent years, been perilously close to Dust Bowl conditions.

Some interesting solutions have been proposed. Academics Deborah and Frank Popper, in an influential paper called 'The Great Plains: From Dust to Dust', which appeared in *Planning* magazine in December 1987, argued for the Great Plains to be returned to grasslands, the state for which it seems best suited – a rich prairie capable of supporting large quantities of game that could be farmed and hunted. The Great Plains, they argue, represents a failed experiment in privatisation

> The federal government's commanding task on the Plains for the next century will be to recreate the nineteenth century, to re-establish what we would call the Buffalo Commons. More and more previously private land will be acquired to form the commons. In many areas, the distinctions between the present national parks, grasslands, grazing lands, wildlife refuges, forests, Indian lands, and their state counterparts will largely dissolve. The small cities of the Plains will amount to urban islands in a short grass sea. The Buffalo Commons will become the world's largest historic preservation project, the ultimate national park. Most of the Great Plains will become what all of the United States once was – a vast land mass, largely empty and unexploited.[8]

The Poppers were seen by Great Plains farmers at the time as out-of-touch East Coast intellectuals and doomsayers. Even in 2009, according the United States' Environmental Production Agency, the Great Plains supplied two-thirds of the country's wheat. It must be remembered that the US wheat crop accounts for roughly 13% of the world's wheat, and roughly 25% of the world's exported wheat.[9] But the unthinkable is happening, and the Poppers now look more like prophets than cranks.

The Tragedy of the Commons

The problem of the fair allocation of limited resources is a very new kind of problem. When people first discovered the underground waters of the Ogallala Aquifer, they marvelled at the potential of this new resource. They did not think about where it came from and presumably assumed that it would never be exhausted; that, like the gentle rain that falls from heaven and the rivers that this feeds, the underground water source would always be there. It's an understandable mistake.

In 1968, the American ecologist, Garret Hardin, wrote a hugely influential paper titled 'The Tragedy of the Commons', which was published in *Science* magazine.[10] In the introduction to this article, Hardin makes a memorable point. He refers to an entirely unrelated article written about the problems created by the nuclear arms race, which was then a seemingly intractable problem faced by the blocs of countries involved in the Cold War. The authors, Hardin noted, reached a brave conclusion: 'It is our considered professional judgment that this dilemma has no technical solution,' wrote the authors of this paper. 'If the great powers continue to look for solutions in the area of science and technology only, the result will be to worsen the situation.'

This was an interesting and prophetic conclusion, which was recalled during the debate about President Ronald Reagan's Strategic Defence Initiative (which became known as 'Star Wars'): the attempt to make America invulnerable to attack by nuclear ballistic missiles that was held by its critics to be both unworkable and also politically destabilising, as it potentially undermined the scary but apparently effective policy of MAD: Mutually Assured Destruction.

The point made by the Cold War authors was entirely sound: that the problem was essentially a human and political problem, and that the only permanent solution could be a moral, not technological, one. In every question about how we should live together on this planet, there are choices that we have to make. There is no technical fix that will take away the need for a moral decision.

Garret Hardin took this as his theme in order to explore the 'tragedy of the commons' – the terrible but unavoidable fact that when a common but finite resource is available to everyone, it will inevitably be over-exploited. Imagine, Hardin says, a piece of common land where many people allow their own animals to graze. Everything goes swimmingly for some time, but a remorseless logic is at work that leads to ruin for all:

> As a rational being, each herdsman seeks to maximize his gain. Explicitly or implicitly, more or less consciously, he asks, 'What is the utility to me of adding one more animal to my herd?' This utility has one negative and one positive component.
>
> 1) The positive component is a function of the increment of one animal. Since the herdsman receives all the proceeds from the sale of the additional animal, the positive utility is nearly +1.
>
> 2) The negative component is a function of the additional overgrazing created by one more animal. Since, however, the effects of overgrazing are shared by all the herdsmen, the negative utility for any particular decision-making herdsman is only a fraction of –1.
>
> Adding together the component partial utilities, the rational herdsman concludes that the only sensible course for him to pursue is to add another animal to his herd. And another; and another.... But this is the conclusion reached by each and every rational herdsman sharing a commons. Therein is the tragedy. Each man is locked into a system that compels him to increase his herd without limit – in a world that is limited. Ruin is the destination toward which all men rush, each pursuing his own best interest in a society that believes in the freedom of the commons. Freedom in a commons brings ruin to all.[11]

You will notice that Hardin, who was a scientist, has slipped into that insidious 'rational agent' way of expressing this very real problem. Nobody that I have ever met addresses this kind of problem by thinking to themselves, 'The positive utility to me of having an extra goat is almost +1, but the negative utility of the overgrazing that this will cause is, personally speaking, a fraction of –1. Therefore, I will graze an extra goat on the commons.' Maybe Hardin met a different kind of person (other scientists, perhaps).

In this ever-recurring scenario, it is almost impossible for any individual to make the right moral decision. It is not that people make a wrong but rational decision, it is not even that they fail to foresee the problems that their individual actions will cause (which is becoming increasingly inexcusable in a world full of information). It is that even if they can see the inevitable and disastrous outcome, it demands a superhumanly self-sacrificing *moral* effort on behalf of any individual not to continue to exploit the resource.

Until disaster strikes, there is, in fact, more grazing available on the commons. A person could put an extra goat, or steer, on that commons and everything would be OK. And if he or she does not put that goat or steer to graze on the commons, then *somebody else will.* A saintly herdsman could choose not to put an extra animal out to graze, only to see his less saintly neighbour do exactly that.

There is another side to this moral conundrum: when we put our extra animal out to graze on the commons, it is not obvious that we are doing harm to anybody else. One cannot steal the grass of the commons, because it belongs to everyone. The act of adding an extra animal does not immediately cause our neighbours to suffer. And so we continue until the commons is overgrazed and there is no grass left for anyone's animals, and the animals all die. 'How can this have happened?' we then wail. We are currently doing this with fish stocks, many species of which are being driven to extinction, while applying the entirely human non-logic of, 'There is still fish to be had, and if I don't catch it, somebody else will.'

The solution to this problem has become, in effect, privatisation. When somebody owns a resource, then they have a vested interest in managing it sustainably: it would be a foolish herdsman who overgrazed his own land, and foolish herdsmen will die out. There are some interesting problems, as you will notice, that are currently being played out on a global scale, about who exactly gets to own things and why, but you will also see that the private ownership scheme really doesn't work with a finite shared resource – like water, or fish, or copper. When China, for example, buys a mountain of copper ore in Peru, it is helping to guarantee its own supply of copper.[12] It is not helping to manage the sustainable use of copper.

In an article about the conservation of water in the Ogallala Aquifer, published in 2003 in the American magazine *Choices: The Magazine of Food Farm and Resource Issues*, the authors wrote:

> Economic efficiency means that resource use should yield the greatest net benefit to society. Allowing individuals to base their resource use on private benefits and costs heightens economic efficiency for many resources. Unfortunately, groundwater is an exception to this rule. Because of its common property attributes, the rate of groundwater use will likely exceed its most economically efficient rate.
>
> The inefficiency of unregulated groundwater use is easy to demonstrate. Because each user holds only the property right for pumping water, rather than the entire bundle of property rights for the water itself, withdrawals are governed by the 'rule of capture'. An individual pays only the pumping cost and not for the value of the water removed from the common pool. The private costs of pumping are therefore less than the social costs of withdrawing water. Excessive pumping is the result.[13]

Or, as I would put it, the individual extracting the water cannot see the harm that he is doing to his neighbour: 'Ain't doing no harm to nobody; just watering my crops.' Or, if the potential harm is pointed out, then self-interest kicks in: 'I've got a family to raise; if I don't draw the water, that other fellow down the road will draw it instead!'

'We Know This Won't Last Forever'

The proposed solution of the authors of the article in *Choices* magazine is to allocate not just pumping rights but 'ownership' rights: water 'deeds' that could also be traded, thereby creating that miracle of the modern world, a *market,* which would presumably regulate itself in that marvellous way that markets are supposed to do. Here's how the proposal would work:

> An irrigator initially may receive deeds for pumping 1,000 acre-feet of water from a given well. If 100 acre-feet are pumped the first year and

> recharge is 25 acre-feet, then deeds for 925 acre-feet remain for the next year. Irrigators could also buy and sell deeds among themselves within prescribed areas.[14]

This raises a worrying scenario: 100 acre-feet are pumped, but only 25 acre-feet are replenished. The authors also note the moral issues of fairness and sustainability: Do the current generation have the right to deprive future generations of the use of resources that we currently enjoy? They notice that the 'water deeds' proposal doesn't quite cover this: although an 'efficient market' in water deeds may help to prevent uneconomic over-extraction, it merely pushes the moral question further back up the decision-making chain. If the water deeds that are issued and sold amount to more extraction per annum than the rate of replenishment, then the aquifer will gradually disappear, efficient market or no efficient market. Somebody, somewhere, has to take the moral decision as to whether we extract water at a sustainable rate or not. Everything else is just a technical response based on that moral decision. At the moment, we still seem to be shirking this moral decision.

An article in the Kansas newspaper, *The Hutchinson News*, reports on a summit meeting in Kansas, on the Great Plains, of 'more than 300 farmers, legislators, professors and agriculture industry representatives' with Sam Brownback, the governor of Kansas. Brownback addressed the problem clearly: 'Without Ogallala water,' he said, 'agriculture and all of its related businesses could not be sustained, manufacturing could not continue, recreational opportunities would diminish and the towns in the area would cease to exist.' Brownback encouraged participants to develop ideas that could be presented to the legislature, and people duly discussed 'the importance of local control, respect for farming heritage, protection of property rights and improvement of irrigation technology.' Ah yes, the improvement of technology. An expert 'Water Information Resource Manager' was wheeled out. He uttered some chilling words: 'We're in a deficit environment in the Ogallala. We know this won't last forever.' The last quote in the article comes from a natural resources economist at Kansas State University. 'If we want to extend the life of the aquifer, some form of restriction or regulation is going to be important,' he said.[15]

Oh no! Restriction or regulation! How un-American! But you will notice that something else seems to have happened, with the chilling finality of a life-support system being switched off. There is no talk in this article of preserving this resource for future generations; none of establishing entirely sustainable farming practices, which would inevitably imply a massive reduction in agricultural output. That won't be on the table at next year's meeting of the Kansas legislature. We have decided, it seems, to deprive future generations of the water in the Ogallala Aquifer for the very human reason that we want it, and want it now. We have decided to 'extend the life of the aquifer', which is a nice way of saying that we have decided to drain it of every last drop of water to sustain, not the aquifer, but our current lifestyles.

So the moral decision has already been taken. At least the farmers and government of Kansas can't insult us all a few years hence by saying that they were blindsided by events. They know what is going to happen, but they're going to do it anyway.

8 THE BLACK DEATH

As a species, we are inevitably blindsided by the onset of epidemics, or even pandemics, affecting whole nations or several nations. We can't be blamed for this: while we are used to the inevitability of individual illness and death in our own lives and in the lives of our families and communities, we cannot foresee that whole societies will be suddenly affected by the same illness and be struck down at the same time. It is, for the vast majority of us, something outside our experience. When this does happen, then, not surprisingly, people feel that the world is ending.

We still (for good reason) look back to the Black Death as the archetypal plague. Modern scholarship has given fresh credence to contemporary medieval reports of a mortality rate of 50% — a figure that had been previously dismissed as the understandable exaggeration of people caught up in events beyond their comprehension. It is genuinely hard to imagine. Think of your own village, town, city, or country. Now imagine that every other person in that entire community has died, suddenly. How does life go on? How do communities and nations stay together?

The bad news is that we will inevitably have to suffer these devastating events, on a more or less apocalyptic scale, for as long as we endure as a species. Our memory of bad times is short; we are an optimistic species. Yet it was only in 1918 — near the end of World War I — that the world was struck by a flu pandemic that, with a horrible irony, not only added to the total fatalities of that war but caused far more deaths than fighting had over the whole four years of that bloody conflict. The total number of deaths in World War I is generally accepted to be around 16.5 million, and some of these deaths were caused, in 1918, not by gunfire or explosion, but by flu. The total number of deaths caused by the pandemic is now estimated to be between 50 and 100 million.[1]

The pandemic came to be known as 'Spanish flu', despite the fact that it had appeared in the US and in other parts of Europe before it appeared in Spain in 1918, simply because Spain was not a combatant in World War I, and so had not imposed press censorship. The countries who were at war were not about to allow their press to tell the enemy that soldiers and civilians were dying in large numbers from an outbreak of a mysteriously virulent influenza virus; and so many people first learned about the disease from reports in Spanish newspapers that the King of Spain, Alfonso XIII, was sick, having succumbed to an illness that was affecting many of his subjects. The disease went on to be truly global in its scope, killing people in every continent.

Going Viral

The most significant thing that our species (*Homo sapiens*) has achieved in its short history has been to create organisations and institutions with life-spans that extend beyond any one individual human life. These organisations keep our collective memory alive and prepare for the future in a way that we short-sighted individuals can never hope to achieve. As a result, fortunately for us, there are people who devote their lives to *not* forgetting about the diseases that have ravaged us in the past. These people are called scientists, and they are underpaid for the essential work that they do.

The onset of a future pandemic is not likely, but certain. To imagine that we will not face some devastating new disease that will affect humanity on a global scale is to believe that the genetic makeup of viruses doesn't change over time or that human ingenuity can devise a rapid cure for all known ills. Viruses can change in small ways every time that they replicate and can also take on elements of the genetic makeup of other viruses. This is where the real risk to humans arises. It is possible to catch a virus from another species when a particular virus is able to 'cross species' (birds and pigs are the most likely sources) and that virus may make us very ill, and even kill us – it is, in fact more likely to make us very ill than a human flu virus, since our immune systems do not recognise it.

But if the virus cannot pass from human to human in the usual way – mainly via coughing and sneezing – then there is no epidemic. We just have to keep away from the source of infection, or keep the source away from humans (1.4 million poultry were culled in Hong Kong after the 1997 outbreak of avian flu in which six people died). The real risk comes when, for example, some unfortunate victim is infected simultaneously by both human and avian flu, and acts as a 'mixing vessel' – a kind of human test-tube – in whom the viruses exchange genetic material. This creates a virus with both avian and human components that can be transmitted from human to human: then we have an epidemic.

Even with the best and most effective vaccines, when an epidemic or pandemic strikes, societies will be faced with very hard choices as to who is actually given those vaccines.

If our goal is to limit the loss of life (an instinctive first reaction), then vaccines must be given to the most vulnerable: probably the youngest and the most elderly – but just as likely people in the prime of life, as some viruses trigger a feedback loop called a cytokine storm in the healthiest (and only the healthiest) immune systems, which can itself be fatal.

If the pandemic is sufficiently severe, and the future of humanity as a whole is suddenly at risk, then we may need to make some harder choices: is our goal to limit the loss of human life or to limit the damage to society? If the latter, then on what basis? Perhaps the economy is what matters: what will allow us to maintain the maximum GDP? Perhaps it is a political calculation: what will help maintain political structures and prevent a descent into anarchy or a takeover of the state by powerful, self-interested forces? Or perhaps these relatively sophisticated concerns will be swept aside by the sheer need to survive as a species: perhaps our decision will be a simple one – that the only people deserving of a vaccine are those who may survive and reproduce. Perhaps anyone over the age of, say, 35 will have to take their chances without the benefit of a vaccine.

We will face these dilemmas at some time in the future, probably soon. We will, despite our best efforts to forecast and prepare, be blindsided by the particular epidemiological problem that confronts us. It is not that we are unaware that we are at risk from an outbreak of bird flu; it is that the business of coping with all of the other problems that life throws at us day to day means that it is difficult for us to be in a constant state of preparedness. The scale of the 1918 Spanish flu pandemic makes it one of the greatest natural disasters in history – though not so great as the Black Death – and yet it is not at the forefront of our minds. We find it hard to put a value on the current risk that we face, because nobody can forecast exactly when the next pandemic will happen. As a result, with impeccable human logic, we decide that we will 'face that problem when we come to it'. This is not a good plan. It is a definite recipe for waking up one day and saying: 'How can this have happened? Why did nobody see this coming? How can we have been so blindsided?'

The Great Plague

In the mid-fourteenth century, the important Genoese trading city of Caffa was besieged twice by the Tartars (Mongols). The Genoese had purchased the city – on the southern coast of the Crimea in the Black Sea – from the Mongols in the late 1200s, after the Mongol hordes had poured out of the East, overrunning Central Asia, the Middle East, and parts of Europe, and made Caffa the administrative centre for all of their Black Sea trade. In 1345, Mongols laid siege to the city that they had previously owned, but were driven off by a relief force from Italy. In 1347, they returned. This time, they were struck down by a terrible and mysterious illness:

> See how the heathen Tartar races, pouring together from all sides, suddenly invested the city of Caffa and besieged the trapped Christians there for almost three years. There, hemmed in by an immense army, they could hardly draw breath, although food could be shipped in, which offered them some hope. But behold, the whole army was affected by a disease which overran the Tartars and killed thousands upon thousands every day. It was as though arrows were raining down from heaven to strike and crush the Tartars' arrogance. All medical advice and attention was useless; the Tartars died as soon as the signs of disease appeared on their bodies: swellings in the armpit or groin caused by coagulating humours, followed by a putrid fever. The dying Tartars, stunned and stupefied by the immensity of the disaster brought about by the disease, and realizing that they had no hope of escape, lost interest in the siege. But they ordered corpses to be placed in catapults and lobbed into the city in the hope that the intolerable stench would kill everyone inside. What seemed like mountains of dead were thrown into the city, and the Christians could not hide or flee or escape from them, although they dumped as many of the bodies as they could in the sea. And the rotting corpses tainted the air and poisoned the water supply, and the stench was so overwhelming that hardly one in several thousand was in a position to flee the remains of the Tartar army. Moreover, one infected man could carry the poison to others, and infect people and places with the disease by look alone.[2]

These words were written by the Italian lawyer, Gabriele de' Mussis, who was alive at the time, in his account of the devastating arrival in Europe of the Black Death.

As the inhabitants of Caffa fled by sea from their noxious city, so they spread the plague throughout Europe. Medical knowledge of the day had no explanation for the transmission of the disease. Illness was thought to result from an imbalance of the four essential 'humours' (fluids) of the body. Bad smells, understandably, were thought to transmit sickness and to upset the natural balance of these humours. God's role in visiting affliction on mankind, which the medieval mind tried always to discern, became more and more inscrutable in the case of this indiscriminate plague. The Christian defenders of Caffa saw that the Tartars had been struck 'as if by arrows from heaven', but they were about to suffer the same fate. They would learn that the disease would spread, quickly and without warning, from boat to shore; from infidel to believer; from parent to child; from the dead to those ministering the corpses. Death, says de' Mussis, 'entered through the windows':

> Among those who escaped from Caffa by boat were a few sailors who had been infected with the poisonous disease. Some boats were bound for Genoa, others went to Venice and to other Christian areas. When the sailors reached these places and mixed with the people there, it was as if they had brought evil spirits with them: every city, every settlement, every place was poisoned by the contagious pestilence, and their inhabitants, both men and women, died suddenly. And when one person had contracted the illness, he poisoned his whole family even as he fell and died, so that those preparing to bury his body were seized by death in the same way. Thus death entered through the windows, and as cities and towns were depopulated, their inhabitants mourned their dead neighbours.[3]

The Black Death, as we now know, did not 'enter through windows': it was spread by fleas, whose main hosts were rodents, especially rats. Its origins appear to have been in central Asia, possibly around the great lake Issyk Kul in modern-day Kyrgyzstan – a key stopover on the Silk Road from China to the West. The disease's original host was a marmot-like rodent.

Environmental changes seem to have forced the rodents into closer contact with humans (folk history about the origin of the plague is full of references to freakish storms, earthquakes and fire storms), and the disease spread from marmots via fleas to rats and humans. Since fleas can live for 80 days without a host – and since the deadly bacterium can survive in flea faeces for weeks – so the increasing mobility of humans with their bedding and clothing began the disease's inexorable spread along the trade routes of mankind.

A flea's bite would transfer the deadly bacterium into the human bloodstream; it would take up residence in the nearest lymph gland and multiply, creating a blistered swelling (a 'buboe' – hence the bubonic plague). Since many flea bites are to the legs, a swelling in the groin was the most common, and most terrifying, symptom of the disease. From its new breeding ground in the lymph gland, the bacterium spread around the body through the bloodstream, infecting vital organs. The victims' bodily fluids gave off a vile, putrid smell: one of the cruellest manifestations of the disease was the disgust it engendered, as well as the terror of infection, driving carers away from sufferers: parents forsook children; husbands recoiled from infected wives.

A Twentieth-Century Plague

At the beginning of this chapter, I wrote that the Spanish flu pandemic of 1918–19 ranked as one of the world's worst natural disasters (which it does) but that it was not so great a disaster as the Black Death. This is true, in terms of the percentage of the world's population killed by both diseases. But to people caught up in the influenza pandemic it seemed as if the Black Death had returned. In many American towns and cities panic set in, made worse by the fact that it was public policy to deny that there was, indeed, an epidemic in America. The public health commissioner of Chicago said, in 1918, 'It is our duty to keep people from fear. Worry kills more people than the epidemic.'[4] It is unlikely that people were prevented from worrying. In Chicago's Cook County Hospital, 40% of all influenza admissions died. In Philadelphia, dead bodies remained for days in houses without being collected. Eventually, trucks and horse-drawn wagons were sent out and the call of, 'Bring out your dead!' was heard on the streets of America in the twentieth century.

As with the Black Death, neighbours refused to help stricken neighbours; a society that prided itself on 'neighbourliness' began to fall apart. The Red Cross in Kentucky reported that people suffering from the disease were starving to death, not because there was no food to be had, but because their neighbours were too frightened to take food to them. Another Red Cross report wrote that, 'A fear and panic of the influenza, akin to the terror of the Middle Ages regarding the Black Plague, [has] been prevalent in many parts of the country.' There were very real fears that society and civilization were on the brink of collapse.[5]

Some smaller, more isolated communities were hit even harder, losing very high percentages of their population. The Fiji islands lost 14% of their entire population in two weeks.[6] One-third of the Inuit community of Labrador was killed, and some villages were wiped out: the village of Okak lost 204 of its 263 residents when the disease arrived in November 1918, carried by a sick crewman from the supply ship SS *Harmony.* By January 1919, every adult male in the village had been killed. As village life ground to a halt, hungry sled dogs attacked human corpses and even the incapacitated sick. Villagers began to shoot the dogs on sight. In January, when the survivors started to believe they really had been spared, they poured petrol on the ground and set fire to it to thaw the frozen soil sufficiently to allow them to bury the dead in a mass grave. Then they put the whole village to the torch and left Okak forever.[7]

The disease itself was astonishingly virulent. Some doctors thought that patients were presenting symptoms similar to dengue fever, cholera or typhoid. Many patients haemorrhaged blood not only from the nose but also from the stomach and intestines, from ears, beneath the skin and the inside of the eyes. Some were partially or even completely paralysed.[8] An American army doctor wrote to a colleague about his experiences in a US Army camp:

> These men start with what appears to be an ordinary attack of *La Grippe* or Influenza, and when brought to the hospital, they very rapidly develop the most vicious type of pneumonia that has ever been seen ... and a few hours later you can begin to see the cyanosis extending from their ears and spreading all over the face, until it is hard to distinguish the coloured men from the white. It is only a matter of a few hours then until death comes.... It is horrible. One can stand it to see one, two or twenty men die, but to see these poor devils dropping like flies.... We have been averaging about 100 deaths per day.... We have lost an outrageous number of nurses and doctors. It takes special trains to carry away the dead. For several days there were no coffins and the bodies piled up something fierce.... It beats any sight they ever had in France after a battle.

There was, however, a glimmer of hope: as the epidemic travelled across America, for example, so it seemed to become less deadly. John M. Barry, author of *The Great Influenza: The Story of the Deadliest Pandemic in History,* notes: 'Cities struck later tended to suffer less, and individuals in a given city struck later also tended to suffer less. Thus west coast American cities, hit later, had lower death rates than east coast cities.'[9] This observation also seemed to hold true for people who were infected later in the same city or general area: people who fell sick four weeks after the epidemic struck an area were more likely to survive than people who fell sick four days after it arrived.

Epidemics come in waves. The first wave of Spanish flu affected very many people, but its effects were mild. When the second wave emerged, the disease was at its most deadly. As the wave continued to spread, so it seemed to lose some of its virulence.

When the second wave of Spanish flu reached Australia in 1919, its effects were nothing like as severe, and the country suffered the lowest death rate of any developed country.[10]

John Barry – who is a writer, not a scientist (though his deep, knowledge of the 1918–19 epidemic has led to his becoming an advisor to the US government, the United Nations and the World Health Organization) – suggests, as a hypothesis, that the virulence of viruses may decrease as they pass through a population. As he writes, 'At the peak of the pandemic ... the virus seemed to still be mutating rapidly, virtually with each passage through humans, and it was mutating toward a less lethal form.' It's a thought from which we can take some comfort, though it seems that the early victims of a pandemic may be condemned to being a heroic first line of defence, taking heavy casualties in order to give others a fighting chance of survival.

Not If, But When

There are three types of influenza virus: A, B and C. The one that mainly affects humans is Influenza B. Influenza B mutates slowly enough to allow most of us to acquire a degree of immunity at an early age, but not so slowly that we can be sure that we will never get the flu again. Nevertheless, its relatively slow rate of mutation and the fact that it affects only a few species (humans, seals and ferrets) limit the risk of an Influenza B pandemic. (Of course, if there were more systematic contact between humans, seals and ferrets, this might no longer hold true.) Influenza C is limited to humans, dogs and pigs, and can produce severe symptoms, but it is not very common.

Influenza A is the most interesting. Every bird in the world is thought to be susceptible to it. Migratory wildfowl carry the virus, but are resistant to it. In the course of their travels they may, of course, transmit the virus to domestic birds, such as ducks and chickens, with which humans have a lot of contact. This would not matter if Influenza A couldn't jump between species.

There are two reasons for this. One is that Influenza A viruses are not very good at repairing the inevitable genetic errors that occur whenever they replicate. As a result, every time the virus replicates, it changes a little. The other reason Influenza A is dangerous is that it can take on bits of genetic material from other viruses. This is known as 'antigenic shift', and it is bad news as it can lead, as we have seen, to a virus with enough 'human' components to be transmitted easily from human to human.

At the moment, the virus seems to be relatively inefficient at transmitting between humans. Nevertheless, the World Health Organization (WHO) has recorded reported outbreaks of H5N1 (or 'Avian flu') in 15 countries since 2003. Across this seven-year period, in China there were 40 cases and 26 deaths; in Egypt, 113 cases and 27 deaths; in Indonesia, 171 cases and 141 deaths; in Thailand, 25 cases and 17 deaths; and in Vietnam, 119 cases and 59 deaths.[11] These are only the reported cases — not all countries have proper surveillance systems in place — and WHO will only include cases where there have been laboratory confirmation of the presence of the virus. Still, the good news is that it is quite clear that this particular strain of H5N1 is not going to cause a pandemic.

The bad news is that another strain almost certainly will. As Dr Hassan al-Bushra, the World Health Organization's regional adviser for communicable diseases surveillance in the Middle East, said in 2006, after an outbreak of Avian flu in Iraq, Egypt and Jordan:

> If people continue to be in contact with [avian flu] and infected by avian flu, at some stage the virus either will mutate into a new form that spreads from human to human, or a new influenza virus will be created through the combination in humans of the bird flu virus with an existing influenza virus. The results of either eventuality would be disastrous. We predict that an influenza pandemic outbreak, which could cross the world in about three months, could end up killing hundreds of thousands of people. Thus the importance of containing bird flu relates more

> to preventing the future outbreak of a new influenza pandemic, rather than to H5N1 itself.[12]

And the really bad news is that experts think that Hassan al-Bushra is being wildly optimistic with his forecast of the number of global deaths. Dr David Nabarro is the Senior System Coordinator for Avian and Human Influenza at the United Nations. His job, as you will have guessed from his job title, is to help to ensure that the UN makes an effective contribution to a future global effort to control a bird flu pandemic. At a press conference in 2005, soon after his appointment to the role, he was reluctant to say that Avian flu would inevitably make the full leap from birds to humans. 'I'm not sure whether "almost certain" is the impression I'd like to have conveyed to you, but it does seem very likely and it would be extremely wrong for me as a public health person to be ignoring this threat.' He was more forthright on the likely impact if this were to happen:

> I'm not, at the moment, at liberty to give you a prediction on numbers, but I just want to stress that, let's say, the range of deaths could be anything from 5 to 150 million.[13]

His job, he went on to stress, was to try to make sure that the figure stayed closer to 5 million than to 150 million.

9 THE BLINDSIDED BRAIN

The fact of 'being blindsided' is not only real, but common and perhaps fundamental to our experience. We make decisions, convince ourselves that they are the result of meticulous, rational thought – and then find ourselves looking back at them and wondering how we could have been so thoughtless or foolish as to ever have thought that the particular decision was right, or that our choice of action was well-considered. Being blindsided so often and so significantly is not something that we can be particularly proud of, but we should perhaps not despair.

The problem, it would seem, is that we make decisions using an astonishingly complex, organic device – our highly-evolved brains – and these brains do not always have the same agenda that we do, particularly when we see ourselves as being modern citizens, consumers, investors and planners.

Fortunately for us, the fields of psychology and neuroscience (which we, as a species, have been clever enough to develop) are beginning to offer us some clear and cogent explanations as to how, and why, we make decisions. Not only that, they are questioning whether the part of our brains that considers itself to be 'in charge', and to be taking carefully considered, rational decisions, can really be considered 'us'.

With this knowledge comes the possibility of reflecting more carefully on the things that influence our decision-making –

things of which we are barely conscious, or not conscious at all – which may enable us to bring these things into consciousness, and to make better decisions in the future.

Fast and Slow Thinking

The psychologist Daniel Kahneman, who won the Nobel Prize in Economics for his work on decision-making and uncertainty, describes in his book, *Thinking, Fast and Slow*, what he thinks recent experiments are telling us about how the brain works. For a great many tasks, our minds make instant decisions without any conscious effort on our part. We instinctively recognise, for example, from a person's face, voice or body language, whether they are angry, happy or sad – and we make predictions about what they are likely to say or do next as a result. We can drive a car without, apparently, thinking about it, unless we are alarmed by some event. We can understand simple sentences and do simple arithmetic. Kahneman calls this 'fast thinking'. Then there are tasks that *do* require conscious effort: performing difficult mental arithmetic; concentrating on one particular voice in a room full of people talking; counting every occurrence of the letter 'a' on this page. This Kahneman calls 'slow thinking,' and it takes physical effort: our heart-rate increases, our muscles tense, our pupils dilate. Because such difficult tasks 'take over' some of the brain's resources, as we shall see in a moment, we are unable to take in during that time everything that is happening around us.

Blind to the Obvious

A remarkable example of this was demonstrated in an experiment conducted by two psychologists, Christopher Chabris and Daniel Simons.[1] Volunteers were asked to watch a video of a staged game of basketball between two teams, and to count the number of passes made by the team in white jerseys, while ignoring the play of the black team. Halfway through the video, a woman dressed in a gorilla suit runs onto the basketball court, waves her arms around and beats her chest in true gorilla fashion, and then runs off the court. About half of the volunteers *do not see the gorilla*. They insist that there was no gorilla. The mental effort of counting the passes by the white team and, especially, of ignoring the black team, blinded them. Their brains were too taken up with the difficult task at hand to register the unexpected – but they were completely unaware of this. As Kahneman concludes, 'We can be blind to the obvious, and we are also blind to our blindness.'[2]

This experiment proves that, in some situations, the mental energy consumed by a difficult task that requires our slow-thinking processes can effectively shut down other brain processes – even such apparently fundamental processes as being surprised by something utterly unexpected in our visual field. This effect is also the basis of the traditional figure of the 'absent-minded professor' – people who are quite literally 'lost in thought', who can be blind to the obvious events taking place around them.

It is, however, the more routine, day-to-day, fast-thinking processes we habitually employ that actually have the most direct relevance to the examples of being blindsided that are examined in this book.

Fast thinking relies heavily on rules-of-thumb, or what psychologists tend to call 'heuristics': decisions and predictions that are based on practical experience, rather than worked out from first principles. This way of making decisions is quick, which is essential for the tasks at hand, and for the vast majority of decisions, this process is likely to be efficient and effective. We are extremely good at assessing other people's moods and their reactions to us. We sense whether they are irritated, or bored, or distracted, and whether they have taken a liking to us or not. We are even better at being afraid: fear is the most important reaction, and it takes precedence over every other response – for obvious reasons. This often gives rise to what we describe as 'sixth sense' experiences: we get a 'bad feeling' about something that we can't explain, and this bad feeling sometimes saves our lives.

A man called Robert Thompson walked into a convenience store in America and felt such an overwhelming sense of fear that he left immediately, without picking up the magazines he had been intending to buy. Minutes later, a police officer entered the store and was shot and killed: he had unwittingly walked in on an armed robbery. Thompson wasn't aware of anything that he had seen that would have alerted him to that fact; there was nothing that would explain his overwhelming sense of fear. Under questioning by Gavin de Becker, an American expert on the prediction and management of violence, Thompson remembered that he had noticed that the storekeeper had glanced at him very rapidly and then switched his focus straight back to the man in front of him at the shop counter. That unnaturally rapid glance is probably the key signal that alerted Thompson to the fact that things were not normal. On further questioning, he recalled that the man at the shop counter was wearing a heavy jacket (perhaps, with hindsight, to conceal a weapon) even though the day was warm, and that there was a car in the parking lot with its engine running and two men inside it. None of these perceptions had entered Thompson's consciousness when he made his decision to leave the store. He walked in; he felt very afraid; and he left.[3]

This is the kind of thing that our fast-thinking processes are very good at, and they were honed to perfection at a time when life was far more straightforward, when fight or flight were our main concerns.

Unfortunately, there are several things that throw fast thinking off track when it makes decisions in this way – things that may have been useful when we were a young species making a living on the African savannah, but which are a problem in the modern world. Things, in fact, that lead us to take decisions that, on later reflection, seem foolish and wrong; decisions that lead to us feeling blindsided. The central paradox is that the rapid, efficient, emotionally driven reactions that helped prevent us from being blindsided on the savannah – the sixth sense that tells us to move out of harm's way before we are even aware that we are in danger, amongst other 'gut reactions' – can so easily lead us to make poor decisions in more complex scenarios. What used to prevent us from being caught unawares is, in modern life, leading us to make poor decisions for reasons that we are not aware of.

Unconscious Influences

One of the more remarkable affects that disrupt our decision-making processes in this way is known as 'priming'. Something that we have just encountered tends to give us a set of expectations that affects what we do next, without our being aware of the fact. If we have just seen the word 'eat', for example, we are more likely to complete the word fragment SO_P as SOUP rather than as SOAP. Conversely, and at a more emotional level, if we think of some action of which we are ashamed, we are more likely to complete the word as SOAP (the impulse to clean ourselves after some action that we regret seems to be entirely real and is known as the Lady Macbeth Effect).

The priming effect can even affect our physical behaviour. A group of students who had been asked to assemble sentences from words associated with old age walked more slowly down the corridor at the end of the experiment, even though they reported that they were not consciously aware that the words they had been working with had any common theme. The idea of age had entered their minds without them realising it, and affected their behaviour.[4]

Another example of things that distort our judgement without our being aware of it is the 'anchor'. Once a figure has been introduced to any debate about numbers, whether or not it has any objective value, we are extremely likely to find that our subsequent judgements are influenced by that original number, which acts as an 'anchor'. The asking price of a house is a good and familiar example. Even professional real estate agents, who professed to have ignored (but of course!) the asking price of various houses during an experiment in which they were asked to give their opinion as to a reasonable buying price and the likely lowest acceptable price for each house in question, were greatly influenced in their estimates by the original asking price.[5] The figures that they proposed were effectively dragged up or down by the level of the initial asking price, regardless of whether the asking price was a good reflection of the market value of the house, and despite their conviction that they, as true professionals, would ignore something as unscientific as the price the vendor happened to have asked for.

In a similar way, a survey of visitors to an exhibition on the environmental damage done by oil tankers in the Pacific showed that they were, in the absence of influencing factors, prepared to donate an average of $64 to save seabirds from the effects of oil spills. These visitors were demonstrating their interest in the issue by attending the exhibition, an interest reflected in their high 'unprompted' level of potential donation. However, if visitors were asked how much they would be prepared to donate prefaced by the phrase, 'Would you be prepared to pay $5 to save seabirds from oil spills…', then the average amount proffered fell to $20. If they were asked, 'Would you be prepared to donate $400 to…', the average amount rose to $143. Same question, different anchor, different result.

The same effect can be seen at work in any auction, where the initial 'estimate' price greatly affects the level of the first bids. On eBay, for instance, the 'Buy Now' price displayed for many items acts as a clear anchor in terms of what would represent a 'good' price.[6]

There are many other things that affect our quick decisions, for example 'availability' (things that have been mentioned recently, and are at the front of our minds[7]); 'affect' (things that we like or dislike, which clouds our rational assessments of their value[8]); and the illusion of causality (we seem to be programmed to assume that event A has 'caused' event B, when in fact they may well be unrelated[9]).

It is easy to see how just a few of these could be enough to create the 'bad decision' that would later result in our feeling of having been blindsided. The decision was made by the fast-thinking system while it was affected by one of its many 'biases and systematic errors' while 'we' (the slow-thinking system) were not aware of the reasons why we made that decision in the first place. As Kahneman points out, we suffer from both our 'excessive confidence in what we believe we know, and our apparent inability to acknowledge the full extent of our ignorance and the uncertainty of the world we live in.'[10]

The Emotional Brain

Another take on how we make decisions is supplied by neuroscience. We like to believe that we make decisions 'rationally', by which we tend to mean that our mental processes have not been influenced by 'emotion'. We know that it is best not to make decisions when we are angry, or upset. We feel that we should make decisions with a clear mind, 'in the light of pure reason', unclouded by emotion. Neuroscience, however, is discovering that what we call 'emotions' represent, in effect, the very hard-wiring of our brains. Emotions can be described as the currency with which our brains do business. This does not mean (of course) that we are not capable of rational thought, but it certainly undermines the notion that we can strip decisions of their emotional content.

Nothing, it seems, comes into our minds without an emotional content attached. The culprits of this 'non-rationality' appear to be the two regions of the brain known as the amygdala. The amygdala play a pivotal role in dealing with incoming sensory stimuli, matching these against our memory of what has happened to us before. And what the amygdala assess is not rational, but emotional. As the psychologist Paul Brown says:

> The amygdala seem to act a kind of guardhouse, assessing every stimulus that hits the brain – whether generated externally (perceptions) or internally (thoughts) – and assigning that stimulus to the correct emotional pathway. The amygdala assess the emotional loading of every stimulus of which the brain is aware in making 'first stage' sense of everything impinging upon us.
>
> The very first thing that the amygdala do is to assess the level of danger or threat: is this a friend or foe? When new stimuli hit us, the amygdala's task is to assign a pathway in terms of the eight basic emotions and in the light of all other prevailing data. Most of this is below the threshold of conscious perception: the amygdala will organise the body's responses within 80 milliseconds if there is threat, whereas the awareness of that doesn't get up into consciousness until about 250 milliseconds. In the presence of danger, the amygdala by-pass everything that might be to do with conscious control and mobilise all body resources within the flight/fight/freeze axes of primary survival responses.[11]

The amygdala don't have time (literally) to spend on rational thought. Our personal experience confirms that in potentially life-threatening situations we do not sit back and have a leisurely think about what to do next. We come to ourselves, as it were, and begin to piece together what has just happened: why it is that we are lying on the ground, screaming and clutching our leg, or why our fists are clenched and there is a red mist in front of our eyes.

More importantly, if the evidence about the way in which our minds react to any kind of stimuli is being interpreted correctly, it seems that *nothing* comes into our consciousness until it has first been ascribed some kind of emotional content. The only exceptions (possibly, but not necessarily) would be the realms of 'pure thought': intellectual exercises that we set ourselves, such as mathematics, philosophy and logic.

Iowa Gambling Task

There is some intriguing experimental evidence to suggest that our 'emotions' are what enable us to make decisions and, indeed, to learn. The now famous psychological study that has become known as the Iowa Gambling Task gave volunteers a notional sum of money and asked them to choose cards from four different packs of cards. Most of the cards gave a money reward; some imposed a penalty. The aim of the game was to end up with the greatest amount of money. Two of the packs gave higher rewards but also included heavy penalties; the other two packs gave lower rewards but also lower penalties. The high penalty packs were the ones to avoid, in order to accumulate the most money, despite the attraction of their higher rewards.

The volunteers were wired up to a skin conductance-measuring device: as we become more stressed or anxious, so we perspire more, imperceptibly but measurably; as we perspire, so the electrical conductance of our skin increases.

After experiencing a few penalties from the high-penalty packs (typically, after choosing about 10 cards from those packs), volunteers demonstrated increased skin conductance response (SCR) whenever they reached out to take a card from those packs. However, when asked what they believed was going on in the game, they reported that they had no idea. This state of affairs – signs of unconscious anxiety when reaching out for cards from those packs but no conscious notion of why they might be 'bad' packs – carried on until, on average, the fiftieth card, at which point some volunteers began to say that they had a 'hunch' that the cards in those packs were bad choices.

It was only at the eightieth card, on average, that people began to say that they understood why the cards in those two packs were bad choices. Some people were never able to express what was wrong with the 'bad' packs, but they continued to show increased SCR and continued to choose advantageously, in terms of the aim of the game.

People, it seems, were making the right choices before they could explain why they were choosing in that way – and, in some cases, even when they did not understand how they were making successful choices for the duration of the game. Yet their emotional system was guiding their actions long before they became aware, even at the 'hunch' level, that there might be a good reason for their actions.

Still more remarkably, some of the volunteers were patients with damage to the prefrontal cortex area of their brains – the area most implicated in decision-making and cognitive behaviour. These patients never demonstrated increased SCR – they showed no signs of nervousness about the good or bad packs. Some of them, nevertheless, figured out that two of the packs were disadvantageous and were able to express this clearly, *yet they continued to choose disadvantageously.*[12] They had worked out what would be a winning strategy, but without the emotional content attached to that knowledge, they failed to act on it. This, it seemed, could be at the heart of why brain-damaged patients struggle with decision-making, socially appropriate behaviour and a range of other issues: it was not that they could not rationally discern the most advantageous course of action; it was that without the emotional 'reward' that accompanies normal decision-making, they would not follow their rational realisation through into action. What, after all, was the point?

Emotions are not only helping us to make decisions before the conscious mind is in a position to make a judgement; they are the very mechanism by which decisions are brought about at all. Without an emotional content, decisions are hard or impossible to make.

Fear and Reward

This is not to say that we cannot be led astray by our emotions: the reward systems that were so well adapted to ensure that we would find food and avoid danger are now affecting our decision-making in far more complex situations – especially with regard to that modern symbol for all things good: money.

Neuroscience reveals the remarkable fact that financial gain stimulates our brains in a way that mirrors the effects of drugs like cocaine: in both cases the 'reward' chemical, dopamine, is released in specific regions of the brain.[13] Making money, as you may have noticed, makes us feel good. This dangerous connection between financial gain and feeling good can lead to obvious behavioural problems. People who make money as the result of risk-taking (like investors) may be driven to take greater risks in search of greater rewards. What is driving them is not their reason, but their emotional response system: they are beginning to crave the dopamine reward that their successful risk-taking receives. Conversely, losing money is experienced as that most powerful of emotions: fear. A degree of fear in financial matters helps us to make sharp, rational decisions – to reduce our exposure to a volatile situation, for example. Extreme fear, however, leads us to make very bad decisions, and would seem to explain the 'panics' with which markets can be seized – a perfect description, since panic is defined as 'unreasoning terror'. When we are frightened but not panic-stricken, our slow-thinking processes are still able to intervene and influence or countermand our fast-thinking responses. But when we are in the grip of fear, we sell assets at fire-sale prices and create rushes on banks, even when this behaviour is most likely to bring about the result that we most fear.

The Left and Right Hemispheres of the Brain

A final insight into our behaviour offered by the discoveries of neuroscience comes from the demonstrable fact of the astonishing and observable differences in the functioning of the left and right hemispheres of our brains. These differences may very well underpin the way we experience reality and explain a great deal of why we behave in the way that we do.

The key contention of this book has been that the events that catch us out and blindside us should not, on any reasonable analysis of the situation, be unexpected. In all the cases explored in this book we have 'been there' and 'done that' before. The problem is that we are constitutionally – or, as will be discussed in a moment, perhaps neurologically – incapable of spotting the wave that breaks over our heads until it is about to do so. We have unjustifiable self-confidence, unreasonable optimism, and an inexhaustible capacity for self-delusion and denial all wired into our brains. It is not that we are incapable of seeing the bigger picture; it is rather that our left hemisphere wilfully refuses to see the bigger picture.

Big Picture, Little Picture

Have you ever noticed how the bird hopping about on your lawn, hoping that the pitter-patter of its feet on the turf will persuade worms that it is raining so that they should come to the surface and be eaten for their pains, is cocking its head to one side? It is part of the charm of birds. It gives them a quizzical look. They look at us, with their head to one side, and seem to acknowledge that it is, indeed, a funny old world. There they are, looking for worms, and there we are, reading a newspaper and drinking tea.

There is a reason they do this, and it is not, sadly, about their personal relationship with humans. Relatively advanced animals (and birds are very advanced, and very intelligent) need to have two ways of apprehending the world. They need to look for food (those worms poking their snouts unwisely above the turf) and they need to keep an eye on the wider world for threats and predators (such as the sudden swoop of a sparrow hawk, or more likely, the sudden pounce of your neighbour's cat). In a broader sense, they need to apprehend the wider, social world: a potential mate; the existing mate and another rather enticing potential mate further down the hedgerow; the flock in which they fly; the field where they forage. Our brains – and the brains of birds and other higher species – have evolved in a strikingly asymmetrical way. Brains have a left hemisphere and a right hemisphere, and the two sides are remarkably different – visibly so, in terms of size and structure; discernibly so in terms of function, as we shall see.

It seems that brains may have evolved divided over the millennia for a very good reason. We need our brains to do two very different kinds of thing at the same time: to focus on the particular and the precise, but also to grasp the wider world in all of its 'otherness' and social complexity. The two sides of the divided brain are connected by a kind of cable called the *corpus callosum*, and the function of this sophisticated bundle of neural fibres is, of course, to allow the two halves to communicate, although, interestingly, its main function seems to be to allow one half of the brain to inhibit the activities of the other.

Two Different Ways of Experiencing the World

Iain McGilchrist, the remarkable polymath who began his academic career teaching English literature at All Souls College, Oxford, but later took up the study of medicine and went on to become consultant psychiatrist at Bethlem Royal Hospital in London and a research fellow in neuroimaging at John Hopkins Hospital, Baltimore, is the author of *The Master and His Emissary: The Divided Brain and the Making of the Western World*. He provides an account of the functions of the left and right hemispheres – or as he would put it, their different ways of experiencing the world (or more precisely, their 'different ways of *being in* the world'[14]):

> In general terms, the left hemisphere yields narrow, focussed attention, mainly for the purpose of getting and feeding. The right hemisphere yields a broad, vigilant attention, the purpose of which seems to be the awareness of signals from the surroundings, especially of other creatures, who are potential predators or potential mates, foes or friends; and it is involved in bonding in social animals.... The right hemisphere

> underwrites breadth and flexibility of attention, where the left hemisphere brings to bear focussed attention. This has the related consequence that the right hemisphere sees things whole, and in their context, where the left hemisphere sees things abstracted from context, and broken into parts, from which it then reconstructs a 'whole': something very different. And it also turns out that the capacities that help us, as humans, form bonds with others – empathy, emotional understanding and so on – which involve a quite different kind of attention paid to the world, are largely right hemisphere functions.[15]

The two hemispheres of the brain should not be thought of as performing different sets of functions, even though they have clear 'specialities'. It became clear, quite early in modern research into brain function, that language was a left-brain speciality: patients who had suffered a left-hemisphere stroke usually lost their capacity for speech. However, it has more recently become clear that the left hemisphere's expertise is in the *syntax* of language: its structure, its nuts and bolts. It is in the right hemisphere that understanding of the whole resides (as opposed to analysis of the particular) and, as a result, it is from the right hemisphere that we get a sense both of context and of non-literal meaning — including metaphor, irony, sarcasm and humour. Everything, that is to say, that is actually interesting.

We can get a glimpse of this strange segregation of the two hemispheres. Presumably, like me, you frequently struggle to find the appropriate word to express yourself more aptly. You rack your brain for a long time, and then give in. Some time later, the precise word for which you were searching 'pops into' your mind. The start of the search sets the left hemisphere off on one of its exhaustive but unintelligent searches. The left hemisphere is obsessed by categorisation; it busily divides the world up into discrete entities and slots them into the appropriate pigeonhole. It is a very valuable *analytical* tool, but it is hopeless at spotting (let alone in dealing with) the strange and even paradoxical similarities between apparently different things. In search of the missing word, the left hemisphere digs further and further into its lexicon of similar words, hoping that the right one will eventually be unearthed. But it is in the right hemisphere that resides the ability to make more tenuous associations, discern shades of meaning and make subtle inferences. When the left hemisphere gets bored of thumbing laboriously through our mental dictionaries in search of the right word, the right hemisphere – which the left hemisphere will have been assiduously preventing from making any contribution – throws up the perfect answer using its more organic, intuitive search methods. Suddenly, the word that was 'on the tip of our tongue' is magically presented to us.[16]

Split-Brain Experiments

The first evidence as to the startling differences between the left and right hemispheres of the brain came as a result of doctors working with 'split-brain' patients – patients who had undergone an operation to sever the channel of communication (the *corpus callosum*) between the two hemispheres, usually in an attempt to alleviate cases of severe epilepsy. This radical surgical procedure was first used in the late 1950s. It was effective in controlling severe epileptic fits by preventing them from affecting the whole brain, and surgeons were relieved and rather surprised by the extent to which their patients were able to lead relatively normal lives after this drastic operation. Nevertheless, the subtle consequences of having the two hemispheres separated gradually became apparent.

Michael Gazzaniga, professor of psychology at the University of Santa Barbara, California, conducted a ground-breaking series of experiments with spilt-brain patients in the 1960s, and was a driving force in developing the field of 'cognitive neuroscience' – a field which, for the first time in history, brought together philosophical explorations of consciousness with the first scientific evidence as to what might actually be going on inside our brains. Gazzaniga's experiments with split-brain patients quickly led to some startling conclusions.[17] Whilst the recovering patients seemed to be the same people – in terms of temperament, intelligence and personality – as they had been before their operation, some interesting minor behavioural differences emerged. For one thing, patients seemed oblivious of physical stimuli on the *left* side of their body: they could brush against objects and not notice. If an object was placed in their left hands, they might deny its presence.

It also became clear that the right hemisphere had some comprehension of words, but no spoken language. When a picture of a spoon was presented to the left hemisphere (via the right eye) or if the patient was allowed to hold a spoon in his or her right hand, but not see it, the patient was able to name the object and describe it, quite normally. When the same picture or tactile experience was presented to the right hemisphere (via the left eye), there was no recognition. It had nothing to say. Gazzaniga and his colleagues began to wonder if the separation of the right hemisphere from its apparently more intelligent partner on the left side of the brain had reduced it to an 'imbecilic' state.

But then they discovered that the right hemisphere was not so stupid after all. If the right hemisphere, having been presented with a spoon, was given a number of non-verbal options with which to respond, it had no problem whatsoever. It could select a spoon with the left hand from among a group of unseen objects. When shown a picture of a cigarette (cigarettes and smoking paraphernalia were more ubiquitous in the 1960s than they are now), the patient could select, by touch, an ashtray from a group of objects that did not include a cigarette: the ashtray was the 'best match'. Although the right hemisphere could not name objects, it was perfectly capable of pointing to a card showing a picture of the object. It could also read words that it could not utter: if the word 'pencil' was flashed to the right hemisphere, the patient could select a pencil from a group of unseen objects.

Cognitive Neuroscience

And then Dr Gazzaniga came to the experiment that changed his life, and led to the development of the new field of cognitive neuroscience. 'It was a great moment', said Gazzaniga. 'I'm not sure I've had such a great moment of a scientific nature since.'[18] In the course of his experiments, Gazzaniga flashed a picture of a snow-covered house to the right hemisphere; the right hemisphere was able to select (with the left hand) an image of a shovel, as the best available match (just as cigarettes were more everyday objects then than they are today, so the link between snow and a shovel is more obvious to the inhabitants of the northern states of the US than it might be to the inhabitants of, say, Spain). When the left hemisphere (which had not seen the image of the snow-covered house) was asked to point to a matching object using the right hand, it was reduced to guessing and scored no better than blind chance.

The next stage of the experiment was to flash a picture of a chicken claw to the left hemisphere at the same time as flashing the picture of the snow-covered house to the right hemisphere. The left hand (right hemisphere) pointed to a shovel and the right hand (left hemisphere) to a chicken. 'I'll never forget the day we got around to asking P.S. [the experimental subject]. "Why did you do that?" said Dr Gazzaniga. He said, "The chicken claw goes with the chicken." That's all the left hemisphere saw. And then he looks at the shovel and said, "The reason you need a shovel is to clean out the chicken shed."'[19]

The left hemisphere, which had no knowledge of the picture of the snow-covered house, created an explanation as to why the left hand (over which it has no control) had pointed to a picture of a shovel. It does so from a position of complete ignorance, shamelessly and with complete conviction. 'It's because you need a shovel to clean out the chicken shed!' it says, with the clear imputation of, 'Don't you get it? Are you stupid or something?'

Right Hemispheres Do Empathy, Left Hemispheres Do Denial

It would seem that it is the right hemisphere that gives us the capacity for empathy, which allows us to understand what other people are feeling. People with right frontal hemisphere damage can lose all understanding of, or interest in, the feelings of others; they have no instinctive grasp of what other people might be feeling, expecting or experiencing, and display indifference to their reactions.

It is the right hemisphere that deals with the subtle messages conveyed by our eyes: patients with right-hemisphere damage sense that other people are communicating something with their eyes, but to them the message is inscrutable. Not surprisingly, it leaves them feeling anxious and paranoid. It is the right hemisphere that deals quite happily with a world that is in constant flux, while the left hemisphere works hard to fix, analyse and categorise that flux – which leads to problems when they stop working together.

What is intriguing – and even amusing – is the extent to which the left hemisphere lives in a state of constant denial about the existence of anything that has to do with the right hemisphere. The right hemisphere receives visual information from the left eye, and the left hemisphere from the right. However, in cases of left-hemisphere damage, the right hemisphere appears to be happy to start accepting information from the right eye as well, and will faithfully reproduce a drawing of an image in its entirety (e.g., a full clock face). But in cases of right-hemisphere damage, the left hemisphere may refuse to acknowledge any information from the eye that it does not control (i.e., the left eye); patients may doggedly reproduce only the right-hand side of an image (e.g., a clock showing only 12 to 6), refusing to acknowledge the existence of the left half.

Some patients may even refuse to acknowledge that the left-hand side of their body exists at all. Since their left arm, for example, does not follow the left hemisphere's instructions, they may deny that they have a left arm. And, the left hemisphere being exceptionally good at making up stories (no matter how far-fetched) to rationalise what it has no knowledge of, will bare-facedly explain that there is another patient's arm in their bed; or their mother's arm; or a dead arm. Some explain that their 'missing' arm has been taken away with the laundry to be washed.[20]

The left hemisphere of our brains appears to be disturbingly keen to deny the existence of the right hemisphere and to invent false narratives about decisions that the right hemisphere has taken, of which the left hemisphere has no knowledge. It appears to be unwilling to admit that it does not, in fact, see the whole picture. It attempts to deny the very existence of the right hemisphere and its more intuitive grasp of the world.

This seems to account for both our tendency to invent plausible explanations about decisions that we have in fact made with little or no conscious reflection, and our experience of being blindsided: of being amazed and disheartened when a decision that we believed had been arrived at after careful deliberation turns out to be foolish. The right hemisphere of our brains, it should be remembered, is concerned with the outer world of friends and predators, with quick decision-making based on learned responses that are designed to keep us alive and help us to find a mate. It has some very interesting parallels with Daniel Kahneman's notion of fast thinking. It is not the system best designed to help us choose what price to pay for a house, which presidential candidate to vote for, or which company shares to buy. A great deal of evidence, however, suggests that we do in fact make these kinds of decisions, not with the kind of detached cost/benefit analysis that we fondly believe we bring to bear on these issues, but using exactly the same mechanisms that we use to distinguish friend from foe: emotional, quick, right-hemisphere, or fast-thinking decisions. Then, perhaps, our left hemisphere provides us with a compelling version of why we have so cleverly made that decision. And then, perhaps, we wake up one day and wonder, 'What were we thinking of?'

Who Are We?

There is one last quirk of the left hemisphere that needs mentioning: it thinks it is 'us'. We saw that Daniel Kahneman thinks that we identify 'ourselves' with our slow-thinking system, but this is rather different: on this left/right analysis, it would seem that we have two slightly warring personalities within our brain/minds: the empathetic right hemisphere and the analytic left hemisphere. Split-brain patients sometimes reported disturbing occasions when their left hand would do something that was beyond their control. If they were choosing something to wear from the wardrobe, for example, the left hand might reach out and grasp some other item of clothing altogether, quite independently, and would not be persuaded to let go. In other more alarming situations the left hand might try to take control of the steering wheel when the subject was driving. What is interesting is that *it was always the left hand*: the right hemisphere, for whatever reason, had chosen some item or some course of action, but the left hemisphere had no knowledge of this. The significance is that the 'narrator' of this story, the person who is experiencing these strange goings on, is the left hemisphere – the hemisphere that does not recognise the left hand as part of 'us'.

The left hemisphere, to begin to conclude, is slightly mad. It experiences the world as a series of disembodied, fragmented snapshots of reality, which it seeks to categorise. It wants control and power, and has no interest in whatever it cannot control. Where something has happened of which it has no knowledge, it will cheerfully concoct some ludicrous story that explains that actually, after all, that was exactly what the left hemisphere had planned to do all along. If something exists over which it has no control, it will shamelessly deny the existence of that thing.

Our right hemisphere (the sane half) is firmly embodied in

the real world. It does not need to embark on difficult philosophical explorations of what it can or cannot know; whether there really is an objective world 'out there'; whether other people are real or mere figments of our imagination. The right hemisphere simply *is*. It grasps the world in all of its fluid complexity; it sees whole pictures; it empathises with other living things; it understands the world, essentially, by means of an emotional response. It experiences the world directly though its actions and this forms the basis for its understanding of the world.

The left hemisphere, in sharp contrast, stands back from the world as it is presented to it by the right hemisphere and attempts to analyse it. It puzzles (like the Enlightenment philosopher, Descartes) over how it can possibly know that the people it sees in the street are not mere machines dressed in clothing, or whether it actually has a body at all. And the problem, as McGilchrist portrays it, is that our analytically oriented left hemispheres are beginning to take over our worldview. We are increasingly seeing our relationship to the world via the fragmented, analytic, 'frame by frame' perception offered by our left hemisphere, rather than with the embodied, empathetic, instinctive perceptions of our right hemisphere. And since the left hemisphere exists in a permanent state of denial, it doesn't even realise that it is taking over, it doesn't share the benefits of the right hemisphere's perception of the world (because it refuses to), and it doesn't understand why, as a result, it feels alienated, anxious and adrift.

Taking Charge

As we struggle towards a more effective way of being in the world, aided by these intriguing insights from the worlds of psychology and neuroscience, it becomes clear that we should, at the very least, not be surprised by our capacity for being blindsided. We experience ourselves as being a distinct mental entity that we like to call 'ourselves' and yet it is increasingly obvious that significant parts of our decision-making process – arguably the most significant parts – are not presented to our conscious minds for examination, and that there might even be something of a disagreement within ourselves as to what would be the best solution to any particular problem.

As a result we wake up, on more mornings than we care to admit to, and think: 'Did we really do that? How could that happen? How can we be so stupid? Why were we so completely *blindsided* by that particular set of events? Why, for goodness sake, didn't we see it coming?'

Despite these embarrassments, we should consider our advantages. We seem to be extremely clever animals, whose behaviour is directed by powerful emotions designed to keep us alive in hostile circumstances. These emotions also drive learning processes of immense subtlety: we are far cleverer than computers, not because we have a better central processing unit, but because ours is driven by emotion; we get better at everything; we learn as we go along, because of our emotions. We should recognise that another of the great advantages of being human – surely the greatest advantage – is that we also have an embedded emotional response that drives us to cooperate, to function as a group, since it is as a group that we are best able to cope with whatever our environment throws at us.

Finally, we must celebrate the relatively recent biological development of the human brain, which has given us such remarkable cognitive abilities, such stunning 'rationality'. But we should break out of the new orthodoxy – the way of thinking that draws an obvious, but mistaken, parallel between the human brain and the computers that the human brain has devised. Just as the Age of Enlightenment's growing understanding of the power of the empirical, scientific method made us believe that all of our thought processes should ideally be 'scientific' in the same way – constantly testing hypotheses, observing the results and drawing conclusions – so the Computer Age seems to have led us to view the brain as a kind of supercomputer, constantly analysing every possible outcome and choosing the most advantageous course of action.

The human brain is not a computer. (If it were, we should perhaps give up the race now and hand over to the machines – they, after all, will run things far more efficiently.) The human brain is much more than a computer. It recognises itself and others. It understands (except in cases of brain damage and defect) that it is embodied in the real world; it has an exquisitely refined sense of what other human beings (and many other mammals) are thinking and feeling. It is not only capable of astonishing feats of computer-like calculation, but of sudden, intuitive leaps of the imagination that reveal whole new ways of interpreting and predicting the world around us.

Most importantly of all, the brain is *social* – it is exquisitely attuned to the complexities of social interaction – and success in complex social interaction is what will allow us to survive and prosper in an increasingly complex world.

It is largely because the brain makes decisions in a social context that so much current thinking, which attempts to analyse human behaviour as if we are all 'independent rational agents', results in our being so frequently blindsided by what people actually do. We are not independent agents and we are not truly rational: there is an emotional component to all of our decision-making (and if there were not, we would be unable to take decisions). This does not just apply to us as individuals, but to governments and international agencies. We are faced by challenging, complex, social issues, and the successful solutions to these issues will be, unsurprisingly, complex and social.

What we experience as rational decision-making is driven by impulses and urges of which we are barely aware: an overwhelming urge to take what is available now before someone else gets it; an inbuilt tendency to follow the herd; a strong sense of what is equitable and fair; an instinct to trust our own group

and to be hostile to outsiders; a poor capacity for rem
ing disasters and planning for their reoccurrence; diffi
envisaging the collective effect of our individual actions. These unexamined motivations are what cause us to be blindsided — to be surprised and distressed, at some future point, by the consequences of actions that we thought we had made rationally and dispassionately.

The route towards a solution lies in an increasing self-awareness of how our brain/mind works and in the embrace of what makes us gloriously, irrationally and emotionally human.

Acknowledgements

This book has been two years in the writing. While it is not quite true to say that empires have risen and fallen, wars have broken out, are still continuing or are stumbling towards some kind of resolution; some tyrants have been toppled – others continue in their tyranny; we have been damaged and alarmed by terrorists, pirates and rioters, and by earthquakes, tsunamis and disease; our world has seemed very insecure – or is, perhaps, merely as insecure as ever.

It was during this period that the idea of 'being blindsided' began to take shape in my mind. The book that I set out to write was far more general; a series of essays, perhaps, about the changes in technology and in society that have impacted on business throughout the ages. As I wrote more, so it became clear to me that there was a pattern to these changes: that we, as a species, were alarmingly prone to deluding ourselves that we were behaving rationally and intelligently until, with the awful benefit of hindsight, we are able to look back and wonder what exactly we were thinking of when we made that particular decision.

I would like to thank my publisher, Martin Liu, for his inspiration, encouragement and forbearance (all of this thinking and writing took longer than planned, as ever) and for his very significant role in the shaping of the book's central argument.

I would also like to thank my editor, Justin Lau, whose clear-sightedness and precision have done so much to bring the ideas in this book into sharper focus.

Finally, I'd like to thank all my family, friends and colleagues, whose ideas and conversation have made such an important contribution to my own thinking, and whose support and encouragement is so essential.

Notes

Chapter 1 | Sooners, Boomers and Boo

1 William Willard Howard. *Harper's Weekly* 33, May 18, 1889; pp 391–394 (www.library.cornell.edu/Reps/DOCS/landrush.htm).

2 Ibid.

3 Ibid.

4 Edward Chancellor. *Devil Take the Hindmost.* London: Macmillan Publishers Ltd, 1999; pp 148–149.

5 Ibid.

6 John Cassidy. *Dot.Con.* New York: Allen Lane, 2002; pp 79–80.

7 Encyclopedia of Ecommerce (http://ecommerce.hostip.info/pages/1034/UUnet-FIRST-COMMERCIAL-ISP.html).

8 John Cassidy, op. cit., pp 80–85.

9 Ernst Malmsten, Erik Portanger and Charles Drazin. *Boo Hoo.* London: Random House, 2002; p 17.

10 Ibid., pp 24–25.

11 Ibid., p 30.

12 Ibid., p 47.

13 Ibid., p 105.

14 Ibid., pp 58–59.

15 Ibid., pp 118–119.

16 Ibid., p 120.

17 Ibid., p 237.

18 Ibid., p 272.

19 Ibid., pp 261–262.

20 Ibid., pp 278–279.

21 Ibid., p 322.

22 Ibid., p 2.

23 'Boo.com Founder Returns to Online Retail with Lara Bohinc', *Daily Telegraph*, 5 September 2011 (www.telegraph.co.uk/finance/newsbysector/retailandconsumer/8445841/Boo.com-founder-Ernst-Malmsten-returns-to-online-retail-with-Lara-Bohinc.html).

Chapter 2 | Bubbles and Crashes

1 William J. Bernstein. *A Splendid Exchange: How Trade Shaped the World*. New York: Grove Press, 2008; p 384.

2 Ibid., p 7.

3 Paul Krugman, 'How Did Economists Get It So Wrong?', *New York Times*, September 2, 2009.

4 Edward Chancellor. *Devil Take the Hindmost: A History of Financial Speculation*. London: Macmillan Publishers Ltd, 1999; p 57.

5 Carmen M. Reinhart and Kenneth S. Rogoff. *This Time is Different*. Princeton, NJ: Princeton University Press, 2009; page xxxiv.

6 Charles Mackay. *Extraordinary Popular Delusions and the Madness of Crowds*. New York: Cosimo Inc., 2008 [1841]; pp 10–12.

7 Ibid., p 11.

8 Ibid., pp 14–15.

9 Edward Chancellor, op. cit., p 61.

10 Charles Mackay, op. cit., pp 28–29.

11 Ibid., p 41.

12 Ibid., p 324.

13 Justin Fox. *The Myth of the Rational Market*. Hampshire, Great Britain: Harriman House, 2009; p 14.

14 Ibid., p 10.

15 See Ellen R. McGrattan and Edward C. Prescott, 'The 1929 Stock Market: Irving Fisher was Right' (www.minneapolisfed.org/research/sr/sr294.pdf).

16 Justin Fox, op. cit., p 204.

17 Ibid., p 201.

18 Ibid., p 253.

19 Ibid., p 202.

20 Ibid., p 207.

21 Alan Greenspan, appearance before Congress Joint Economic Committee June 1999; quoted in Michael Zandi, *Financial Shock.* New Jersey: Pearson Education Inc, 2009; p 70.

22 See Joseph Schiller (www.irrationalexuberance.com/definition.htm). Schiller, Professor of Economics at Yale University, had met Greenspan two days before the latter's speech and admits saying at the time that markets were 'irrational' but does not believe that he coined the phrase 'irrational exuberance' used soon afterwards by Greenspan. However, Schiller did choose the phrase as the perfect title for his book about the dot-com bubble, *Irrational Exuberance.*

23 Jonah Lehrer, 'When we're cowed by crowds', *Wall Street Journal,* May 28, 2011 (online.wsj.com/article/SB10001424052702304066504576341280447107102.html).

24 See Daniel Kahneman, *Thinking, Fast and Slow,* Allen Lane, 2011; p 119ff.

25 See Joseph Stiglitz. *Freefall: Free Markets and the Sinking of the Global Economy.* London: Penguin Group, 2010; pp 241–243.

26 Joseph Stiglitz, op. cit., p 240, quoting the work of Professor Franklin Allen of the Wharton School of Pennsylvania and Douglas Adam of New York University.

Chapter 3 | The Science of Desire

1 Earnest Calkins, 'Consumptionism', *Printer's Ink,* May 22, 1930, p 52; quoted in Mark Crispin Miller's introduction to the 2007 reprint of Vance Packard, *The Hidden Persuaders,* Brooklyn, NY: Ig Publishing, 2007 [1957], p 20.

2 Clyde Miller, *The Process of Persuasion,* quoted in Packard, op. cit., p 154.

3 Mark Crispin Miller's introduction to Packard, op. cit., p 20.

4 Vance Packard, op. cit., p 131.

5 Ibid.

6 Stuart Heather, 'Libido can rule when the ego goes shopping', University of Melbourne's *UniNews* Vol 12, No 22, 15 December 2003 (uninews.unimelb.edu.au/news/1091/).

7 Vance Packard, op. cit., pp 148–149.

8 Ibid., p 34.

9 John E. Hollitz, Eisenhower and the Admen: The Television 'Spot' Campaign of 1952, *The Wisconsin Journal of History*, Vol. 66, No. 1 (Autumn 1982), p 36 (www.jstor.org/stable/4635688).

10 Ibid., p 35.

11 Ibid., p 39.

12 Ibid., p 39.

13 Republican Party pamphlet, quoted in ibid., p 34.

14 John E. Hollitz, op. cit., pp 37–38.

15 Ibid., pp 38–39.

Chapter 4 | New Lamps for Old

1 *Daily Mail*, Aug 1, 2007 (www.dailymail.co.uk/news/article-472044/Illegal-heading-Killer-20mph-petrol-driven-rollerblades.html).

2 Bethany McLean and Peter Elkind. *The Smartest Guys in the Room*. London: Penguin Books, 2004; pp 28, 31.

3 Ibid., p 35.

4 Ibid., p 36.

5 Ibid., p 60.

6 Ibid., pp 38, 105.

7 'Enron's internet monster', BBC News, Nov 30, 2001 (news.bbc.co.uk/1/hi/business/1684503.stm).

8 'A matter of principals', *The Economist*, 28 July 2001 (www.economist.com/node/674210).

9 Ibid.

10 'Enron's internet monster', BBC News, op. cit.

11 'A matter of principals', *The Economist* op. cit.

12 'Q&A with Enron's Skilling', *BusinessWeek*, Feb 12, 2001 (www.businessweek.com/2001/01_07/b3719010.htm).

13 Quoted in William A. Bratton, 'Enron and the dark side of shareholder value' (papers.ssrn.com).

14 'Q&A with Enron's Skilling', *BusinessWeek*, op. cit.

15 McLean and Elkind, op. cit., p 223.

16 Bratton, op. cit.

17 'At Enron, "The Environment Was Ripe for Abuse"', *BusinessWeek*, Feb 25, 2002 (www.businessweek.com/magazine/content/02_08/b3771092.htm).

18 McLean and Elkind, p 56.

19 United States of America v. Jeffrey K. Skilling (www.scribd.com/doc/52458966/Fifth-Circuit-Skilling-Decision-06-20885-CR1-wpd).

20 McLean and Elkind, p 299.

21 Ibid., p 301.

22 Bratton, op. cit., p 1.

23 Baruch Lev. 'Where have all of Enron's intangibles gone?' *Journal of Accounting and Public Policy* 21 (2002), pp 131–135 (pages.stern.nyu.edu/~blev/docs/).

24 'How Enron's directors made millions', *Telegraph*, Jan 27, 2002 (www.telegraph.co.uk/finance/2750772/How-Enrons-directors-made-millions.html).

25 McLean and Elkind, op. cit., p 404.

26 Ibid., p 410.

27 'Enron to "file for bankruptcy"', BBC News, Nov 30, 2001 (news.bbc.co.uk/2/hi/business/1684010.stm).

28 'Enron debacle forces audit rethink', BBC News, Dec 5, 2001 (news.bbc.co.uk/1/hi/business/1692778.stm).

29 McLean and Elkind, op. cit., p 38.

30 CNBC Portfolio's 'Worst American CEOs of All Time' (www.cnbc.com/id/30502091?slide=19).

31 Baruch Lev, op. cit., pp 131–135.

32 Ibid., p 163.

33 Joseph Stiglitz. *Freefall*. New York: Allen Lane, 2010; p 253.

Chapter 5 | The Gunfight at the OK Corral

1 Gavin Hewitt, 'Filming a revolution', on Gavin Hewitt's Europe, BBC News (awww.bbc.co.uk/blogs/thereporters/gavinhewitt/2009/11/filming_a_revolution.html).

2 'Todesopfer an der Berliner Mauer', Chronik der Mauer (www.chronik-der-mauer.de/index.php/de/Start/Index/id/593792) (in German).

3 Julia Barbara Hansen, master's thesis, University of Colorado, 1937. Quoted in Terry L. Anderson and Peter J. Hill. *The Not So Wild, Wild West.* Stanford, California: Stanford University Press, 2004; p 125.

4 Ibid., p 128.

5 Terry L. Anderson and Peter J. Hill. *The Not So Wild, Wild West.* Stanford, California: Stanford University Press, 2004; pp 111–112.

6 Carol M. Miller, 'The St. Scholastica Day Riot: Oxford after the Black Death', Tallahassee Community College (organizations.ju.edu/fch/1993miller.htm).

7 Sewell Chan, 'Remembering the '77 blackout', *New York Times,* August 20, 2011 (cityroom.blogs.nytimes.com/2007/07/09/remembering-the-77-blackout/).

8 'The Blackout: Night of Terror', *Time Magazine,* July 25, 1977; pp 2–3 (www.time.com/time/magazine/article/0,9171,919089-1,00.html).

9 Quoted in London's *Evening Standard,* 9 August 2011, p 11.

10 en.wikipedia.org/wiki/File:Ownwspok.jpg

11 Statement from Wyatt Earp, November 17, 1881 (www.tombstone1880.com/archives/wyatt.htm); the McLaury's surname is misspelled in the testimony as 'McLowry'.

12 *Denver Republican,* May 14, 1893; quoted in Ben T. Traywick, 'Wyatt Earp's Thirteen Dead Men', *Tombstone News,* September 8, 2011 (thetombstonenews.com/wyatt-earps-thirteen-dead-men-p1467-84.htm).

13 Jonathan Rowson, *Transforming Behaviour Change: Beyond Nudge and Neuromania* (www.thersa.org/projects/social-brain/transforming-behaviour-change).

Chapter 6 | Weapons of Mass Financial Destruction

1 Justin Fox. *The Myth of the Rational Market.* Hampshire, UK: Harriman House Ltd, 2009; p 194.

2 John Birger, 'What onions teach us about oil prices', *Fortune,* June 27, 2008 (money.cnn.com/2008/06/27/news/economy/The_onion_conundrum_Birger.fortune/).

3 Carmen M. Reinhart and Kenneth S. Rogoff. *This Time is Different.* Princeton, NJ: Princeton University Press, 2009; p 210.

4 Joseph Stiglitz. *Freefall: Free Markets and the Sinking of the Global Economy.* New York: Allen Lane, 2010; p 2.

5 Howard Davies. *The Financial Crisis.* Cambridge, UK: Polity Press, 2010; p 161.

6 In 2003, Robert Lucas of the University of Chicago, in his presidential address to the American Economic Association, declared that the 'central problem of depression-prevention has been solved, for all practical purposes, and has in fact been solved for many decades'. Cited in Paul Krugman, 'Fighting off the Depression', *New York Times,* Jan 4, 2009.

7 Stephen A. Ross, 'Options and Efficiency', *Quarterly Journal of Economics,* Feb 1976. Quoted in Justin Fox, *The Myth of the Rational Market.* Hampshire, UK: Harriman House, 2009; p 150.

8 'Buffett warns on investment "time bomb"', BBC News, Mar 4, 2003 (news.bbc.co.uk/1/hi/2817995.stm).

9 Joseph Stiglitz, op. cit., p 86.

10 Michael Lewis. *The Big Short.* New York: Allen Lane, 2010; p 17.

11 Joseph Stiglitz, op. cit., p 86.

12 Michael Lewis, op. cit., pp 23–24.

13 Joseph Stiglitz, op. cit., p 5.

14 Susanne Craig and Deborah Solomon, 'Bank Bonus Tab: US$33bn', *Wall Street Journal,* July 31, 2009; p A1 (online.wsj.com/article/SB124896891815094085.html).

15 Paul Krugman, 'How Did Economists Get It So Wrong?', *The New York Times Magazine,* Sep 2, 2009; p MM36 (www.nytimes.com/2009/09/06/magazine/06Economic-t.html?scp=1&sq=How%20did%20economists%20get%20it%20so%20wrong&st=cse).

16 Stephen Foley, 'US house price fall beats "Great Depression slide"', *The Independent on Sunday*, June 1, 2011 (www.independent.co.uk/news/business/news/us-house-price-fall-beats-great-depression-slide-2291491.html).

17 Michael Lewis, *The Big Short*, p 129.

18 Joseph Stiglitz, op. cit., p 93.

19 Michael Lewis, op. cit., p 51 note.

20 Ibid., p 51.

21 In the case of credit default swaps (CDSs) on mortgage bonds, as opposed to those on bonds issued by a single corporation, the matter of 'default' was not so cut and dried as default by a corporation: individual borrowers within the pool of loans would default one by one. Rather than the owner of the CDS having to wait for payment when every single mortgagee had defaulted, it was agreed by the International Swaps and Derivatives Association (ISDA) that payment to CDS owners would be made incrementally, based on the level of borrowers' defaulting. See Michael Lewis, op. cit., pp 48–49.

22 Ibid., p53.

23 Jesse Eisinger and Jake Bernstein, 'The Magnetar Trade: How One Hedge Fund Helped Keep The Bubble Going', *ProPublica*, April 9, 2010 (www.propublica.org/article/all-the-magnetar-trade-how-one-hedge-fund-helped-keep-the-housing-bubble).

24 Michael Lewis, op. cit., pp 77–78.

25 David Paul, 'Credit Default Swaps, The Collapse of AIG, and Addressing the Crisis of Confidence', *Huffington Post*, October 11, 2008 (www.huffingtonpost.com/david-paul/credit-default-swaps-the_b_133891.html).

26 BBC News, Aug 8, 2011 (www.bbc.co.uk/news/business-14451682).

27 David Paul, 'Credit Default Swaps', op. cit.

28 See Joseph Stiglitz, op. cit. p 169ff.

29 Alan Kohler, 'A Tsunami of Hope or Terror?', *Business Spectator*, November 19, 2008 (www.businessspectator.com.au/bs.nsf/Article/A-tsunami-of-hope-or-terror-LHRJP?OpenDocument).

30 Ibid.

31 'Goldman Sachs: Fabrice Tourre's private emails', BBC News, Apr 27, 2010 (news.bbc.co.uk/1/hi/business/8646487.stm).

32 Laurence Knight, 'Have Goldman Sachs charges opened floodgates?', BBC News, April 27, 2010 (news.bbc.co.uk/1/hi/business/8646728.stm).

Chapter 7 | Dust Bowl and the Dirty Thirties

1 'Ogallala Aquifer', in Water Encyclopedia (www.waterencyclopedia.com/Oc-Po/Ogallala-Aquifer.html).

2 *Campbell's 1907 Soil Culture Manual*, pp 13–14 (www.archive.org/stream/campbellssoilculoocamprich#page/no/mode/2up).

3 Timothy Egan. *The Worst Hard Time*. New York: First Mariner Books, 2006; pp 35–36.

4 Ibid., p 58.

5 Ibid., p 121.

6 Ibid., p 138.

7 Ibid., p 151.

8 Deborah Epstein Popper and Frank J. Popper, 'The Great Plains: From Dust to Dust', *Planning* magazine, December 1987 (www.lacusveris.com/The Hi-Line and the Yellowstone Trail/The Buffalo Commons/From Dust to Dust.shtml).

9 'The US produces about 13% of the world's wheat and supplies about 25% of the world's wheat export market. About two-thirds of total US wheat production comes from the Great Plains (from Texas to Montana).' (www.epa.gov/agriculture/ag101/cropmajor.html — as updated 10 September 2009)

10 Garret Hardin, 'The Tragedy of the Commons', *Science Magazine*, 13 December 1968; Vol. 162, no. 3859 (www.sciencemagazine.org).

11 Ibid., pp 1243–1248.

12 'Peru's copper mountain in China's hands', BBC News, 17 Jun 2008.

13 Jeffrey M. Peterson, Thomas L. Marsh and Jeffery R. Williams, 'Conserving the Ogallala Aquifer: Efficiency, Equity and Moral Motives', *Choices Magazine*, February 2003 (www.choicesmagazine.org/2003-1/2003-1-04.htm).

14 Ibid.

15 *The Hutchinson News*, 17 August 2011 (hutchnews.com/Todaystop/BC-KS--Aquifer-Conservation-1st-Ld-Writeth-20110722-16-26-38).

Chapter 8 | The Black Death

1 John M. Barry, '1918 Revisited: Lessons and Suggestions for Further Enquiry', in Stacey L. Knobler, Alison Mack, Adel Mahmoud and Stanley M. Lemon (eds), *The Threat of Pandemic Influenza: Are We Ready? Workshop Summary*. Washington, D.C.: The National Academies Press, 2005; p 58 (www.nap.edu/openbook.php?record_id=11150&page=1).

2 Rosemary Horrox. *The Black Death*. Manchester: Manchester University Press, 1994; p 17.

3 Ibid., pp 1–19.

4 John M. Barry, op. cit., p 65.

5 Ibid., p 65–66.

6 Ibid., p 61.

7 Newfoundland & Labrador Heritage (heritage.nf.ca/law/flu.html).

8 John M. Barry, op. cit., p 60.

9 Ibid., p 63.

10 Ibid.

11 'Cumulative Number of Confirmed Human Cases of Avian Influenza A/(H5N1) Reported to WHO' (www.who.int/csr/disease/avian_influenza/country/cases_table_2010_12_09/en/index.html).

12 IRIN interview with WHO experts Hassan al-Bushra and John Jabbour (web.archive.org/web/20060407052900/http://www.alertnet.org/thenews/newsdesk/IRIN/e83d17668fc60eb55518a76c1de858fd.htm).

13 Press conference by UN system senior coordinator for Avian, human influenza, 29 September 2005 (www.un.org/News/briefings/docs/2005/050929_Nabarro.doc.htm).

Chapter 9 | The Blindsided Brain

1 Christopher Chabris and Daniel Simons. *The Invisible Gorilla and Other Ways Our Intuition Deceives Us*. London: HarperCollins, 2011.

2 Daniel Kahneman. *Thinking, Fast and Slow.* London: Allen Lane, 2011, p 24.

3 Gavin de Becker. *The Gift of Fear: Survival Systems That Protect Us From Violence.* Boston: Little Brown & Co., 1997; pp 27–28.

4 Daniel Kahneman, op. cit., pp 52–56.

5 Ibid.

6 Ibid., pp 123–125.

7 Ibid., pp 129–136.

8 Ibid., p 12.

9 Ibid., pp 74-78.

10 Daniel Kahneman, op. cit., p 14.

11 Quotation from personal correspondence with Professor Paul Brown. See also Paul Brown, Tara Swart and Jane Meyler. 'Emotional Intelligence and the Amygdala', *NeuroLeadership Journal,* Issue 2, 2009 (www.neuroleadership.org).

12 Antoine Bechara, Hanna Damasio, Daniel Tranel and Antonio R. Damasio. 'Deciding Advantageously Before Knowing the Advantageous Strategy', *Science Magazine,* 28 February 1997: vol. 275 no. 5304; pp 1293–1295 (www.sciencemag.org).

13 Andrew Lo, *Fear, Greed and Financial Crises: A Cognitive Neurosciences Perspective* (www.argentumlux.org/documents/Lo__2011__-_Fear__Greed__and_the_Financial_Crisis-_A_Cognitive_Neurosciences_Perspective.pdf), p 15.

14 Iain McGilchrist. *The Master and His Emissary: The Divided Brain and the Making of the Western World.* New Haven and London: Yale University Press, 2010; p 31.

15 Ibid., pp 27–28.

16 Ibid., pp 41–42.

17 See Michael Gazzaniga, 'The Split Brain in Man' (bernard.pitzer.edu/~hfairchi/pdf/psychology/GazzanigaSplitBrain.pdf).

18 Carl Zimmer, 'Scientist at Work: Michael Gazzaniga', *New York Times,* May 10, 2005.

19 Ibid.

20 Ibid., pp 49, 67.

Bibliography

Anderson, Terry L. & Peter J. Hill. *The Not So Wild, Wild West.* Stanford, California: Stanford University Press, 2004.

Barrionuevo, Alexei. 'Ex-Enron Chief Denies Shift of Contracts', *New York Times,* 1 Apr 2006.

Barry, John M. '1918 Revisited: Lessons and Suggestions for Further Enquiry', in Stacey L. Knobler, Alison Mack, Adel Mahmoud and Stanley M. Lemon (eds), *The Threat of Pandemic Influenza: Are We Ready? Workshop Summary.* Washington, D.C.: The National Academies Press, 2005.

Bechara, Antoine, Hanna Damasio, Daniel Tranel & Antonio R. Damasio. 'Deciding Advantageously Before Knowing the Advantageous Strategy', *Science Magazine,* 28 Feb 1997, vol. 275, no. 5304, pp. 1293–5.

Becker, Gavin de. *The Gift of Fear: Survival Systems That Protect Us From Violence.* Boston: Little Brown & Co, 1997.

Bernstein, William J. *A Splendid Exchange: How Trade Shaped the World.* New York: Grove Press, 2008.

Bratton, William W. 'Enron and the Dark Side of Shareholder Value', *Tulane Law Review,* May 2002, p. 39.

Brown, Paul, Tara Swart & Jane Meyler. 'Emotional Intelligence and the Amygdala', *NeuroLeadership Journal* 2, 2009.

Campbell, H.W. *Campbell's 1907 Soil Culture Manual.* Lincoln, Nebraska: The Campbell Soil Culture Co., 1909 (www.archive.org/stream/campbellssoilculoocamprich#page/no/mode/2up).

CASSIDY, JOHN. *Dot.Con*. New York: Allen Lane, 2002.

CHABRIS, CHRISTOPHER & DANIEL SIMONS. *The Invisible Gorilla and Other Ways Our Intuition Deceives Us*. London: HarperCollins, 2011.

CHAN, SEWELL. 'Remembering the '77 Blackout', *New York Times*, 20 Aug 2011.

CHANCELLOR, EDWARD. *Devil Take the Hindmost: A History of Financial Speculation*. London: Macmillan Publishers Ltd, 1999.

CRAIG, SUSANNE & DEBORAH SOLOMON. 'Bank Bonus Tab: US$33bn', *Wall Street Journal*, 31 Jul 2009.

DAVIES, HOWARD. *The Financial Crisis*. Cambridge, UK: Polity, 2010.

EGAN, TIMOTHY. *The Worst Hard Time*. New York: First Mariner Books, 2006.

EISINGER, JESSE & JAKE BERNSTEIN. 'The Magnetar Trade: How One Hedge Fund Helped Keep the Bubble Going', *ProPublica*, 9 Apr 2010.

FAMA, EUGENE F. 'Random Walks in Stock Prices'. Quoted in Justin Fox, *The Myth of the Rational Market*. Hampshire, Great Britain: Harriman House, 2009.

FOLEY, STEPHEN. 'US House Price Fall Beats "Great Depression Slide"', *The Independent on Sunday*, 1 Jun 2011.

FOX, JUSTIN. *The Myth of the Rational Market*. Hampshire, Great Britain: Harriman House, 2009.

GAZZANIGA, MICHAEL. 'Consciousness and the Brain' (www.bio.brandeis.edu/bauer/1999/gazzaniga.html).

GAZZANIGA, MICHAEL. 'The Split Brain in Man' (bernard.pitzer.edu/~hfairchi/pdf/psychology/GazzanigaSplitBrain.pdf).

HARDIN, GARRET. 'The Tragedy of the Commons', *Science Magazine*, 13 Dec 1968; vol. 162, no. 3859, pp. 1243–8.

HEATHER, STUART. 'Libido Can Rule When the Ego Goes Shopping', University of Melbourne's *UniNews*, vol. 12, no. 22, 15 Dec 2003.

HOLLITZ, JOHN E. 'Eisenhower and the Admen: The Television "Spot" Campaign of 1952,' *The Wisconsin Journal of History*, Vol. 66, No. 1 (Autumn 1982), p 36 (www.jstor.org/stable/4635688).

HORROX, ROSEMARY. *The Black Death*. Manchester: Manchester University Press, 1994.

Howard, William Willard. 'The Rush to Oklahoma', *Harpers Weekly* 33, 18 May 1889; pp. 391–4 (www.library.cornell.edu/Reps/docs/landrush.htm).

Kahneman, Daniel. *Thinking, Fast and Slow.* London: Allen Lane, 2011.

Knight, Laurence. 'Have Goldman Sachs Charges Opened Floodgates?', *BBC News*, 27 Apr 2010.

Knobler, Stacey L., Alison Mack, Adel Mahmoud & Stanley M. Lemon (editors), *The Threat of Pandemic Influenza: Are We Ready? Workshop Summary.* Washington, D.C.: The National Academies Press, 2005.

Kohler, Alan. 'A Tsunami of Hope or Terror?' *Business Spectator,* 19 Nov 2008.

Kohler, Alan. 'The Terror Beneath the TARP', *Business Spectator,* 11 Feb 2009.

Krugman, Paul. 'Fighting Off the Depression', *New York Times,* 4 Jan 2009.

Krugman, Paul. 'How Did Economists Get It So Wrong?', *New York Times,* 2 Sep 2009.

Lehrer, Jonah. *The Decisive Moment.* Edinburgh: Canongate Books Ltd, 2009.

Lehrer, Jonah. 'When We're Cowed by Crowds', *Wall Street Journal,* 28 May 2011.

Leung, Rebecca. 'Enron's Ken Lay: I Was Fooled', CBS's *60 Minutes,* 11 Feb 2009.

Lev, Baruch. 'Where Have All of Enron's Intangibles Gone?' *Journal of Accounting and Public Policy* 21 (2002), pp. 131–5.

Lewis, Michael. *The Big Short.* New York: Allen Lane, Penguin Group, 2010.

Lo, Andrew. *Fear, Greed and Financial Crises: A Cognitive Neurosciences Perspective* (www.argentumlux.org/documents/Lo__2011__-_Fear__Greed__and_the_Financial_Crisis-_A_Cognitive_Neurosciences_Perspective.pdf).

Mackay, Charles. *Extraordinary Popular Delusions and the Madness of Crowds.* New York: Cosimo Inc., 2008 [originally published 1841].

MALMSTEN, ERNST, ERIK PORTANGER & CHARLES DRAZIN. *Boo Hoo.* London: Random House, 2002.

MCGILCHRIST, IAIN. *The Master and His Emissary: The Divided Brain and the Making of the Western World.* New Haven and London: Yale University Press, 2009.

MCGRATTAN, ELLEN R. & EDWARD C. PRESCOTT. 'The 1929 Stock Market: Irving Fisher was Right' (www.minneapolisfed.org/research/sr/sr294.pdf).

MCLEAN, BETHANY & PETER ELKIND. *The Smartest Guys in the Room.* London: Penguin Books, 2004.

MILLER, CAROL M. 'The St. Scholastica Day Riot: Oxford After the Black Death', Paper presented at the Florida Conference of Historians 1993 (organizations.ju.edu/fch/1993miller.htm).

PACKARD, VANCE. *The Hidden Persuaders.* Brooklyn, NY: Ig Publishing, 2007 [1957].

PAUL, DAVID. 'Credit Default Swaps, The Collapse of AIG, and Addressing the Crisis of Confidence', *Huffington Post,* 11 Oct 2008.

PETERSON, JEFFREY M., THOMAS L. MARSH & JEFFERY R. WILLIAMS, 'Conserving the Ogallala Aquifer: Efficiency, Equity and Moral Motives', *Choices Magazine,* Feb 2003.

POPPER, DEBORAH EPSTEIN & FRANK J. POPPER. 'The Great Plains: From Dust to Dust', *Planning* magazine, Dec 1987.

REINHART, CARMEN M. & KENNETH S. ROGOFF. *This Time Is Different.* Princeton, NJ: Princeton University Press, 2009.

ROSS, STEPHEN A. 'Options and Efficiency', *Quarterly Journal of Economics,* Feb 1976. Quoted in Justin Fox, *The Myth of the Rational Market.* Hampshire, UK: Harriman House, 2009.

ROWSON, JONATHAN. *Transforming Behaviour Change: Beyond Nudge and Neuromania* (www.thersa.org/projects/social-brain/transforming-behaviour-change).

SIMPSON, JOHN. 'Peru's "Copper Mountain" in China's hands', *BBC News,* 17 Jun 2008.

STIGLITZ, JOSEPH. *Freefall: Free Markets and the Sinking of the Global Economy.* New York: Allen Lane, 2010.

WEBB, ALEX. 'Boo.com Founder Returns to Online Retail with Lara Bohinc', *Daily Telegraph,* 5 Sep 2011.

ZANDI, MICHAEL. *Financial Shock*. New Jersey: Pearson Education Inc, 2009.

ZIEGLER, PHILIP. *The Black Death*. Stroud, Gloucestershire, UK: Alan Sutton Publishing Ltd, 1991.

ZIMMER, CARL. 'Scientist At Work: Michael Gazzaniga', *New York Times*, 10 May 2005.

About the Author

JONATHAN GIFFORD is a businessman, historian and author, whose writing focuses particularly on the human aspects of leadership and management.

After reading philosophy at the University of Kent at Canterbury, Jonathan worked for a number of major media organisations, beginning his career at the *Guardian* newspaper in the 1970s. He went on to work for the *Sunday Express*, the *Mail on Sunday*, and later for BBC Magazines, where he launched the award-winning *BBC History Magazine* in 2000. He is a director of the marketing consultancy Bluequest Media and lectures in advertising and marketing at the European Communications School in London.

Jonathan is the author of *History Lessons: What Business & Management Can Learn from the Great Leaders of History,* and *100 Great Leadership Ideas.* He lives in Oxfordshire with his wife and children.

www.jonathangifford.com